HARRY C. TREXLER
LIBRARY

PARENTS FUND
1988 - 1989

MUHLENBERG
C O L L E G E

THE COSTS OF
ECONOMIC GROWTH

Also by E. J. Mishan

Welfare Economics: Ten Introductory Essays
21 Popular Economic Fallacies
Welfare Economics: The deVries Lectures for 1968
Economic & Technological Growth: The Price We Pay
Cost-Benefit Analysis
Making the World Safe for Pornography, and Other Intellectual
Fashions
Elements of Cost-Benefit Analysis
The Economic Growth Debate: An Assessment
What Political Economy is All About
Economic Efficiency & Social Welfare
Pornography, Psychedelics & Technology
Introduction to Normative Economics
Economic Myths and The Mythology of Economics

THE COSTS OF
ECONOMIC GROWTH

REVISED EDITION

···

E. J. Mishan

PRAEGER

Westport, Connecticut
London

Published in the United States and Canada by
Praeger Publishers, 88 Post Road West, Westport, CT 06881,
an imprint of Greenwood Publishing Group, Inc.

English language edition, except the United States and Canada,
published by Weidenfeld & Nicholson, England

First published 1993

Library of Congress Cataloging-in-Publication Data

Mishan, E. J. (Edward J.), 1917–
    The costs of economic growth / E. J. Mishan.—Rev. 2nd ed.
        p.   cm.
    Includes bibliographical references and index.
    ISBN 0–275–94703–3 (alk. paper)
    1. Economic development.   2. Great Britain—Economic policy—1945–
I. Title.
    HD82.M513   1993
    338.941—dc20   93–19231

Library of Congress Catalog Card Number: 93–19231

ISBN: 0–275–94703–3

Printed in Great Britain

Contents

Contents

Preface to the Revised Edition

On a re-reading of the first edition of my *Costs of Economic Growth* written a quarter of a century ago, I became prey to ambivalent emotions. For were this first edition to be reprinted today without alteration it would, I believe, be as relevant to our times as it was when it first appeared – apart, that is, from a few pages in the original Chapter 2 bearing on the then government's wayward monetary and fiscal policies. In that respect I have to confess (to my shame perhaps) that I could not altogether repress some feeling of satisfaction. Events had indeed vindicated my forewarnings. At the same time it was impossible to avoid a sense of dismay at the continuation over the same period of almost all the untoward trends, environmental and social, singled out in the original volume – and this despite the public's growing awareness of environmental problems over the past two decades.

This fact itself – the tardiness of the response of governments to the manifest spread of environmental degradation – recently excited my curiosity and was responsible for an article in the *National Westminster Bank Review* (May 1990) which has become the basis of Part VI. There, in addition to some obvious updating in the light of more recent global perils, I had occasion again to touch on the urban traffic congestion and the devastation being wrought by unchecked jet tourism. And in the process of elaborating and rearranging the arguments, it seemed a good idea to follow this with a Part VIII that addressed itself to the seemingly insoluble social problems generated by the advance of science and technology. Since it is more difficult to bring these human and social consequences of economic progress into relationship with 'the measuring rod of money', they receive much less systematic attention than the more tangible physical effects.

Those who have read the first edition of the book will notice another feature of the revised edition: the insertion of Part IV in the attempt to persuade readers, especially those who tend to be impressed by official estimates of economic growth, that the calculated figures for the growth over time of real per capita income are entirely compatible with a secular decline in human welfare. (Again I am indebted to the editors of the *National Westminster Bank Review* for permission to draw on my 1984 article.)

Although for the most part the first edition was well received, there was the occasional note of dissent which (uncharitably) I attributed more to the reviewer's ideological convictions than to a considered assessment of my arguments. Certainly a dissenting opinion that does not take issue with the arguments strikes one as being little more than a knee-jerk reaction to the conclusions reached. And it is not unknown for book reviewers to make use of the opportunities provided chiefly for airing their own private philosophies or credos.

Be that as it may, it is as well to affirm that the touchstone throughout the essay is that of the welfare of ordinary human beings. Thus the judgements I make are not value judgements: they are judgements of fact – the question being whether this or that development contributes to the good life on any reasonable definition. Contrary to the allegations of some careless referees, there is no looking back to some mythical golden age and no attempt to show that the 'old days' in any particular country were in all respects better than the present. On the other hand, I do try to convince the open-minded reader that if the criterion is human welfare then, since the turn of the century, and more certainly since World War II, the changes that have taken place in Western Europe and North America have, on balance, been for the worse and are unlikely to get better.

Most people living today can have no recollection of what life was like before World War II. And those old enough to remember are apt to overlook the fact that, say, during the interwar period (1919–39) nearly all the abrasive features of modern times were then scarcely known. True, unemployment in Britain during the thirties averaged about 2 million, yet (not surprisingly) prices remained stable and the country did not have to put up with exorbitant wage-claims each year. Nor was it continually worrying about its position in the economic-growth league or perpetually agonising about the surrender of its sovereignty to a European Union.

In those innocent days the word environment was regarded as a literary term. The idea of a nuclear holocaust belonged to science fiction. The destruction of the world's rain forests, the dissipation of the ozone layer, the greenhouse effect were unimagined. There was no anticipation of ecological damage to be wrought by acid rain, by chemical pesticides and artificial fertilisers nor, for that matter, of oil spills, polluted beaches, contaminated coastal waters, 'dead lakes', rivers thick with scum and effluent, and land-fills and ponds of toxic wastes. Battery hens and factory farms were unheard of: farming had not yet become agribusiness.

The suburbs were quiet and pleasant. Nobody's ears were assailed by low-flying aircraft or the neighbours' stereophonics, nor indeed by screaming chainsaws and long-wailing lawn-mowers. In English seaside resorts it was still possible to smell the salt sea air. The Mediterranean coastline had not yet been wrecked by 'development' and the waters were clear and fit to bathe in.

People were spared the current obsession with 'racism' and 'sexism'. The traditional consensus about morality and property, about language and culture, had not yet been fractured. Broken marriages, school-girl pregnancies, and abortions were the exception: the 'one-parent family' had not yet made its debut into society. Militant homosexuality, 'gay hot lines' in phone books, and 'gay' bars, were yet to emerge – along with endemic outbursts of 'queer-bashing'. The implacable antagonisms of today between 'pro-life' and 'pro-choice' factions, between research scientists and the 'animal rights' movement, between the porno barons and steamy media sex on the one hand and, on the other, infuriated parents and conservative thinkers, were unknown. Explicit depiction of sexuality and sadism were not then available to the public at news-stands and video shops.

Television was scarcely known and computers were not a commercial proposition. Consequently, there was more informal hospitality and less haste. The Christmas season began in December and not, as now, in September. What we now call 'junk mail' scarcely existed. There was no interminable waiting one's turn on the phone, no queuing to reach check-out counters of supermarkets. Willing and knowledgeable shop assistants were in plentiful supply, as also were reliable craftsmen: the 'cowboy' plumber, builder, etc. had yet to emerge on the scene.

Traffic congestion in the cities, car-parking problems, miles of 'tailbacks' along the highways were not then familiar features of life. Nor were soccer hooliganism, race riots, or battles with the police. Above all, people could walk along the streets in comparative safety any time of the day or night: 'mugging' and street-rape are distinctly postwar phenomena.

One could go on. But enough has been said about the absence in the interwar period of so much that plagues us today to make us wonder whether the rise in material standards over the last half century was worth it. To be sure, the statement itself assumes that the emergence of these latter-day afflictions is linked in some way with technical innovation and the spread of industrialisation that are essential characteristics of modern economic growth. One of the main tasks of this volume is therefore to make it abundantly clear that such an assumption is wholly warranted: that the process of economic growth in the West necessarily generates a formidable range of untoward social consequences.

The fact that certain ideas or themes appear in more than one chapter or in different parts of the book may not be attributed entirely to absent-mindedness. Apart from the rhetorical requirements of emphasis, a particular theme may appear in different contexts and give rise to different implications. The invention of the airliner, for example, along with the technical advances that increased its speed and range of travel while lowering its real cost have several effects that are relevant to the economic growth debate. The impact on the physical environment is taken up in Part VI, whereas the conflicts of interest arising from mass tourism or the South-to-North migration are addressed in Part VII. Again such conflicts are among those (also mentioned in Part VII) that lead to state intervention and regulation, so diminishing individual freedom.

Apart from elaborating some of the proposals – such as the enactment of a charter of amenity rights and state initiative in the provision of separate amenity areas – that I put forward in the first edition with the aim of making life more bearable for many people who feel trapped within the suffocating pressure of the modern world, I have found it impossible to end on an optimistic or even a hopeful note. As I see it, the growing desolation of our planetary home is only temporarily obscured by the clamour, the frenzy and the conflicts that – as indicated in the text – arise as the inevitable by-products of an expanding technology. And I hasten to add that this desolation encompasses also the spiritual desolation in the West that is the legacy of a triumphant science.

One longs for a miracle, an unambiguous manifestation of the divine, a mystic light spreading over the universe, the voice of God speaking to us from the clouds. But until that day dawns, we remain orphans of the Enlightenment vainly seeking fulfilment in secular pursuits – the pursuit of power, pleasure, excitation – destined to live our lives without faith or purpose.

Previsions of the future further ahead than is foreseeable might only change the nature of the gloom. Although I once did so in an earlier article, I do not speculate in this volume about the chance of the human adventure culminating in a decisive struggle between consumer interest on the one hand and the interests of the scientific community on the other.

The business community thrives on expanding markets which depend not only on per capita purchasing power but also on the size of the world population. At the time of writing, this population exceeds 5 billion, and is growing by about 100 million a year. And though, in the absence of disasters (discussed in the text), the annual increase of population will grow, it cannot grow large enough for the business world. To the scientific community, on the other hand, the greater the world population the greater the diversion from its prime objective of probing ever deeper and ever farther into the secrets of the universe. For the larger the world population, the larger its absorption of the planet's resources and the greater its demand for energy and for space in the day-to-day production-consumption process, which may properly be regarded as a process of transforming the earth's material resources into waste – liquid, solid and gaseous waste.

The rational scientist is bound to see this process also as a drag on its own manpower and ingenuity, diverting its pursuit of knowledge toward the gratuitous task of maintaining an outsize population. From a strictly scientific perspective then over 99 per cent of the world's population is expendable, cluttering up the planet, voraciously consuming its resources, inevitably destroying thousands of species of flora and fauna each year, and deflecting the enterprise and energies of scientists from their prime purpose.

Should the scientific community ever come to dominate society – owing to a collapse of civil government or a universal panic following a sequence of global catastrophes – priority would be given to a rapid diminution of world population, an objective that could be humanely accomplished within two generations through the use of chemical means to prevent human reproduction. History as we know it would come to an end and the age of pure science would dawn.

Fascinating though it may be, I have resisted the temptation to speculate about such possible futures in the present volume, restricting myself, as in the original volume, to the more immediate and pressing issues connected with modern economic growth.

The reader or the reviewer who has the time and patience to compare this new edition with that which appeared in 1967 will notice some differences in style and manner. Conscious as I was when writing the text of the original edition about the attitude of some of my colleagues at the London School of Economics, who were wont to view my occasional attacks on the economic-growth establishment during the sixties as an amiable eccentricity, I sought to guard my flanks against possible counter-attacks. Although it cannot be said that in this new edition I have thrown caution to the winds, my arguments are on the whole less elaborately qualified.

True, my critique of economic growth in Book 1 is again developed (with the exception of Chapter 10) almost entirely within the accepted framework of economic presuppositions – the framework about which the academic discipline known as welfare economics, or normative economics, has grown. (The student who is curious to know how much can be said about social welfare by mainstream economists is referred to my *Normative Economics*.) For even within this accepted framework of economic premises and relationships – and limiting the objective of the analysis to ways of expanding the individual's area of choice – the common rationalisations for continued pursuit of economic growth do not stand up to close scrutiny.

Turning to the many consequences of economic and technical growth that cannot be properly accommodated within the conventional framework of economic assumptions, on the principle that 'discretion is the better part of valour' I relegated my arguments to what I called 'A Digression' of about forty pages on the 'More Intimate Reflections on the Unmeasurable Consequences of Economic Growth'. Since that time my courage has grown and I am now intrepid and rash enough to devote the whole of Book 2 to a more systematic and detailed arrangement of considerations that bear on what we are wont to call the Quality of Life. It is in Book 2 then that the reader is impelled to reflect not only on the ambient physical environment but also on the changing social environment in which he is immersed. He is to address himself to the more important consequences upon the aspirations, the character and, ultimately, the emotional fulfilment of ordinary people that flow, not only from growing material abundance, but more particularly from the rapidity of technological change and from the sort of innovations both in consumer goods and services and in production and business methods that are necessarily brought into being by modern economic growth.

Clearly the considerations broached in this exploratory venture are more speculative and more far-ranging than those discussed in Book 1. They certainly cannot count on the support of the conclusions reached in a number of technical papers published in the professional journals. But even if my interpretation of current trends and my manifest scepticism about the value of economic growth are open to challenge, there can be no doubt whatever that the issues raised in Book 2 are the crucial ones in any debate about the sort of civilisation we should strive for and the sort of civilisation that is in fact taking shape.

The four appendices that appeared in the original volume have been retained, although that on the balance of payments has been somewhat truncated in the interests of accessibility. They may not all be equally intelligible to the layman, but then they are not really necessary to the arguments in the text. Their chief purpose was and is that of persuading mainstream economists who might glance through the book that if my critiques of the advantages of free trade, of the benefits of private transport, or of the familiar scepticism about long-term technological unemployment depart in some respects from the usual propositions that draw on standard economic postulates, they do none the less deserve serious consideration.

For the younger economist – or at least for one who has not read the first edition of this volume – a word of explanation may be necessary since he will not find references in the following pages to the popular idea of sustainable economic growth.

As a result of the initial ferment produced by the simple 'dynamic' models of Harrod and Domar in the late forties, there emerged a number of relatively primitive growth theories in the fifties such as those contrived by Swann and by Solow. In due course these were followed by more developed equilibrium, or 'golden', paths of economic growth pioneered by Phelps and others. As could have been anticipated, more theoretically sophisticated models were constructed later, including multi-sector models, in which environmental and other constraints were introduced. And if the history of economic theory since World War II offers any guide to papers yet to be written, the increasing scope for mathematical virtuosity may be depended upon to direct the energies of the profession into elaborating yet more complex constructs.

The relevance of such models of sustainable economic growth to future developments, or to the course of human welfare in the coming years, is academic in both senses of the word. The purpose of these models is that of explicating the relationship of a few 'key' parameters, which parameters themselves define the character of the model that will ensure the continuation of the growth process (the simpler models, for example, may include the savings ratio, the rate of return on capital, the rate of technical progress, the rate of population growth, each of them perhaps related to other variables). But otherwise, such models do no more than reveal the conditions under which a constant (or other) rate of economic growth can be maintained indefinitely – always assuming, of course, that the model constructed is erected on the chief economic variables.

Although such analysis is of great interest to some economists, these theories of sustainable growth have little to offer the nation's policy makers since the influence that the latter can exert on these 'key' parameters is in any case very limited. For one thing, although the trends over the past forty years or so, with respect to population growth, the rate of saving, the rate of technological growth, in any one country, have varied significantly, nothing can be said with confidence about the future. We cannot predict the pattern of innovations very far ahead, and we may well encounter diminishing returns to technical research in the more important sectors of the economy.

Secondly, the consequences that emerge from the introduction of innovations, both in production and consumption, tend to react sooner or later, and usually adversely, on net productivity. More important, however – and as will be described at length in the following pages – the chief innovations since the turn of the century have the most potent and far-reaching effects on the quality of our lives. And it is the nature of these consequences, arising as they do from the growth of science and technology, that is the subject matter of my thesis.

The preceding paragraph should act as a caveat about the meaning of economic growth in the title, but it can bear emphasis.

When writing the first edition of the book in 1966, unemployment was not high, and though financial editors habitually made invidious comparisons between the UK economy and those of other European countries, our growthmen were for the most part sanguine about the future. But although I was not concerned then with the prospects for employment, I later realised that my use of the term 'economic growth' could be misinterpreted. At various conferences my alleged views occasionally came under attack by economists (who apparently had not read the book, or not read very far) speaking eloquently about the costs of *not* growing – arguing (correctly) that a stagnating economy would sharpen the conflict between capital and labour, would spread despondency, social misery, political instability, and so on.

Such misinterpretation arising from the title of my book is no less likely at a time when the second edition is scheduled to appear, at a time when unemployment in Britain is close to three million, the economy in the dumps, the immediate prospects bleak, and the government loathe to stimulate the economy by increasing public expenditure.

Let me make it clear then, first, that as it happens I am as much concerned as any other economist about the current magnitude of the depression and, like others, I also have my own explanations and nostrums (some of which are ensconced in appendices A and B). But the unemployment problem does not excite my attention in the text itself. There I am chiefly occupied in addressing an entirely different problem: that of the effects on our welfare of sustained secular growth irrespective of whether the economy is booming or slumping. More explicitly, I am concerned with the manifold consequences bearing on the quality of life of continued technological growth over the foreseeable future.

In order then to avoid being distracted from the thesis being propounded, the reader is advised to assume throughout the existence of a steady and tolerable level of employment and a satisfactory distribution of income. Indeed, if my arguments are valid, the untoward consequences that stem from technological growth operate continually over the future even under the most favourable economic circumstances imaginable.

I follow tradition in acknowledging that my intellectual debts are many. In what is intended to be a popular exposition, however, I feel no obligation to give chapter and verse, and no compunction about plagiarising freely from many of my earlier works. I should have been glad to have acknowledged the help given by colleagues, but this new edition has been written during my retirement and, therefore, without the benefit of their comments and advice that I once enjoyed. The charitable reader will perhaps bear this fact in mind if occasionally he stumbles across an obscure passage or stylistic infelicity. Finally I wish to record my indebtedness to Miss Marianna Tapas at the London School of Economics, who typed the finished draft and in the process corrected an embarrassing number of grammatical errors, and also to the editors of the *National Westminster Bank Review* for permission to draw on some of the material in my articles of 1984 and 1990.

E. J. Mishan
August 1992

Introduction

I

Contrary to their fashionable phrases about the need to face change, those who proclaim themselves to be in the vanguard of new thought generally prove to be in the iron clutch of economic dogma, much of it provided by famous economists of the past as a guide to policy in a world different from our own. Free trade, free competition, sustained economic growth, the free movement of peoples – these were, for Britain at least, the dominant economic aspirations of the nineteenth century. Nor were they entirely irrelevant after the turn of the century. Indeed, one might subscribe to such docrines without self-deception until the close of the Second World War. For it was only after the first phase of the postwar recovery of Europe that one could descry the shape of things to come and, in that vision, doubt the relevance of these once-emancipating liberal doctrines to the momentous developments being wrought in our lives by the increasing pace of science and technology. The more salient among these developments are (1) the unprecedented expansion of the human species, with ecological consequences we are only beginning to perceive, (2) the growing speed of technological advance and, as a corollary, the growing speed of obsolescence of skills, of knowledge and of culture, both esoteric and popular, and (3) the postwar surge of affluence in the West, much of it channelled into communications, in particular the mushroom growth of television, automobile ownership, air travel and mass tourism, phenomena that over a few short years have created a complex of urgent problems. Although the suddenness of these developments has caught us off our guard, one might have thought that a modest concern with the welfare of society would have suggested the wisdom of setting aside inherited dogma and challenged us to think about what is taking place around us.

There may well be good explanations why this has not yet happened. It is possible that our forms of government are better adapted to a more leisurely age, one in which social grievances could be redressed and problems met as they arose. Significant events, one felt assured, took time to shape themselves. Institutions need only change through the slow accumulation of knowledge and experience. As for the physical environment about us, it could be depended upon to hold its form for many years. Thus men conditioned themselves to detect in the passage of events familiar patterns and parallels, and lulled their apprehensions whenever catastrophe appeared imminent with aphorisms about the illusion of change and about the basic sameness of the world in spite of appearances to the contrary.

Moreover, no provision is made, nor perhaps could it be made, for the sort of training that might fit a man to think about and judge the effects on the welfare of ordinary people of a gathering eruption of science and technology in pressure sufficient to splinter the framework of our institutions and to erode the moral foundations upon which they have been raised. In the course of his work a person of trained intelligence has little incentive to turn his mind to such tremendous questions. Whether working in the physical or social sciences, those scholars who are not struggling abreast of the cumulating literature in their chosen field are struggling for recognition chiefly by attempting to publish original scientific work – an aim that is facilitated not by broadening but by narrowing yet further the focus of their enquiries. Economists are not excepted. Although many are interested in more than mathematical refinement and generalisation for its own elegant sake, they do not tend to wonder aloud whether, for instance, the last few decades of material growth in the West have, on balance, further promoted the happiness of mankind. Such speculation, they might suppose, is better relegated to the amateur debating society. The world has more important matters to attend to. Such broad questions cannot, in any case, be systematically discussed using simply the purely technical apparatus of the social sciences; nor can they be discussed without the frequent invocation of 'value judgements'. And any social scientist who will dare to go far in offending against custom and usage must be prepared to bear the withering scorn of those of the fraternity who have been more zealous in safeguarding their methodological chastity.

II

Whatever the explanation, we live in paradoxical circumstances. Notwithstanding the fact that bringing the Jerusalem of economic growth to England's green and pleasant land has so far conspicuously reduced both the greenness and the pleasantness, economic growth still remains the most respectable catchword in the current political vocabulary. Even the younger men of today, struggling for the reins of power, habitually disregard, in their diagnoses of the times, the new sources of social conflict and social discontent emerging around us. They continue to give expression to the basic doctrines of their fathers and spin rhetoric out of the growth theme in blithe unconcern for the spreading jungle of problems stemming directly from the material prosperity of the last four decades. They persist in minting phrases combining 'new' and 'change', 'modern' and 'dynamic', as though these were cardinal virtues, and in effect offer us all salvation by science – and via more exports. One factor that enables them to get away with their routine push-and-shove exhortation to the public is the postwar 'discovery' of that latest addition to the armoury of the Establishment, the economic index – a remarkably simple thing in itself, a mere number in fact, yet one that is treated with unabashed reverence. Apparently one has but to consult it to comprehend the entire condition of society. Among the faithful, and they are legion, any doubt that, say, a four per cent growth rate, as revealed by the index, is better for the nation than a three per cent growth rate is near-heresy, tantamount to a doubt that four is greater than three. Such a doubt is not much worse than the doubt that economic growth itself, like the growth of knowledge, is 'on balance' a good thing. None the less, since many of the influences on our well-being (and possibly the major influences) – and here we are to be concerned wholly with well-being, with welfare, satisfaction or happiness, possibly not measurable but certainly meaningful – do not lend themselves easily to the number system, it is not hard to show, as I propose to do in the following chapters, that doubts about a positive connection between social welfare and the index of economic growth are amply justified.

Some of these influences, however, have not been entirely ignored by the profession, though I shall suggest that the extent of their impact on social welfare has been grossly underestimated. The nature of these influences is indicated in the economist's standard critique of a perfectly competitive system whenever it is regarded as promoting an ideal allocation of resources. Since the turn of the century they have been systematically treated under the heading of external dis-economies – or 'spillover effects', to use the more popular jargon adopted by economists.

There are other criticisms, however, or misgivings at least, that go far beyond those that may be comprehended by spillover effects. These other criticisms do not depend for their validity and force upon the particular institutions by which a society allocates its growing resources and distributes its products. The economic growth of an affluent society under the direction of a highly centralised planning commission would be no less vulnerable to such criticisms than would a decentralised and free enterprise system.

It would have been a pleasing intellectual exercise to have formalised these latter criticisms, if only to contain them within the field of economics and thereby to strengthen their appeal to my colleagues. But it cannot really be done. The economist who is sympathetic to my views may have to accept many arguments that cannot be tucked comfortably into some corner of any structure of welfare economics.

III

What I wish to be concluded might usefully be summarised here: that the popular postwar dichotomy drawn between the 'conservatives' on the one hand and the 'progressives' on the other – or, to vary the terminology, between the traditionalists and the old school on the one hand and the 'modernisers' and 'pacemakers' on the other – has served to confuse the chief issue that confronts us: that of seeking to adjust the environment to gratify man's nature or, instead, that of adjusting man's nature to an environment determined predominantly by 'efficiency considerations', that is, by technological advance.

One could, of course, decide to use words differently and, therefore, to agree that the issue is that between 'facing change' and 'going on in the same old way', provided that we dissociate 'facing change' from the inertia of mere momentum and, more specifically, from the orthodox measures that invariably feature on the agenda of our would-be 'pacesetters' – increasing competition, pushing exports, increasing technological efficiency and above all, of course, faster economic growth. For those who, from habit as much as conviction, hanker after these things, who are impatient to hustle us into the future, painful though it may be, are not, on an alternative use of language, facing the twentieth century at all. They are merely trimming their sails to the winds of fashion. The phrase 'facing the twentieth century' might better refer to the need, in the face of a new and incalculable power of the rising technology, to surrender the simple faith in the beneficence of industrial progress guided only as it is by ancient presumption in favour of liberal economic doctrines. Stated more positively, the younger generation will be facing the future with honesty only when it brings itself to face the strain of thinking through the consequences, tangible and intangible, certain and speculative, of the current drift into the future and, in doing so, recognises that in the new world the old liberal economic harmonies are not to be found; that so many painful choices have to be made, and that in some cases the need of men and the needs of technology may prove to be irreconcilable.

I am far from being unaware that many of my arguments will not stand up to so-called scientific scrutiny; that many assertions are made without the attempt to present evidence. For this I hold the present state of knowledge to be at fault, not my arguments. Owing to the speed with which events have overtaken our analytic and statistical techniques, we have not yet evolved methods for estimating the more outstanding spillovers of the postwar era. Yet such is our perverse faith in figures that what cannot be quantified is all too often left out of the calculus altogether. There is apparently a strong prejudice among research workers against admitting that the unmeasurable effects are likely to be more significant than the measurable ones. In many cases, therefore, the conclusions reached on the basis of these measurable effects only are unwarranted.

Be that as it may, since there does not appear much likelihood of our being able to estimate these growing spillovers, or 'social costs' as they are sometimes called, in the near future, it is more urgent that they be brought to the attention of the public in the most graphic manner rather than have writers relegate them to apologetic footnotes. The undeniable fact that no estimates have been made, or are likely to be made shortly, about the magnitude of some of the more untoward social effects need not intimidate the economist from occasionally respecting the plain and inescapable evidence of his own senses. Nor should such a fact prohibit his reasoned conjectures about the future if present trends remain unchecked.

IV

As for those consequences of rapid technological advance that do not, even in principle, lend themselves easily to measurement, one cannot await the advent of a more accommodating methodology before considering them in earnest, since they seem yet more portentous than those which are measurable in principle. Here the appeal to the reader must of necessity be in terms of familiar experience and intuition. It should be clear that it would not have been possible to write Part VI if I had had to submit to the self-denying ordinances of the good economic theorist: that tastes be accepted as data and that people's choices are final. For pure economic analysis, whatever is the nature or standards of the observed wants of people, or whatever people become under the impact of commercial or technological developments, is a matter of complete indifference. Such indifference, however, or rather irrelevance, need not become a part of the convictions of the practising economist. Indeed, if he is seriously concerned with human welfare, the effects of existing economic organisations and the kinds of technological innovation on standards of taste, on norms of behaviour and on the character of people are of primary importance.

Of course, anyone may assert, in an outburst of promiscuous detachment, that a fondness for *The Adventures of Superman* is to be respected no less than a fondness for Milton's *Paradise Lost*; that a marked preference for the strains of 'Jive at Five' is not to be ranked below Beethoven's 'Pastoral' Symphony. One may assert it. But in fact nobody really believes it. Nor do we act as though anybody really believes it.

We are not at all surprised to learn about a boy who once doted on *The Adventures of Superman* becoming disenchanted with the book as he grew older, and moving on toward an appreciation of, and perhaps an enthusiasm for, *Paradise Lost*. The reverse would not be credible. We should be stupified to learn of a lover of Shakespeare's or Milton's poetry turning for greater fulfilment to *The Adventures of Superman* – unless it was also pointed out that he was entering his dotage. In sum, we do rank taste – whether always correctly or not – along the scale of better or worse. And should society ever cease to do so, consistency would require also that art, music, literature cease to be taught.

Again, it may be asserted – especially when considering the possibility of some unfortunate development – that future generations might not mind living under conditions that are repellent to us; that they will, after all, have become adjusted. Perhaps they will. But the pertinent question is whether human adaptation to the development in question is one that enhances the experience of life or otherwise. That we tacitly reject this argument whenever it touches our immediate concerns is borne out by our response to any current abuse. Apparently no one thinks it fit to propose that an existing social evil be left unremedied until such time as people have become callous, hardened or corrupt enough as no longer to care about it.

V

Without my being reckless enough to list some of the necessary conditions for the good life in Part VII, I should have been unable to reinforce and to illustrate further my general thesis. So if it were true that people were in fact adapting themselves successfully to the requirements of a rapidly advancing technology and to the sorts of goods it promoted, it might also be true that, in consequence, they were moving away from the good life. The possibility that, in the process of becoming more productive and more innovative, man will unavoidably become less sensitive, less articulate, less poetic, less serene – though content to remain so – cannot be excluded.

So far, however, men have not been remarkably successful in adapting themselves to our new runaway world. Casual evidence suggests that momentum is being maintained at a high cost in terms of nervous strain and anxiety. It also suggests that the civilisation of the West carries with it the seeds of its own disintegration, a thesis adumbrated in Part VIII.

I shall not pretend that my incursion into this faintly charted territory in Parts VII and VIII has been uncongenial, and there may well be places where the flow of ideas has carried the argument a little further than can be comfortably sustained by the current evidence. On the whole, however, it has been worthwhile if only for the opportunity it afforded of giving systematic expression to my own misgivings about the sort of world that technology is shaping for us. But I also confess that I entertain the hope that, before putting the book down, some readers may be persuaded to contemplate the future with less complacency than they possessed before picking it up.

BOOK ONE

The Economic Consequences

PART I

....

Economics: Choice or Necessity?

1 Growthmania

I

Revolutions from below break out not when material circumstances are oppressive but, according to popular historical generalisation, when they are improved and hope of a better life is in the air. So long as toil and hardship was the rule for the mass of people over countless centuries, so long as economic activity was viewed as a daily struggle against the niggardliness of nature, men were resigned to eke out a living by the sweat of their brows untroubled by visions of ease and plenty. And although economic growth was not unheard of before this century – certainly the eighteenth-century economists had a lively awareness of the opportunities for economic expansion, through innovation, through trade and through the division of labour – it was not until the recent postwar recovery turned into a period of sustained economic advance for the West, and the latest products of technological innovation were everywhere visible, and audible, that countries rich and poor became aware of a new phenomenon in the calendar of events, since watched everywhere with intentness and anxiety, the growth index.[1] While his forebears thought themselves fortunate to be directly employed, the European worker today expresses resentment if his attention is drawn to any lag in his earnings behind those of other occupations. If, before World War II, the nation was thankful for a prosperous year, today we are urged to chafe and fret on discovering that other nations have done perhaps better yet.

Indeed, with the establishment of the National Economic Development Council in 1962 economic growth became an official feature of the Establishment. To be *with* growth was manifestly to be 'with it' and, like speed itself, the faster the better. And if NEDC, or 'Neddy' as it was affectionately called, was to be superseded, it would be only to make way for larger and more forceful neddies. Since then, though

---

[1] Like a national flag and a national airline, a national plan for economic growth is deemed an essential item in the paraphernalia of every new nation state.

3

more particularly in the sixties and seventies, every businessman, politician, city editor or writer impatient to acquire a reputation for economic sagacity and no-nonsense realism was busy shouting 'giddy-up' in several of two-score different ways. If the country was ever uncertain of the ends it should pursue, that day has passed. There may have been doubts among philosophers and heart-searching among poets, but to the multitude the kingdom of God was to be realised here, and now, on this earth; and it was to be realised via technological innovation, and at an exponential rate.

Even today, its universal appeal exceeds that of the brotherhood of man, indeed it comprehends it. For as we become richer, surely we shall remedy all social evils; heal the sick, comfort the aged and exhilarate the young. One has only to think with sublime credulity of the opportunities to be opened to us by the harvest of increasing wealth: universal adult education, free art and entertainment, frequent visits to the moon, a domesticated robot in every home and, therefore, woman for ever freed from drudgery; for the common man, a lifetime of leisure to pursue culture and pleasure (or, rather, to absorb them from the ubiquitous television screen); for the scientists, ample funds to devise increasingly powerful and ingenious computers so that we may have yet more time for culture and pleasure and for scientific discovery.

To be sure, additional items of public concern – environmental devastation, soaring crime rates – have made their way into the nation's political agenda over the past few years. Yet, it is argued, priority must still be accorded to economic growth. For without the additional wealth provided by economic growth, we shall be unable to invest in the resources necessary to improve the environment and, more generally, the quality of life. In sum, there can be no real alternative to economic growth.

II

But to be tediously logical about it, there is an alternative to the postwar growth-rush as an overriding objective of economic policy. One may concede the importance of economic growth in an indigent society, or in a country with an outsize population wherein the mass of people struggle for bare subsistence. But despite ministerial twaddle about the efforts we must make to 'survive in a competitive world', Britain is just not that sort of country. Irrespective of its 'disappointing' rate of growth, or the present position of the gold reserves, it may be reasonably regarded, in view of its productive capacity and skills, as one of the more affluent societies of the West, a country with a wide margin of choice in its policy objectives. And it is palpably absurd to continue talking, and acting, as if our survival – or our 'economic health' – depended upon that extra one or two per cent growth. At the risk of offending financial journalists and other fastidious scrutinisers of economic statistics, whose spirits have been trained to soar or sink on detecting a half per cent swing in any index, I must voice the view that the near-exclusive concern with industrial growth is, in the present condition of Britain, unimaginative and unworthy.

The reader, however, may be more inclined to concede this point and to ponder on a more discriminating criterion of economic policy if he is reminded of some of the less laudable consequences of economic growth over the last forty years.

Undergraduate economists learn in their first year that the private enterprise system is a marvellous mechanism. By their third year, it is to be hoped, they have come to learn also that there is a great deal it cannot do, and much that it does badly. For today's generation in particular, it is a fact of experience that within the span of a few years the unlimited marketing of new technological products can result in a cumulative reduction of the pleasure once freely enjoyed by the citizen. If there is one clear policy alternative to pressing on regardless, it is that of seeking immediate remedies against the rapid spread of disamenities which now beset the daily lives of ordinary people. More positively, there is the alternative policy of transferring resources from industrial production to the more urgent task of transforming the physical environment in which we live into something less fit for machines perhaps, but more fit for human beings.

Since I shall illustrate particular abuses of unchecked commercialism in later chapters and criticise them on grounds familiar to economists, I refrain from elaboration at this point. However, it is impossible not to dwell for a moment on the most notorious by-product of industrialisation the world has ever known: the appalling traffic congestion in our towns, cities and suburbs. It is at this phenomenon that our political leaders should look for a really outstanding example of postwar growth. One consequence is that the pleasures of strolling along the streets of a city are more of a memory than a current pastime. Lorries, motor-cycles and taxis belching fumes, filth, stench, snarling engines and unabating visual disturbance have compounded to make movement through the city an ordeal for the pedestrian at the same time as the mutual strangulation of the traffic makes it a purgatory for motorists. The formula of mend-and-make-do followed by successive transport ministers is culminating in a maze of one-way streets, peppered with parking meters, with massive signs, detours, and weirdly shaped junctions and circuses across which traffic pours from several directions, while penned in pedestrians jostle each other along narrow pavements.

Towns and cities have been rapidly transmogrified into roaring workshops, the authorities watching anxiously as the traffic builds up with no policy other than that of, on the one hand, spreading the rash of parking meters to discourage the traffic, and, on the other, of accommodating it by road-widening, tunnelling, bridging and patching up here and there; perverting every principle of amenity a city can offer in the attempt to force through it the growing traffic. This 'policy' – apparently justified by reckoning as social benefits any increase in the volume of traffic and any increase in its average speed – would, if it were pursued more ruthlessly, result inevitably in a Los Angeles-type solution in which the greater part of the metropolis is converted to road space; in effect a city buried under roads and freeways. The once-mooted alternative – 'traffic architecture' based on the principle of multi-level separating of motorised traffic and pedestrians, following the Buchanan plan of the early sixties – may be an improvement compared with the present drift into chaos, but it would take decades to implement, would cost the earth, and would apparently remove us from contact with it. The more radical solution of prohibiting private traffic from town and city centres, resorts and places of recreation can be confidently expected to meet with the organised hostility of the motoring interests and 'friends of freedom'. Yet, short of eating the heart out of our towns and cities, there is no feasible alternative to increasing constraints on the freedom of private vehicles.

III

Other disagreeable features may be mentioned in passing, many of them the result either of wide-eyed enterprise or of myopic municipalities, such as the postwar 'development' blight, the erosion of the countryside, the 'uglification' of coastal towns, the pollution of the air and of rivers with chemical wastes, the accumulation of thick oils on our coastal waters, the sewage poisoning of our beaches, the destruction of wildlife by indiscriminate use of pesticides, the change-over from animal farming to animal factories, and, visible to all who have eyes to see, a rich heritage of natural beauty being wantonly and systematically destroyed – a heritage that cannot be restored in our lifetime.

To preserve what little is left will require major legislation and strong powers of enforcement. But one cannot hope for these without a complete break with the parochial school of economics that has paralysed the mind of all governing authorities since the industrial revolution. It will require a new vision of the purposes of life to stand up to the inevitable protests of commerce, of industry, and of the financial journalists; protests that employment, expansion, exports – key words in the vocabulary of the parochial school – will be jeopardised if enterprise is not permitted to develop where profits are highest.

What has caught us off our guard is the unprecedented speed and scale of the material transformation. Such is the expanding reach of modern technology, such the opportunism of corporate enterprise, that the waste products of expanding industry, which for thousands of years were absorbed into the cycle of nature, are now issuing forth in such volume that our planet will be uninhabitable if trends continue. And though we are all environmentalists now, our attention is continually being distracted either by technological wonders or by official economic imperatives. Our vision is distorted, and we do not clearly perceive the growing incongruity of our economic and ecological objectives. We do not pause to reflect on the generations it would take to undo the damage wrought since the turn of the century – to regrow the forests over the millions of acres stripped of timber; to purify rivers and lakes of accumulated chemicals and sewage; to revive the once-abundant wildlife of the African continent; to restore to its original magnificence several thousand miles of Mediterranean coastline ruined in the postwar tourist spree; to cleanse the atmosphere of millions of tons of floating pollutants and of an uncertain but increasing amount of radioactive matter. Thus, it is not the limit of material resources that will eventually check the 'sustainable economic growth' we have come to accept as a proper and realisable goal of economic policy. After all, there are incalculable mineral reserves under the ocean bed or, for that matter, in the earth's crust less than a kilometre beneath the surface. What is going to check our Rake's Progress – our expansionary exuberance – is the carrying capacity of the earth's atmosphere, the exhaustion of the regenerative powers of its soil, the frailty of its ozone mantle, the extinction of life in its oceans.

At times one detects a residual complacency, promoted by economists imbued with the virtues of competitive enterprise and inadvertently, perhaps, fostered by those historians whose cultivated detachment forbids their being ruffled by current events. Rather than project uncouth trends, they respond to present dangers by observing patiently that similar alarums were sounded in ages gone by. Did not Malthus warn the world of the destructive pressures of population growth at the close of the eighteenth century, and this when the population was a small fraction of what it is today? Science, like love, will surely find a way! As for the disappearance of the woods, or of the countryside? Go back a century and we shall find men lamenting the vanishing countryside! Go back to the eighteenth century, or back to the seventeenth, and again we shall find men who despise the new towns and bemoan the passing of rustic virtues. *Ergo*, nothing has really changed: current alarms are groundless.

The trick is to find a precedent, or contrive one if need be, and apparently any current danger is effectively exorcised. And, to conclude, since we have managed somehow to escape global disaster so far, we have every reason to be optimistic about the future.

IV

Our political leaders, nearly all of them, have visited the United States, Japan and Germany, and all of them seem to have learned the wrong things. They have been impressed by the efficient organisation of industry, the high productivity, the extent of automation, and the new one-plane, two-yacht, three-car, four-television-set family. The spreading suburban wilderness, the near traffic paralysis, the mixture of pandemonium and desolation in the cities, a sense of spiritual despair scarcely concealed by the frantic pace of life – such phenomena, not being readily quantifiable, and having no discernible impact on the reserves of foreign currencies, are obviously not regarded as agenda.

Indeed, the jockeying among party leaders for recognition as the agents of modernisation, of the new, the bigger and better, is one of the sadder facts of the postwar world, in particular as their claim to the title rests almost wholly on a propensity to keep their eyes glued to the speedometer without regard to the direction taken. Our environment is sinking fast into a welter of disamenities, yet the most vocal representatives of the main political parties cannot raise their eyes from the trade figures to remark the painful event.

V

In the endeavour to arrest this mass flight from reality into statistics, I hope to persuade the reader that the chief sources of social welfare are not to be found in economic growth *per se*, but in a far more selective form of development which must include a radical reshaping of our physical environment with the needs of pleasant living, and not the needs of traffic or industry, foremost in mind. Indeed, in the later chapters I shall argue that the social process by which technological advance is accommodated is, in any case, almost certain to reduce our sources of gratification.

Before launching into the main themes, however, something must be said about the myth which persuades us that, as a nation, we have no real choice; that living in the twentieth century, we are compelled to do all sorts of things we might otherwise not wish to do. Since childhood, all too many of us have lived in awe of the balance of payments, and having accepted the growth imperative, we have also unthinkingly come to link faster growth with an improved balance of payments, a proposition for which there is no economic warrant.

Enough will be said in the following chapters to indicate that there is a great deal more choice in our domestic affairs than is usually conveyed by the newspapers, enough at least to free us from the imagined compulsion of having to expand rapidly, and from popular fears of 'not surviving', or 'being left behind in the race', or 'stagnating in an amiable backwater', *ad nauseam*. Having pushed aside such bogies, we are free to examine the rationale of the market mechanism in order to explain how the persistence of commercial habits of thought is responsible for the creation of so much 'diswelfare'.

2 The No-Choice Myth

I

Let us begin by being platitudinous to the point of remarking that all three possible goals of long-term policy – (1) economic growth, (2) a more equitable distribution of the national product, and (3) improved allocation of our national resources – play some part in the complex of existing economic policy. Differences of opinion may therefore be attributed to differences in emphasis. For many years now the emphasis has been almost entirely on growth, whereas one of the themes of this essay is that it ought to be almost entirely on improving the allocation of our existing resources. It is the task of these first chapters to persuade the reader of the urgent need for this shift in priorities.

Before inspecting these long-term goals more closely, let us distinguish them from the perennial concerns of the day-to-day running of the country which too often appear wholly to absorb the energies of the government. These routine preoccupations, which go to fill the financial columns of our newspapers and are the subject of innumerable reports, are three in number: (a) the maintenance of a high level of employment, (b) the stabilisation of the level of prices, and (c) the promotion of a favourable balance of payments. Insofar as we succeed in these objectives we refer to the economy as 'healthy' or, better yet, 'sound'. Certainly it would be reckless to ignore the indices of the current performance of the economy. Any time that (a) a large proportion of the voluntary labour force is without employment, or (b) an initially suppressed inflation has slipped its restraints and a distrust of the currency is spreading, or (c) there is no reasonable prospect of paying for the inflow of goods from abroad, a sense of crisis impends and there is warrant enough for temporarily overlooking long-term goals in the immediate attempt to return the economy to a more acceptable norm in any of these respects. The economy may be likened to an engine whose smooth functioning is indicated by governors labelled 'employment', 'price stability' and 'balance of payments'. Obviously any poor performance calls for repairs; and it is the task of a good mechanic to avoid breakdowns and ensure the good condition of the engine. But keeping the engine trouble-free is not an end in itself. The engine drives a vehicle, and the speed of the vehicle to some extent, and the direction it takes, to a greater extent – long-term policies – are what really matter.

Since national self-castigation, in all economic matters at least, has been in high fashion since World War II, one must risk the charge of unpardonable complacency by the reflection that our postwar record – apart from inflation which was rather high in the seventies – has not been so bad after all. Although we were prone to more industrial unrest, we enjoyed high levels of employment until the eighties. If frequently troublesome, the balance-of-payments position was never such as to cause great hardship. And though there seems to have developed a constitutional convention (upheld by the opposition party in Parliament) of continually deploring the country's rate of economic growth and of observing how far it lags behind those of our European competitors, if we can bear with this mortifying statistic we may live quite comfortably.[1]

It should be evident, at any rate, that the attention paid to these auguries of economic malaise is excessive when compared with a more sober appraisal of our long-term prospects. One explanation of the popular fascination with economic indices – with the monthly ups and downs of employment, trade, interest rates, inflation rates, output, sales and the like – among economic journalists is surely that an aptitude for summarising official figures, and for the uttering of warnings whenever there is a 'wrong' movement in the graphs, is not a difficult one to master.

The knowledge that several hundred financial journalists and government officials pursue this hobby – tabulate figures (to the nearest million), construct charts, and spin endless columns of verbal statistics – is something we might continue to put up with were it not for the fact that the fascination with 'index economics' distracts attention from the broader aims of economic policy, and tends to become a substitute for them. We become so preoccupied with the

---

[1] Not every kind of growth index, however, would place Britain near the bottom of the list. Much would depend upon the base period adopted, the length of the period chosen, the goods included and their relative weights in the index. If frequent tea-breaks and other manifestations of disguised leisure are regarded as *goods* – and economics suggests they be so regarded – their conceivable quantification and inclusion in any index of output per capita might go some way to enhance Britain's comparative performance.

ups and down of the indices that we fail to raise our sights to the larger issues that confront us. Continuously arguing about and tinkering with the economic engine, we have only afterthoughts to spare for the rapid and visible changes taking place about us. In the event, there is no general awareness among the public of the range of significant social choices facing it.

Admittedly the economic engine does not turn very smoothly, but the trouble is not that satisfactory living standards are in jeopardy. The trouble is an incipient source of instability that was commonly referred to as 'the revolution of rising expectations'. This postwar phenomenon, however, is universal and has been responsible for the wage-push inflation that is afflicting all the industrial nations in varying degrees, not least Great Britain – notwithstanding which the quaint notion persists that the sovereign remedy for all our economic troubles, including inflation, is that of faster economic growth.

And misled by, or heedless of, this transparent economic fallacy, successive governments, in a bid for electoral support, have gone out of their way to implant expectations of continuously rising living standards. Having assiduously sown the seeds of rising expectations for more of 'the good things in life', we perforce reap the harvest of rising wage claims and rising prices. The resulting slow but uninterrupted inflation over the last half century or so has itself imparted to the economy a psychological momentum: workers, managers, bankers, professional men, shareholders, all anticipate rising incomes and prices to continue over the future notwithstanding anything governments may do.

II

For all that, the belief persists that faster economic growth is the solution of last resort to our chronic economic infirmities. If only we can somehow get Britain 'moving' fast enough, inflation would cease to plague us and the balance of trade would return to equilibrium. Indeed there is a two-way misconception inherent in the current views of the major political parties: (1) faster economic growth will enable us to overcome both rising prices and insufficient exports, and (2) any success in increasing exports or in restraining prices improves our overall growth performance. Thus an increase in exports appears both as a precondition and also as an effect of faster economic growth. For such economic relationships there is no economic warrant (see Appendix A).

This is the circle of reasoning within which we have been confined during the postwar period and which is predominant in official quarters. It is a circle of reasoning that seems to leave us little choice. We appear to be caught in a treadmill, wherein we must press harder if we are to 'keep up in the race', or even to survive. Yet, if the truth must be told, there is no economic warrant for such constricting beliefs. We have only ourselves to blame if our no-nonsense patriots have mesmerised us over the years into this unrelenting frame of mind.

With the rapid growth in the popular channels of communication it is more true than ever before that the sheer weight of reiteration rather than the power of reason influences the attitude of the public. A simple term such as 'growth potential' is loaded with compulsion: it suggests that waste is incurred whenever we fail, as invariably we do, to realise this potential growth. It is an apt term for the technocratic view of things that envisages the country as some sort of vast power-house with every grown man and woman a potential unit of input to be harnessed to a generating system from which flows this vital stuff called industrial output. And since this stuff can be measured statistically as GNP (Gross National Product), it follows that the more of it the better. Viewed as power-houses for producing GNP, certain countries appear to perform better than Britain. It is obvious, therefore, that we must make every endeavour to catch up. Moreover, other countries use more engineers and more PhDs per million of population than we do. Also they have a higher productivity. It follows that we *need* x per cent more engineers and y per cent more PhDs. To continue, steel output could, if we tried hard, rise to z million tons by the year 2000, as much as is used per capita in the US today. In consequence, we *need* to expand steel capacity at w per cent per annum. Again, in order for every family in Britain to have its own motor-car by 1995, we need to expand the motor-car industry at v per cent per annum. With such 'needs of industry' to be met we shall require increased commercial transport and, therefore, increased imports of fuel. Extrapolating the demand for electricity to the end of the century, we find it can be met only by expanding capacity by 40 per cent, which requires £30 billion of new investment. Consequently we *need* to work harder in order to pay for our *needs*. And so we go on, slipping from implicit choices to explicit imperatives.

What choice have we but to return to the treadmill?

This is a sad state for any nation to be in, and in an affluent society surpassingly strange: to have come this far into the twentieth century with economists interpreting the alleged increase in our real income as 'enrichment' or, more sagaciously, as 'an extension of the area of choice', and then to be told almost daily that we have no choice; that if we are to pay our way in the world we must work ever harder. This is enough surely to tax the credulity of any being whose judgement has not yet been swept away by torrents of economic exhortation.

But of course we have a choice, a wide range of choice! One of the main purposes of this volume is to uncover the kinds of choices that face us, or any modern community, and to make it apparent that the so-called policy of economic growth as popularly understood is hardly more than a policy of drifting quickly – of snatching at any technological innovation that proves marketable with scant respect for the social consequences.

In the formulation of the ends of economic policy the word *need* is not to be invoked. Markets do not *need* to expand – although, of course, businessmen dearly like to see them expand (whether through increasing per capita income, increasing domestic population or increased immigration). It is quite possible to arrange things so as to produce a good deal fewer gadgets and instead to enjoy more leisure. And, although blasphemous to utter, it is also possible to train fewer scientists and engineers without our perishing from the face of the earth. Nor do we *need* to capture world markets in the hope of being able to lower costs; or to lower costs in the hope of capturing world markets. We can, while acting as rational beings, deliberately choose to reduce our foreign trade and in some lines, therefore, to produce smaller quantities at a somewhat higher cost.

We can cut down on newspaper advertisement and conserve forest-lands[2] – a thought which raises the question: why are such choices not offered to us? A short answer is that the market is a low-cost mechanism of choice only for 'private' goods such as cars, watches, wallpaper and thimbles. Goods which simultaneously benefit a large number of people – so-called 'collective goods' such as parks, street lighting, drains, museums, monuments – present difficulties in the decisions for producing them and, once produced, in pricing their benefits to the public. For lack of an effective mechanism of public choice, decisions about the creation of collective

---

[2] It has been estimated that each Sunday issue of the *New York Times* devours the equivalent of 150 acres of forest. If there were some institutional mechanism offering readers the alternative choice, one Sunday at least, of a jointly held area of 150 acres of forest-land for their future recreation, they might well choose it.

goods tend to be made by governments which, in deference to the taxpayer, are generally guided by inapplicable commercial principles.

We can even decide to reduce the strains of competition and opt for an easier life. All these choices and many others can be translated into perfectly practicable alternatives whenever public opinion is ready to consider them. And I have no objection to our bright young men dubbing all suggested alternatives to the sweat-and-strain doctrine as 'irresponsible' provided they agree to use the word *want* instead of *need*. This simple switch of words will serve to remind us that policies radically different from those we habitually pursue are actually open to us all the time – though some people may well feel uncertain of, or disapprove of, some of their consequences.

III

Appendix A, on the balance of payments, is written for the reader who is still the victim of the common but vague notion that the so-called pressures of world competition virtually compel us to treat economic growth, and therefore investment in plant and equipment, as a top priority.

It may be omitted on the first reading, however, as it forms something of a digression from the mainstream of the argument. Needless to say, my sympathies are with the ordinary citizen who can hardly fail to be influenced by the disproportionate attention paid to foreign trade, who is subjected mercilessly to fallacious official pronouncements about the importance of working harder if we are 'to pay our way in the world', or for whom it is laid down that unless we grow faster we shall run further into international debt.

Misconceptions such as these render the public that much more vulnerable to the monotonous chorus of the established enlightenment to the effect that we have no choice but to thrust ahead at all cost. They make the public more resigned, therefore, to bearing with the proliferation of disamenities and hazards that have resulted from its tacit acceptance of wholly commercial criteria now in favour – currently sanctified in Britain by frequent invocation of the euphemism, 'the enterprise culture'.

3 Choice in Economic Policy

I

In the light of the preceding remarks let us reconsider the question of emphasis among the three components of long-term economic policy:

(1) *Economic Growth*. Though no economist who has studied the relation between economics and social welfare would endorse a policy of economic growth without an embarrassing amount of qualification, the profession as a whole behaves as if, on balance, it was a good thing. This attitude may spring from the impatience with quasi-philosophical enquiries that unavoidably call into question the usefulness of much of the highly skilled economic research currently undertaken. But there is room also for rationalisation. One of the more obvious pretexts for pressing on regardless is the existence of poverty in the greater part of the world: in Asia, in Africa, and in large parts of South America. There are pockets of degrading poverty even within the wealthy countries, though, as indicated earlier, their continuation may be attributed ultimately to political prejudices, not to economic necessity.[1]

Now if the rich countries, in response to a moral challenge, sought to convert themselves into an arsenal to provision the hungry areas of Asia and Africa, a case could be made for retaining economic growth as the chief goal of economic policy for some considerable time. But though magniloquence on the foreign aid theme marks all fitting occasions, the scale of such aid to poor countries in the postwar period is more suggestive, to use Professor Bauer's words, of 'conscience money' than of moral commitment. Bearing in mind that the total aid

---

[1] If within these wealthy countries the public conscience is unperturbed by the existence of a small minority of very poor people, many of whom are too old or too sick to take care of themselves, we might as well admit it. It is hypocrisy to pretend that the only way to help them is to create more wealth by growing faster when, in fact, the share of the underprivileged minority in the annual increment of output is negligible.

provided by any one of the industrialised countries seldom exceeds one per cent of its GNP, one has to reject this rationalisation out of hand.

The belief that only a faster economic growth will enable any country to 'pay its way in the world', or that faster growth generates more exports, hardly stands up to analysis, as indicated earlier.

We fall back then on the more popular and explicit belief that a per capita rise in real income is a good thing in itself; that in expanding the range of opportunities for ordinary people it increases their welfare. It will not, however, be difficult to uncover serious weaknesses in this common presumption, enough at any rate to warrant a conclusion that economic growth *per se* is a component of policy on which the least emphasis should be placed if we are interested primarily in social welfare.

Indices of economic growth may measure, in a rough sort of way, the increase in a country's gross productive power. But no provision is made in such indices for the 'negative goods' that are also being increased; that is, for the increasing burden of disamenities in the country. Nor can they reveal certain imponderable but none the less crucial consequences associated with the indiscriminate pursuit of technological progress, about which much will be said in Part VII. Indeed, the adoption of economic growth as a primary aim of policy, whether it is urged upon us as a moral duty to the rest of the world or as a duty to posterity, or as a condition of survival, seems on reflection as likely to add at least as much 'ill-fare' as welfare to society. Certainly there can be no purely economic justification for a policy of growth *per se*. The simple view that it 'enriches' society, or that it expands the range of choice open to mankind, stands up neither to argument nor to the facts of common experience – unless, of course, words such as 'enrich' or 'choice-expansion' are made to carry the same meaning as an increase of productive potential which is, roughly, what the index of productivity seeks to measure.

If, however, we are concerned with social welfare in the ordinary sense, the only legitimate procedure is to consider consequences of each and every economic reorganisation entailed by the growth process, in the endeavour to determine which, on balance, are beneficial and which are not. It may justly be protested that this is impracticable; that we cannot foretell the consequences, tangible and intangible, of the economic and social reorganisations resulting from a succession of interdependent technological innovations. However, we can make some attempt to sort things out. Thus, we put aside until later the more general reflections on certain potent, albeit intangible, factors. In the meantime we consider the sorts of welfare criteria by which economists have sought to justify the adoption of one policy as against alternative policies. The scope for such criteria is admittedly restricted, as we shall presently see, but the notions on which they are raised help to orient our thinking. Moreover, in circumstances where their application may be admitted, they can be very revealing. In particular, they enable us to point up some of the chief sources of 'ill-fare' that remain uncorrected under present institutions.

Indeed, we might go so far as to suggest that economic growth *per se* should be jettisoned as an independent goal of policy. For if we are concerned primarily with social welfare, those forms of economic growth that meet our welfare criteria will in any case be approved and adopted, the remainder being rejected: thus, sources of 'worthwhile' economic growth will continue to be sought after.

II

(2) *A more equal distribution of real income* has long been recognised by Western societies as one of the chief aims of economic policy. While, in general, any change in the pattern of prices – prices of goods and/or of productive services – makes some people better and others worse off, the most effective short-run method for redistributing real income is the levying of highly progressive income taxes and capital taxes, while making freely available to all the greater number of services provided by the government.

On the assumption that the structure of ability in the UK is more equally distributed than the structure of disposable incomes, policies for expanding educational opportunities have long-run effects in equalising earning power. Since much has already been done in Britain along these lines, it would be useful, before moving on, to take stock of our present position.

The official statistics available, however, are unreliable in so many aspects that any conclusion about the trend of income distribution over the last two decades must be treated with a degree of caution that effectively forbids any presumption one way or the other. The common impression that there is greater social and economic equality today than there was, say, in the thirties is formed from several developments. (a) The extension to every employed person since 1948 of national insurance and the provision of a national health service covering every person in the country. Today about 40 per cent of the

Government's current expenditure is on social services, compared with about a quarter in 1920; and this over a period that has seen public expenditure increase from 20 per cent of the net national expenditure to something approaching 50 per cent. (b) A doubling in the average standard of living since the war – much of this economic gain taking tangible shape as a widespread ownership of consumer durables such as motor-cars, washing machines, television sets, refrigerators, vacuum cleaners and the like. (c) The maintenance during the postwar period until about 1980 of a high level of employment with unusually good opportunities for unskilled and juvenile labour – an era that seems to be coming to a close. (d) A gradual extension to all social groups in the community of higher education over the last four decades.

For all that, existing inequality of wealth still appears quite striking. The top 5 per cent still takes about a quarter of the national income, and about two-thirds of the total income from property. None the less, the inspiration towards a greater degree of equalisation does not, or should not, draw its strength only from a sense of unfairness or envy on contemplating the figures at the top end of the scale. After all, one can envisage a society having a small proportion of very rich families, withal a comfortable standard of living for the remainder.

This is not the condition in Britain, however. Despite the extension of welfare services and the increase in pensions and unemployment benefit since the war, the position at the lower end of the scale is anything but reassuring. The official income figures are not very helpful since the breakdown is by person and not by family, and many of the poor do not earn any income in the official sense.

Putting this hard-core poverty into a special category since, in the absence of direct concern by the state, it is not likely to disappear of itself over the foreseeable future, and turning to the remainder of the community, one might hazard the guess that the movement towards increasing equality will continue for some time as the advantages of being born into wealth are increasingly offset by the educational opportunities being opened to young people in every social and income group. The one major contingency that can upset these sanguine expectations is that of an unemployment crisis within the next few years caused by the rapid adoption of automation in industry and commerce.[2] Looking beyond such a crisis and farther into the

---

[2] Since there is a prevalent belief that technological innovation cannot cause unemployment, Appendix B is devoted to a cursory analysis of this possibility.

future when such educational policies as we are now pursuing will have established a thoroughgoing meritocracy – one in which those born into talent (instead of wealth) will inherit top positions, and those found wanting will be relegated to the bottom of the social hierarchy – it cannot be foreseen whether disposable incomes and wealth will be more equally distributed than they are today. But there is no reason to suppose that the distributional structure of gross income, once it comes to reflect the distribution of native ability, will be any less unequal than it is under the existing system.

III

(3) Leaving out the problem of hard-core poverty in Britain, one should not expect any great accession of social welfare from attempts to accelerate the trend towards a more equal distribution of disposable income and wealth. In contrast, one may anticipate immediately perceptible benefits from the introduction of legislation to curb the chief sources of disamenity that afflict our daily lives. In order, however, to make a respectable economic case for such legislation, we need first to make explicit the economist's notion of an ideal allocation of resources – ideal, however, only within a restrictive framework which we adopt provisionally. It will then become apparent that private enterprise, working within the framework of current institutions at least, has no tendency to bring about this ideal allocation.

Private enterprise, when working smoothly, does have the virtue of using variations in prices and outputs to match supplies to amounts demanded; the smoother it is working the faster are shortages and surpluses eliminated. The mechanism is simple: if a shortage appears in any good its price tends to rise, so acting to ration the limited supplies. But the profit of producing that good also rises, which brings about an expansion of its output and overcomes the initial shortage. If, on the other hand, there is a surplus of any good on the market, the profit on its production falls, which brings about a reduction of output, thus eliminating the initial surplus. A good deal of so-called economic planning does no more than utilise methods for anticipating future excess demands and supplies in the various sectors of the economy, and, where necessary, take measures to reduce the consequent periods of maladjustment. This is an extremely useful task, yet a subsidiary one insofar, at least, as it is more desirable that the economy should move in the right direction – towards an 'ideal' or 'optimal' allocation – than that it should merely move more quickly and, possibly, in the wrong direction. At any rate, the principles on which an improvement in resource-allocation may be determined are logically prior to, and may be treated in separation from, the question of speed of adjustment. It will be simpler, therefore, if we put aside this speed-of-adjustment aspect of the problem, in order to focus attention on the allocation problem – on the 'optimal' set of outputs and prices; those towards which, on broadly accepted economic criteria, the economic system 'ought' to be moving at any moment.

The principle that a good should be produced if, and only if, its value to society exceeds its costs of production suggests that production of any good should be expanded until its value (which declines with the increase in output) is no longer greater than its 'marginal cost' – the addition to total cost incurred in producing one unit more of the good in question. The principle thus extended is commonly known as *marginal-cost pricing* since (if the units of output are small enough) the 'optimal' output is reached by producing to the point at which the market price is equal to marginal cost.

If the reader accepts that – within the standard framework of economic assumptions – an optimal or ideal output is one that meets the marginal-cost pricing rule he can move on to Part II wherein those additional social costs that escape the economic calculus are brought into the picture.

Readers who are uncertain or unconvinced of the economic rationale of marginal-cost pricing may turn first to Appendix D.

PART II

....

Market Failure

4 The Spillover Enemy

I

Economists are as aware as most people that the operations of an industry, or the activities of ordinary persons, may have a variety of important effects on the profits of other industries or on the welfare of other people, which effects are partly or wholly disregarded by the industry, or persons, generating them. Moreover, the effects in question can confer benefits on other industries, or persons, or else inflict losses on them. Owing to the current state of technology and its development, however, these repercussions are more likely to be damaging than otherwise.

They are popularly referred to as 'spillover effects', or simply 'spillovers', and the economist is concerned with them simply because the price system fails to take account of their effects on the profits and on the welfare of others. They are not included in the costs of production of those industries that generate them. Neither then do they enter the set of prices that would be thrown up by perfectly competitive markets. And since prices are the signals by which the resources of the economy are allocated, a failure of the signals leads to a failure in the allocation of resources.

Before elaborating on the significance of spillovers, however, it is necessary to distinguish them clearly from the familiar economic repercussions that arise from the essential interdependence of all prices and quantities of goods, which interdependence is a characteristic of any well-functioning market system. In principle, the distinction is straightforward: within an interdependent economic system, every effect – every bit of good or 'bad' generated – registers and enters into the set of market prices. Only the effects from spillovers escape capture by the resulting set of prices.

To illustrate the interdependence of a segment of the economy in the *absence* of spillovers, we can imagine a spontaneous increase in the public's consumption of liquid milk. Within a short period, the

22

increased quantity of milk produced will tend to raise its price. But a rise in the cost of liquid milk will raise the price of butter, so reducing the demand for butter which, in turn, will act to increase the demand and price of margarine and other fats that are substitutes for butter. Furthermore, the prices of beef, leather and other goods will be affected as the economic system adjusts itself to the initial growth in the demand for milk.

The dairy farmers, however, ignore all such repercussions that arise from their endeavours to increase the amount of milk produced. And, indeed, so long as all the relevant economic data enter the calculus, as they do in a well-functioning market, no other action is called for, or warranted. Generally, every initial change in consumer demand, or any change in technology, produces innumerable adjustments, large and small, throughout the whole economy, adjustments that are wholly warranted under a well-functioning and competitive market system.

In contrast, however, and as already indicated, spillovers are distinguished by their being, unwarrantably, left out of the economic calculus from the start. Of course, it happens innocently enough. There is no malice aforethought. For example, machines properly employed to produce specific kinds of goods may also produce incidentally some quite unwanted side effects. But whereas the goods that are purposely produced by the industry have a price, or positive market value, the incidental 'bads' that are unintentionally generated do not have a *negative* market value as they should. In other words, while the recipient of the manufactured goods is willing to pay for them, the recipient of the incidental 'bad' that is also produced in the industrial process receives no compensation from the industry for having to put up with it. The damage suffered goes unrecorded. And insofar as it remains unrecorded, the computed value of the net aggregation of goods produced over the year – say the net national income – will overstate the true value. To calculate the true value we should have to subtract from this computed value that sum of money which would exactly compensate those who suffer from the incidental damages.

This sort of disjuncture or 'market failure' is at the heart of the matter. A simple illustration would be that of a manufacturer of vacuum cleaners whose factory chimney produces a great deal of smoke. Proper economic accounting would require him to calculate not only the value of the goods (the vacuum cleaners) produced, but also the value of the bads (the damage caused by his smoke). Certainly this smoke damage suffered by others constitutes a cost to society. It follows, then, that the value to society of the complete range of his products – in this case, the vacuum cleaners along with the smoke damage – will be lower than the market value of the vacuum cleaners alone by the cost of the smoke damage inflicted on others.

If now the manufacturer is compelled to pay compensation for the damage caused in operating his factory[1] or, alternatively, to pay for the installation of effective anti-smoke devices, he would have to reduce his output of vacuum cleaners. For only by restricting their sale will their price become high enough to cover the resulting rise in unit costs.[2]

II

Why is it that the notion of spillovers has not been brought more forcibly to the attention of the public? There may be more than one reason, and it will be revealing to discuss those which come to mind.

First, the response of the growth-minded business economists to the allegation of damaging spillovers is to counter with the assertion that there are also many favourable spillovers. A perfume factory, for example, may sweeten the air in the vicinity. Bees raised for honey may fertilise the fruit trees of a neighbouring orchard. The construction of a dam might improve the fishing upstream. The value conferred on others by these beneficial spillovers would then have to be added to the market value of the commercial products in order to obtain their true value to society.[3]

The argument as it stands is certainly valid. But the extent and magnitude of such beneficial spillovers make no difference whatsoever to the main argument. For whether or not the economy is adjusted to the incidence of favourable spillovers, it still follows that

[1] The idea suggests an alternative method to that of *subtracting* the costs of the damage from the market value of the vacuum cleaners: namely, that of *adding* these costs to the commercial costs of production in order to obtain the true or *social* costs of production. Either method of correction will do – though, obviously, we cannot employ both methods simultaneously. In the following pages, we shall favour the latter method as, perhaps, being more direct for most applications.

[2] If the cost of anti-smoke installation were an overhead cost, one that did not vary with the number of vacuum cleaners produced, the manufacturer's unit cost would remain unchanged, and he would have no incentive to reduce his output. His profit, however, would have fallen by the cost of the anti-smoke device. Allowing that the vacuum-cleaner industry were competitive, a number of manufacturers would have to drop out before those remaining would again be able to make normal profits. Again, therefore, the output of vacuum cleaners would have to be reduced.

[3] Alternatively, the value of the incidental benefits enjoyed by others could be *subtracted* from the commercial costs to yield the true or social cost. As for the *outputs* of industries having favourable spillovers, by symmetrical reasoning they should be expanded.

outputs have to be contracted in those industries producing damaging spillovers.[4] The extent of the resulting improvement in allocation depends entirely on the incidence and magnitude of the damaging spillovers that are corrected in this way, quite independently of whether corrections are made for the favourable spillovers.

Secondly, the academic economist tends to concentrate largely on spillovers within an inter-industry context, the favoured examples being those spillovers produced by one firm or industry that fall on another firm or industry. The reason for this bias may be historical. The originator of the idea, Alfred Marshall, confined himself to the beneficial effect conferred on an industry as a result of an additional firm entering that industry. In any case, these inter-industry spillovers are easier to calculate than those which fall upon the public at large, and schemes for mutual adjustments are more feasible as between organised groups than as between an unorganised public and the industry in question.

Thirdly, the academic economist, until very recently at least, regarded these spillovers as only one among several factors that prevented the emergence of some kind of ideally functioning economy. What is more, he tended to look upon them more as an obstacle to theoretical generalisation than as a social menace. Familiarity with the spillover concept, and its frequent treatment in the professional literature, may have imparted a feeling that the matter was well under control. Thus many economists continued to ignore events taking shape around them, immersing themselves instead in the intellectual fascination of complex mathematical models or the problems involved in the general solutions of optimal systems.

Fourthly, there is the undoubted difficulty in measuring the kinds of damage that are suffered by the public at large. The smoky factory chimney is so popular a classroom example of spillover suffered by the public simply because it appears to limit itself to the dirt spread within the locality. The additional costs of keeping clothes clean in the smoke-polluted area can be approximately estimated, and added to the unit commercial cost of the product. Again, the costs of water pollution by one or more factories are also amenable to calculation whenever the authorities have estimates of consequent losses suffered by other industries making use of the same body of water. But all too many of the major social afflictions such as industrial noise, dirt,

---

[4] There may also be cases in which both positive and negative spillovers are generated in the production of the one sort of good. The effects will then partly cancel out, leaving a net negative or net positive effect in the calculation.

stench, ugliness, urban sprawl and other features of modern living that jar the nerves or impair the health – to say nothing of ecological damage or global peril – are difficult to measure and to allocate among the different sources: which is no reason, of course, for treating them with resignation.

This last sentence above should serve to assure that the reader is not misled by some of the homely examples used earlier into believing that spillovers are not among the more important problems facing society. Every environmental problem today, indeed every ecological problem, may properly be regarded as an example of (uncorrected) spillover effects. Moreover, the economic literature on spillovers throws much-needed light on the feasibility or otherwise of the various remedial strategies.

III

A final explanation of why the concept of spillover effects has not, until very recently at least, been brought more forcibly to the attention of the public and of governments is the conviction among the pro-market school of economists, whose influence is (at the time of writing) on the ascendant, that there is generally no good case for governments to take action. Given time enough for private economic arrangements to be made, things will sort themselves out: economic resources will tend to move toward a satisfactory allocation. Government intervention, on the other hand, will (such economists allege) dampen enterprise, reduce efficiency and extend bureaucracy.

Since this conviction that, in general, competitive markets are better able to cope with spillovers than are governments is widely held among economists and Western governments, it warrants more extended treatment.

A cynical view is that the crux of the pro-market economist's argument takes its rationale from that of the protection racket. By paying some agreed sum to the criminal gang the potential victim is left unmolested – an arrangement which has the virtue of leaving both him and the gang better off than if, instead, he refused to pay up. The private arrangements that are made to deal with spillover effects follow the same logic and, apparently, produce the same felicitous outcome. Thus, my neighbour and I may both be made better off if I am able to bribe him to refrain from using his diesel power-saw on Sunday afternoons. Again, the owner of a plant that uses the waters of a stream to produce soft drinks might well attempt to bribe a corporation that proposes to establish a soap-producing factory upstream to refrain from pouring its effluent into the otherwise clear waters. Such arrangements, if carried out and maintained, can properly be viewed as economic improvements inasmuch as all parties concerned are made better off by such voluntary agreements than they would be in the absence of the agreements.

The pro-market economist is always good enough to recognise the possibility of some difficulty here which, not surprisingly however, he neatly turns to his advantage. In the simple examples above, it was seemingly practicable for the victim to buy himself relief from the nuisance or prevention of the damage. It becomes less practicable as the numbers involved increase. For example, it may well be that the largest sum each family in the neighbourhood of an airport would be willing to pay to induce the airport authority to site the airport elsewhere would amount, in aggregate, to a sum of money that is more than enough to compensate the airport authority for the anticipated loss in moving to the next-best site. Indeed, this sum could be very much larger than any conceivable gain the airport authority could hope to secure over the future. Certainly, then, an economic improvement would ensue provided the transaction took place.

But the initiative for bringing about such a mutually beneficial arrangement may not exist in the circumstances. And even if it did, the total cost of estimating and ensuring a fair contribution from each of a score or more thousand families could be prohibitive. In the event, such potential economic improvements would not in fact be realised, and the airport would remain on its existing site.

True enough, agrees our pro-market friend. But that is exactly how it ought to be. For those costs of estimating and securing a fair contribution from each of these families, and also the costs of negotiating with the airport authorities, are not by any means simply book-keeping or imaginary costs. They are real costs in that they entail time, effort and resources. If, therefore, they were to be incurred in making effective this arrangement, their magnitude would swamp the potential gains from moving the airport to another site. The result would be a net economic loss.

Let us formalise the logic of the above example by using the term *transactions costs* to comprehend all the costs incurred by the parties concerned in negotiating, implementing and, if necessary, maintaining a mutually beneficial arrangement.

Now, in the complete *absence* of transactions costs, the existence of any uncorrected negative spillover would always offer opportunities for mutually beneficial arrangements. Thus with zero transactions costs, enlightened self-interest would suffice to deal with all spillovers by bringing about voluntary re-arrangements that are effectively economic improvements. And in such a hypothetical zero-transactions-costs world, the magnitude of the benefits, shared as they are among all parties to the new arrangement, may be referred to simply as the *net benefits*.

It follows, therefore, that only where the magnitude of these net benefits exceeds that of the transactions costs can a mutually beneficial arrangement result from voluntary agreements in dealing with a spillover.

According to pro-market argument, the world we live in is such that wherever a large number of people are involved in an endeavour to curtail the damaging effects of some negative spillover this crucial condition is (alas!) not met. Transactions costs prove to be too heavy, and there is then no economic warrant for taking any action. This is hard doctrine – which is perhaps why economists take joy in articulating it. Yet it is surely unassailable – at least it is if we go along with the implicit premises of the argument which, as we shall see in the following chapter, turn on a legal foundation.

In the meantime, let us give brief consideration to at least three objections to the pro-market response to spillovers.

First, most of the larger spillovers affecting neighbourhood amenity and health are suffered by the lower-income groups and the poor; those in fact who are least able to move away to a more desirable residential area.

The social injustice that may arise from general acceptance of pro-market doctrine may be further compounded by social inequity. For even where voluntary arrangements are economically feasible (where transactions costs are low enough), it would seem to be quite unfair that victims of spillover effects should be made either to suffer the full effects of the damage wrought on their lives or property, or else to limit the damage by paying to the perpetrators of it an appropriate sum.[5] Admittedly, the damage inflicted on others is incidental rather

---

[5] Not all adverse spillovers are to be regarded as inequitable. An inevitable characteristic in the post-industrial countries, where material values predominate and where inordinate expectations are encouraged, is dissatisfaction with one's estate and envy of others. Such envy of others' status, achievements or property does come under the definition of spillovers. But it is hard to sympathise with those prone to this vice to the extent of proposing they be compensated for the mortification they suffer as a result of the success of others.

The contribution an economist can make to society's welfare should be guided in some measure by the values common to that society. Utilitarianism may have to defer to ethics.

than deliberate. But then – and this is another objection – there is no incentive under this proposed *status quo* for those who are responsible for the spillovers in the first place to seek ways to minimise them. Quite the contrary, for since the payment that can be exacted will depend upon the extent of the nuisance or damage, there is something to be gained in surreptitiously increasing it.

Finally, as will be made clearer in the following chapter, the transactions costs involved in reaching agreements to curb spillover effects within the market sector of the economy can be unnecessarily heavy. If this is the case, then within that sector, and pending new institutional mechanisms, many potential economic improvements continue (unnecessarily) to remain unrealised.

Bearing in mind these objections to the market solution to spillovers, we shall now move on to explore two alternative but related approaches to a more comprehensive solution to spillover problems: (1) the scope for enactment of what I shall call 'amenity rights' which is discussed in the next chapter, and (2) the extension to the environment of the concept of 'separate facilities' which is the subject of Chapter 6.

5 The Institution of Amenity Rights

I

The competitive market has long been recognised as an inexpensive mechanism for allocating goods and resources over time with tolerable speed and efficiency. Yet once the production of *bads* (noxious spillovers) has begun increasingly to accompany the production and consumption of goods, it is necessary to face the fact that there is a serious failure of the market mechanism. It should be emphasised, however, that the failure is not to be attributed to the market itself, but to the legal framework within which it operates. In particular, we must remind ourselves that what constitutes a cost to a commercial enterprise depends also upon the existing law. If, for example, the law countenanced slave labour, the cost of that labour would be equal to the costs involved in either buying or capturing a person and of maintaining him thereafter at a standard necessary to enable him to discharge his 'duties'.

How then may the law be altered to cope with those spillovers that are most responsible for spreading disamenity?

As far as private industry is concerned, the alteration required of the existing law is clear. For private enterprise, when it troubles to justify itself, does so on the grounds that the value of what it produces exceeds the cost it incurs: in short, benefits exceed losses. But what count as costs under the law and what *ought* to be counted as costs is just what is in issue.

A great impetus would doubtless take place in the expansion of the X industries if, for example, they were allowed freely to appropriate the land or property belonging to people within the Y group. Even if this licence extended to them were bought off by the Y group, the X industries would be richer by the amount paid to them. And, incidentally, one could be sure that if, after the elapse of some years, the government sought to revoke this privilege accorded to the X industries, there would be an outcry followed by a determined campaign alleging that such arbitrary infringement of their rights would inevitably stifle progress, jeopardise employment and, of course, lose the country valuable export markets.

Although the example is far-fetched it is entirely fitting. For private property in this country has been regarded as inviolate for centuries. Even during a national emergency, a government appropriating private property is obliged to compensate the owners. It may be alleged that the compensation paid was too much or too little. But it would not occur to the government simply to confiscate private property.

In proposing an extension of this principle of compensation, we have to bear in mind significant facts about allocation. Clean air, clean water, quiet, are indeed scarce goods, far scarcer than they were before World War II, and sure to become scarcer in the foreseeable future. There is no economic warrant, therefore, for allowing them to be treated either by producers or consumers as though they were free goods – that is, as though they were so abundant that their depletion would make no difference to anyone.

Indeed, if we could imagine a world so fashioned that, say, clean air and quiet took on a physically identifiable form, one that allowed them to be transferred between people, we should be able to observe whether a man's quantum of either had been appropriated or damaged by someone else, and if so we should be able to institute legal proceedings. The fact that the universe has not been so accommodating in these respects does not in any way detract from the principles governing the allocation of scarce resources. One has but to imagine a country in which men were legally invested with property rights to privacy, quiet, and clean air – simple things, but for many indispensable to the enjoyment of life – to recognise the extent of the compensatory sums that would perforce have to be paid to them by modern industries. Many industries would have to close down or else to operate at levels below those which would prevail in the absence of such legislation. And the magnitude of such compensatory payments would also act as an incentive for industry and transport to seek technical and other ways of reducing their spillovers.

In the particular example used in the preceding chapter, the airport authorities would be compelled, under our proposed law, fully to compensate all victims of aircraft noise in the vicinity. In order to remain viable, the airport may have to cut down the number of flights, to require that aircraft be fitted with noise-reducing devices, to ban all night flights, or to do all three. Even these measures may not suffice, and the airport may have to close down – there being no way it can adjust so that its revenues cover all its social costs. Under the new law, then, the airport would be revealed as uneconomic.

II

The consequence of legal recognition of such rights in one form or another – let us call them *amenity rights* – would be far-reaching. The use of so humble an implement as the motorised lawn-mower, leaf-blower, chain-saw or any other modern garden accessory would come into conflict with such rights. The noise produced in using one or other of these motorised garden implements is generally heard by scores of other families who, of course, may also be enthusiastic gardeners. If they are all satisfied with the current situation, or could come to agreement with one another, well and good. But once amenity rights were enacted, no person would be liable at any time to suffer unwanted noise against their will nor, for that matter, any spillover effects of another's activity.

It may well be that the sum which would adequately compensate the victim of the noise or other spillover (always assuming he tells the truth) would exceed that which the offender is able to afford. In such a case, the activity in question must be deemed uneconomic: the garden enthusiast would have to make do with a hand lawn-mower – at least until such time as manufacturers discovered means of effectively silencing the din. It is important to note, however, that the manufacturers would have the strongest incentive for investing in research for this purpose, for under the new legislation the degree of noise-elimination would be a big factor in its marketability.

Admittedly there would be difficulties wherever actual payments had to be made, say, to thousands of families disturbed by aircraft noise. Yet once the *principle* of amenity rights were legally recognised, a rough estimate of the magnitude of the aggregate of payments necessary to maintain the welfare of the number of families affected would be entered as a matter of course into the economic calculation. And unless these compensatory payments could also be covered by the proceeds of the airport authority (allowing for adjustments in number of flights, routes, times, etc.), there would be no *prima facie* economic case for maintaining the airport.[1]

---

[1] It can be argued that the victim of a spillover, instead of honestly estimating the minimum sum that would reconcile him to bearing with the nuisance, might submit a much higher sum and that, therefore, the aggregate social cost derived by consultation with the victims would be wholly unreliable. Exactly the same may be said of landowners whose consent is required in order to lay a railway line. And just as a body of law has evolved to determine just compensation for surrender of the rights of way, so will the courts discover ways of giving effect to citizens' rights under amenity legislation.

The concept of amenity rights can be brought into relation with traditional ideas about industrial expansion. From time to time the courts give voice to the doctrine that in the ordinary pursuit of industry a reasonable amount of inconvenience has to be borne with. The one defect of this otherwise judicious doctrine lies in the tacit acceptance that the costs of such inconveniences are to be borne by the victims. Where such inconveniences are slight, or of short duration, this tacit understanding can be justified: the costs of implementing amenity rights would exceed the small benefits. But in a world where the inconveniences caused by spillovers are becoming increasingly less bearable, legal recognition of amenity rights puts a new edge on the interpretation of the word 'reasonable'. Thus, if, by now having to include in its costs the sums necessary to compensate those suffering the inconvenience – or else to include additional expenses incurred in eliminating the inconvenience – an existing service cannot be profitably continued, the inconvenience caused has now to be deemed *unreasonable*. And there should be no difficulty in persuading the owners of the service in question that the incidental inconvenience generated is unreasonable since, under amenity legislation, they would be unable to cover their full costs.

A government may continue to claim that certain services, say, particular airline services, should be maintained in the national interest even though social costs cannot be covered by revenues. But it would now have to think twice before recourse to such facile formulae since it would be required by amenity legislation to vindicate its claim about the high value to the nation of such services by paying to the owners a direct subsidy to enable them to cover the full social costs.

III

At this stage it is important to make clear that two principles are served by amenity legislation, those of economy (discussed above) and equity. In the examples above, the principle of economy would be served provided only that the enterprise were compelled to include in its costs a sum equal to the required compensation for any (residual) disamenity – that is, even if the victims themselves received no compensation whatever. For this compensatory sum can properly be regarded as the relevant social value, or price, of the scarce resource – be the scarce resource quiet, or clean air or water – being used in the area: a scarce resource that, in the absence of legislation, would be treated as an abundant resource, or free good.

But insofar as such legislation also confers *amenity rights* on the citizen he is indeed entitled to compensation. Such entitlement serves the principle of equity. For the loss of welfare suffered by a citizen in consequence of the process of production (or consumption) of a good is clearly not of the citizen's making: he is but an unwitting victim of the activities of others.

It can, of course, be argued on economic grounds that arrangements for estimating and paying compensation can be costly. But the objection can only be tentative. Once such entitlements were legally established, the initial transactions costs would decline over time as experience brought into being appropriate institutions and procedures for estimating and distributing compensation.

What is of prior importance, however, is that the ethical and economic principles served by a bill of amenity rights be accepted by law in the first instance. Once accepted, it will not overtax the wit of man to devise the machinery necessary to implement the new legal rights. But there should be no doubt in our minds that such legislation would have the most drastic effects on private enterprise which, for too long, has been able to ignore an incalculable amount of overspill damaging the health and amenity of the public at large. As we are now aware, for many decades and without giving it a thought, private firms have been poisoning the air we breathe, polluting lakes and rivers with their effluents, and destroying the peace and quiet of millions with innovations that range from motorised garden implements to motorcycles, from transistors to private planes.

Placed in proper perspective, then, the proposal in this chapter has to be understood, not as an attack on the enterprise economy or on the competitive market, but as *a radical alteration of the legal framework within which private enterprise operates specifically in order to direct its drive and energy toward ends that accord more closely with the interests of society*. Indeed, such legislation would provide industry with the pecuniary incentive necessary to undertake continued research into methods of removing all potential and existing spillovers that afflict modern life.

IV

The social advantage of enacting amenity legislation is reinforced by a consideration of the regressive nature of the spillovers affecting our living conditions. Among the advantages of wealth are the opportunities for escape to more congenial environs. The richer a man, the wider his choice of neighbourhood and area. If the neighbourhood he lives in appears to be sinking in the scale of amenity, he can move to a quieter or cleaner area. If he has to be in the city occasionally, he can select a suitable town house, secluded perhaps, or made soundproof, and spend his leisure in the country or abroad. In contrast, the poorer a family, the smaller its opportunity for moving from its present locality. For all practical purposes it is 'stuck' in the area and must put up with whatever damage is inflicted upon it. And generalising from the experience of recent years, one may depend upon it that it will be the neighbourhoods of the working and lower-middle classes that will suffer most from the increased construction of highways, ring-roads, road-widening schemes, city beltways, and such development that tends to concentrate the traffic and thicken the pollution.

Thus the recognition of amenity rights would also have favourable redistributive effects on the welfare of society. It would promote not only a rise in the standards of the urban and suburban environment from which all would benefit, it would raise them most for lower income groups that have suffered more than others from unchecked 'development' since the fifties.

V

Finally, in any practical appraisal of this proposed legal innovation, we remind ourselves of the point made in the preceding chapter, that the magnitude of transactions costs in making new economic arrangements does, at present, build inertia into the *status quo*. To recapitulate briefly, the existence of net benefits from the curtailing of adverse spillovers is not, under the current dispensation, a sufficient condition for intervening in market solutions – as pointed out by pro-market economists. It is also necessary that the transactions costs incurred in making this potentially beneficial change be smaller than this calculated net benefit. In effect, such transactions costs appear to act as a barrier to economic improvements that could be made by removing or reducing spillovers.

But it is essential to understand, in this connection, that the effect of this transactions-cost barrier on economic activity depends directly upon the law's investiture of rights. Under existing laws, adherence to economic principles would clearly require a continuance of the *status quo* whenever transactions costs exceeded in magnitude the potential net social benefit calculated as the most the victims could pay to curtail spill over *minus* the market losses sustained in doing so. And, indeed, since under the existing law it is the victims of the spillovers who have to bear the transactions costs, they will not, in fact, be able to negotiate with the industry responsible if such costs exceed their anticipated net benefits from reducing the spillovers. In all such cases – and they are likely to be the important cases – the existing market solution continues to prevail.

The picture is quite different, however, if a bill of amenity rights were writ into the Constitution. For then these same transactions costs act, instead, as a barrier to the spillover-activity. True, where transactions costs are small relative to the net benefits of introducing the spillover-activity, the incentive to produce an optimal output will continue to exist, just as it would under the existing law.[2] But for those cases in which the transactions costs exceed the magnitude of those net benefits that are realised in an optimal position then – in direct contrast to the outcome under the existing law (no reduction whatever in the spillover activity) – no spillovers whatever will be generated for the simple reason that it will no longer be profitable for the industry to produce any of the output at all.

Since the transactions costs are likely to be relatively large for all environmental spillovers, which tend to affect large numbers of people or the public in general, the proposed change in the law is a radical one: *for the pattern of production of the whole economy will be very different according as the existing law or the amenity law prevails.* Under the existing law, it will tend to be uneconomic to curtail environmental spillovers – as, indeed, pro-market economists have argued. Under the proposed amenity law, in contrast, it will tend to be uneconomic to operate industries and generate environmental spillovers.

In sum, under existing laws the proliferation of adverse spillovers takes refuge behind the barrier of transactions costs. Under the proposed law, it is the citizens' amenity that is protected by this barrier.

Over time, of course, changes in population, in tastes and in technology may diminish some of the transactions costs and may raise the net benefits associated with optimal positions of industrial activities under either law. And wherever the latter exceed the former,

---

[2] Although, in the text, reference is usually made to an optimal *output*, an industry need not restrict itself to output changes, for it has recourse to other methods of reducing spillovers, such as moving its site or changing its technology. In general, it will find it less expensive to reduce spillovers by combining the different methods. (The economics student interested in the analysis is referred to my article, 'What is an Optimal Level of Pollution?', *Journal of Political Economy*, 1974.)

optimal arrangements will come into being. But the converse is just as likely. In a world where new environmental hazards come to light each year, therefore, there is nothing to be gained by delaying the introduction of amenity legislation.

It remains to remind ourselves that, whatever the outcome, only under the proposed amenity legislation is the equity principle met: the victims of spillover effects are adequately compensated.

VI

Before ending this chapter, we consider briefly the circumstances in which – for some time at least – complete prohibition of the spillover activity in question is the only prudent policy.

To be sure, an interesting outcome arising from the enactment of amenity rights would be the complete prohibition of each of a number of clearly defined disamenities in the absence of consent among all parties affected. It is this mutual consent that is the operative attribute. If, for example, the owner of a diesel-saw can afford to bribe all the families within earshot of his tree-sawing activities to consent to them, at least during certain hours, then each person would be made better off than he would be under a complete noise-prohibition. Again, if speed-boat enthusiasts could afford to bribe all those who objected to the disturbance not to invoke the law, all would be better off than if the ban against noise were enforced within the locality.

Thus, for those spillovers involving noise, visual disturbance or invasion of privacy, within a particular locality, a waiver of the relevant amenity rights contingent upon the consent of all affected citizens clearly entails an economic improvement. But there can be other sorts of spillovers for which such a consensus to waive the contingent prohibition does not confer an economic improvement.

First, there may be insufficient information on the range of consequences flowing from the spread of a particular spillover. A citizen who agrees to put up with this kind of spillover in return for a payment may be doing so in ignorance of the risk to which he exposes his person and his family and also an unknown number of people. For example, the unpleasantness he experiences inhaling a mixture of air and exhaust fumes could be only a fraction of the damage inflicted on his health and property. Similar remarks are pertinent to other forms of air pollution, to effluents poured into rivers and lakes, to nitrates in the soil, to the discharge of oil on the high seas, to the use of chemical fertilisers and pesticides and to the radioactive wastes of nuclear reactors.[3] In such cases, the immediate impact on his well-being may be slight compared with the increasing risk over time to his health and to his life. To add to the difficulty, an objective assessment of the risks may not be available at the time, even if he were able to evaluate them. (We shall return to this problem in Part VI.)

Secondly, there are many spillovers that are experienced not only by today's generation but also by future generations. Some of the effects mentioned above can be included also in this type of spillover. Other examples are the spillovers associated with mass tourism, the irrevocable destruction of places of rare beauty and magnificence. Not only is the present generation denied the opportunity of such enjoyment and solace, but so also are future generations. In such cases the state, in its role as custodian of the future, may be obliged to overrule the immediate interests of the existing generation.

---

[3] Wherever there is life, radioactive substances are absorbed into the biological cycle. Within hours of the depositing of radioactive wastes in water, the bulk of them can be found in living organisms. Plankton, algae and many sea animals have the power of concentrating these substances by a factor of a thousand, and in some cases even of a million. As one organism feeds on another, the radioactive materials climb up the ladder of life and find their way back to man. No chemical reaction, no physical interference, only the passage of time reduces the intensity of radiation once it has been set going.

6 The Introduction of Separate Areas

The most effective way of dealing with the riot of spillovers that have spread over the country since World War II, and one that underwrites other proposals, is the enactment of a comprehensive charter of amenity rights, all of them enforceable in the courts. Other than the two special categories mentioned in the preceding chapter for which complete prohibition is the only practical solution, no qualification need be admitted. Whatever the particular facts, the enactment of amenity rights will effectively protect the interests of those who suffer the disamenities produced by spillovers. And if, as suggested earlier, these rights are subject to a waiver-by-consent clause – allowing the victims of some local form of nuisance the option of agreeing to waive such rights in return for compensation or other arrangement – then all concerned are better off than if amenity rights were used to prohibit completely that particular nuisance.

Nor need there be any provision for those cases in which different people react differently to some feature. It may well be that some people have no objection to the noise of engines operated by others: they may even revel in them. It may also be the case that there are people so habituated to gaseous air that they would feel faint and dizzy when breathing fresh air in the country. And it is far from unlikely that the postwar period has spawned people so accustomed to the sound of radio and television that their nerves would be on edge if they remained long in quiet surroundings. Such people might well choose to take up residence along traffic-infested roads and to take their recreation along transistorised beaches. But whatever the facts, and however one judges the character of such people, wherever it was practical to implement the waiver-by-consent clause, economic improvements would be registered also in those cases in which the reactions of one group are the opposite of another group in the same area.

If, for example, half the people along a stretch of beach enjoyed the sound of transistors and the other half detested it, a decision could not be reached by voting as this would result in a tie. Once the law guarantees quiet, the transistor enthusiasts could try to purchase a licence to play their transistors from the other group. Certainly if the transistor fans were rich and the anti-transistor fans were poor, they would succeed in coming to an agreement, in which case everyone would be as well or better off than he would be if, instead, the complete prohibition remained in force.[1]

But we may be able to go one better. If, beginning from the arrangement just described, the stretch of beach were separated into two sections, one being set aside for the transistor fans, the other for the sole use of those who seek quiet, there would be a further economic improvement. The latter group would continue to enjoy peace and quiet, as they are entitled to under the amenity charter, whereas the transistor fans may now enjoy their transistors without being obliged to make any payments for the privilege.[2]

Thus, provided there is no feature requiring a uniform arrangement within the area, we can do better for the population in question by providing separate areas for groups with conflicting tastes or wants.

II

Familiar instances of already-existing separate-area or separate-facilities solutions include the provision of separate smoking and non-smoking compartments in railway coaches and, in some cinemas, smoking in the balcony but not in the stalls. Pedestrian pavements and, less commonly, bicycle paths can be placed in the same category. Other instances, some homely, some political, will come to mind. But wherever it is practicable, a separate-facilities solution increases social welfare beyond the level that can be reached by a common-to-all optimal arrangement within a single area.

The economic advantage is buttressed by two others:

(1) In a swiftly changing world, traditions have no time to take root.

---

[1] If, however, the initial situation was such that those who enjoyed their transistors were few in number or, on the average, poorer than the anti-noise group, they would be unable to reach agreement. In that case, the existing prohibition has to be regarded as optimal, there being no possible pecuniary arrangement that would make them all better off.

[2] A more formal analysis for the economics student will be found in my article, 'Pareto Optimality and the Law', *Oxford Economic Papers*, 1967.

There is apt to be less agreement than hitherto on the constituents of a good life. It is altogether possible that many people today enjoy the more hectic life offered by a sprawling metropolis, dented by enclaves of culture and entertainment, along with the traffic fumes, the din and the tawdry façades – notwithstanding which a sizeable proportion of the urban population would be glad to forgo the remaining advantages of city life in exchange for a quiet environment within a country setting, at least if the quiet environment could be guaranteed. If so, it would be politically simpler to encourage the creation of separate areas than to reach agreement about some ideal form of urban life, even supposing there were the political will to implement it.

(2) Apart from political expediency, there are humanitarian arguments to reinforce the economic ones. There are a growing number of people today – call them eccentric, hypersensitive, perverse, immature, neurotic, if you wish – who find particular features of modern urban or suburban society jarring, abrasive and generally hard to bear with. For some it is the growing sense of isolation which paradoxically increases along with the means of communication; for others it is the pressure of 'keeping up with the machine'; for yet others, there is the sense of futility or despair at the spreading wilderness of steel and concrete.

Our technically triumphant civilisation currently offers them no permanent escape – no alternatives other than perhaps wandering off to India in a mad moment, repeatedly falling sick, feeding off tranquillisers, or joining the drug cult. A variety of separate and viable areas within which the seemingly annoying or persecutory features of the Machine Age were excluded, and within which more benign features could be incorporated, appears to be an economically feasible proposition, and one which an affluent society – currently so concerned with animal rights and animal welfare – ought also to offer to its hapless human members.

III

It is of some interest to realise that if, indeed, amenity rights were to be enacted, the ordinary working of the market itself would tend to promote the creation of separate areas. If, for example, the majority of people dwelling within a large area preferred to live without an automobile while the majority in a different area preferred their automobiles, motoring would turn out to be much cheaper in the latter area inasmuch as the compensatory payments for infringing amenity rights would be smaller there (assuming the waiver-by-consent arrangement were implemented). Consequently motorists will have an inducement to move from the former area to the latter – which makes it yet cheaper per motorist to drive within the latter area, and so on. Over time it becomes increasingly expensive for the remaining drivers in the former area, and increasingly inexpensive for the growing number of drivers in the latter area. In this way, and without in any way interfering with people's choices, the tendency for the former area to become an automobile-free area is actuated by the enactment of amenity rights.

Indeed, organised motoring organisations would find it profitable to purchase large areas of country (compensating the anti-automobile inhabitants either for moving elsewhere or for putting up with the nuisance) within which motoring enthusiasts could pursue their favourite pastime, unobstructed by speed limits if they wish, and dwell together in roaring harmony.

On the same principle, airlines would have the strongest incentive to avoid flying over areas where opposition to aircraft noise was greatest and to concentrate flights over those areas in which compensatory payments were lowest. Provided that opinion for and against a given spillover varied from area to area, this tendency toward the creation of separate areas would grow, particularly in cases where the parties causing the spillover were highly organised, as indeed are the motoring and airline interests.

Notwithstanding the operation of such a tendency in the presence of amenity rights, there is no reason why the state should not also take the initiative in providing separate areas in order to meet the wants of those for whom quiet, clean air and a greener environment are highly valued, especially when we bear in mind that it might do so without prejudice to others who 'couldn't care less'. Even if it transpires, which I very much doubt, that people who value these amenities are only a small minority, a genuine commitment to the principle of amenity rights warrants the creation of separate areas designed specifically for their welfare.

In fact, now that science has succeeded in launching us into the supersonic era it is of the utmost urgency that governments set aside large areas free of all aerial disturbance. For the longer the delay the greater becomes the apparent dependence of the economy on such flights. The more are industrial operations re-scheduled to the new transport speeds, and the closer the integration of supersonic flights with all other forms of transport, the more massive becomes the build-up of vested material interests.

IV

If, within the United States, reservations were eventually set aside, as a matter of justice, for those American Indians who wanted to be no part of the white man's civilisation, such an act of justice should be extended to those citizens today who dearly wish to opt out of the 'high tech' economy, or at least out of some of its more vexatious characteristics. Far more than any imaginable access of material goods, social welfare could be significantly enhanced by providing a variety of separate areas, so offering the community a wider choice in respect of environmental desiderata. And if within so small a country as Britain, the reservation of viable areas, conveniently located yet free from aircraft and other engine noises, appeared to be unfeasible on ordinary commerical criteria under the existing law, the provision of these amenity areas would be entirely feasible under an effective system of amenity legislation.

In the meantime regional authorities could make a start, not only by encouraging the growth of pedestrian precincts within towns and cities, but also by setting aside residential areas through which no motorised traffic is permitted to pass. Speed-boats should be prohibited on the more beautiful lakes and lochs, and along the coastal waters of seaside resorts. Municipalities also have an important environment role to play in keeping shopping areas, city squares, cathedral precincts and other places of architectural splendour or historic interest free from motorised traffic, so enabling the public to stroll about at ease and enjoy the sights undisturbed by clamour, fumes and visual distraction.

And surely such proposals are reasonable enough in themselves without labouring their economic rationale under one sort of legal framework or another. No enthusiastic pacemaker need feel himself deprived if such urban amenities were provided, or if some areas in Britain were set aside for the comfort and pleasure of the more sensitive or eccentric of his fellow citizens.

It may, however, be emphasised that such areas would not all display the same features. Opportunity should be provided for a wide range of experiment in communal living. Indeed, there can be no objection either to developing, specifically for enthusiastic motor-cyclists and other speed fans, areas within which they could spend hours driving through at full throttle without any risk of annoying those whose tastes run to other things. At the other extreme, residential areas could be planned for the more conservative groups of people glad to live without the aid of motorised contrivances, and for those who would prefer the use only of horses and horse-drawn vehicles as the means of transport. In between, there could be plenty of choice, some such areas having no more than ample pedestrian precincts or traffic-free shopping islands; others permitting only public electrically-powered transport on their roads; yet others prohibiting all types of motorised vehicles – or prohibiting them between certain hours – and possibly prohibiting also television sets in the endeavour to encourage community life and restore a tradition of informal hospitality.

Finally, all such amenity areas would have a direct rail link to one or more of the larger towns, so enabling the residents to commute to work on weekdays – although, of course, the wishes of the residents themselves would always be taken into consideration. And it goes without saying that the government has a crucial role to play in providing constitutional guarantees that no development will be permitted to take place, and no aircraft permitted to fly, close to the amenity area. The government will also be responsible for extending internal security and other public services to the area.[3] Any objection by an existing government that these and other capital costs would be heavy has to reckon with the enactment of the citizens' charter of amenity rights. Under this legislation, all such costs would fall on the public at large inasmuch as it is clearly the existing structures and infrastructure that deprive the citizens of the amenity that is now rightfully theirs.

V

Business economists have ever been glib in equating economic growth with an expansion of the range of choice facing the individual: they have failed to observe that as the carpet of increased choice is being unrolled before us by the foot, it is simultaneously being rolled up behind us by the yard. In the absence of new legal constraints and institutions, we are being compelled willy-nilly to move into the uncertain future that commerce and technology fashions for us without appeal and without redress. In all that contributes in trivial

[3] There should be no problem in determining the size and number of any particular type of amenity area. Larger numbers of people per square yard opting for type A area compared with type B would be taken as an index of the greater popularity of the former, and measures would be taken to increase the size and/or number of A-type areas until some equilibrium were established. Provided there is imagination in the design of amenity areas and initiative in their provision, the whole enterprise will be guided effectively by market forces – by demand and supply conditions.

ways to his satisfaction, the things in which modern business excels –
new models of cars and computers, prepared foodstuffs, plastic *objets
d'art*, an increasing variety of telephonic and electronic gadgetry –
man has ample choice. In all that is beginning to destroy his
enjoyment of life, he has none. The environment about him can grow
ugly, his ears assailed with impunity, and smoke and foul gases
exhaled over his person. Whether he is indifferent to such an assault
on his amenity, whether he suffers it stoically, whether he is furious,
there is little he can do about it under the present dispensation.

Under such circumstances, then, the familiar rationale that such
discomforts are merely the costs of progress quite misconstrues the
issue. For it suggests that in some sense the workings of the market
strike a balance that results in a social net gain; it suggests that there is
a sort of *quid pro quo* in which certain conveniences are surrendered in
exchange for the manifest benefits vouchsafed to us by economic
progress. For such a belief, there is no warrant. If, indeed, each one of
us agreed to accept the incidence of the bads (or adverse spillovers) in
order to have the opportunity of buying the goods in question, the
costs-of-progress argument might be justified. But since there is in
fact no economic mechanism that offers to us this overall or package
choice, the argument has to be rejected. True, each of us may attach
quite different weights to the goods and bads simultaneously being
produced. Not every reader can be expected to share the author's
disrelish for much of the stuff produced by modern industry. But
whatever one's personal evaluation of the net package provided by
industry he has no choice but to accept it. In other words, the
accompanying bads are not chosen by him: they are forced upon him.
And this form of coercion, though admittedly not deliberate, affronts
or should affront the liberal conscience.[4]

In sum, extension of choice in terms of environmental amenity is
one of the really significant contributions to social welfare that is
immediately feasible. As suggested, however, it is not likely to be

---

[4] Indeed, the standard liberal justification of a good pricing system is based on the belief that it is
truly an instrument of personal freedom of choice. It is said to enable people to choose among
individual goods, and at supply prices that reflect their real resource cost to the economy. But if bads
are also being produced, symmetrical reasoning would require an extension of the pricing system in
order to allow each of us to choose which particular bads, and how much of each, to absorb at the
going price offered for their absorption. If this expansion were possible, and were adopted, then
indeed the pricing system of the competitive market would be an instrument of personal freedom of
choice.

As mentioned above, however, the existing economic system is one that forces people to absorb
the incidental bads. A vital area of choice is not being made available and, therefore, there can be no
presumption that, on balance, each or any of us becomes better off over time.

brought about for any but the rich by market forces working within the existing legal framework. Political initiative is necessary to provide the ordinary citizen with an effective range of environmental choices. And, as argued in this chapter, legal introduction of amenity rights is the instrument which would touch off government and private enterprise in the creation of a diversity of amenity areas offering to all men those vital environmental choices that have been denied them for so long.

PART III
....

Transport and the City

7 Dereliction of the City

I

The advantages of the city are too obvious to dwell upon. Regarded as a centre of commerce, it attracts buyers and sellers from all over the country by offering a wide range of specialised services. In the past the city was also a centre of intellectual and artistic achievement. And today only the city or metropolis can provide a sophisticated public that is large enough to provide daily audiences for symphony orchestras, operas, ballets, and a variety of theatres, museums and galleries. Returning to more mundane matters, there can be additional advantages in that the operation of such public services as water, gas, electricity and administration generally, show appreciable economies of scale. Such economies of scale, however, are not unlimited. In the absence of other considerations, a certain size is reached at which all such economies are fully exploited – after which it is no longer possible to lower the marginal cost of any service by increasing the size of the city, whether size is measured by area, population or wealth.

But even assuming these economies to be substantial, there are countervailing diseconomies of scale. The larger the city the more time and resources have to be spent on the movement of goods and people. The growth of building densities adds further to the volume of traffic and therefore to its congestion.

It might be thought that in some providential manner all this 'comes out in the wash', the right size being determined by a balance of forces in which the increasing economies of scale are offset by the increasing diseconomies. Alas, things do not work out that neatly. Whatever the equilibrium of forces at work, it is not one that issues in a city of optimal size. In fact there is an asymmetry in their operation as a result of which the city tends to be larger than an optimal or ideal size. For the economies of large-scale organisation are generally apparent and often calculable, and therefore there are incentives for

47

their exploitation by private and public enterprise. Indeed, the more obvious economies associated with a metropolitan area such as London – the availability of specialised personnel, accessibility to market and technical information, the provision of finance and other facilities – are apt to be overrated today. In contrast, the impact of additional population in adding to the traffic, to the noise and grime, and to the time spent commuting, to say nothing of the greater strain on people's health, is not taken into account by commerce and industry.[1]

II

There are other considerations. The extent of the damage inflicted by traffic congestion, even when restricted to the damage inflicted on the people immediately involved, tends to be underrated by a public which habitually thinks in terms of an average rather than in terms of a *marginal* concept. A familiar example illustrates the crucial difference. In a compartment of the corridor coaches still used by British Rail, three persons can sit comfortably on either of the seats facing each other. The addition of another usually results in all four persons sitting a little too close for comfort. The additional man, in reaching a decision whether or not to stand or sit, need only weigh the advantage to himself of sitting wedged between two persons as against standing. He need take no account of the increased discomfort of the other three – which, however, enters into the *marginal* cost. Were he compelled to take into consideration the inconvenience borne by the other three, say, by compensating each of them, he might choose instead to stand all the way rather than sit.

The same principle is at work on the roads. Suppose that each hour no more than about one thousand cars can drive comfortably down a given stretch of road. This fact does not, however, prevent additional cars from using the road. Once the number exceeds a thousand, each additional car driver contemplating the use of the road need reckon only the incipient congestion that he himself will experience. But if, for argument's sake, we assume that every other motorist (experiencing the same incipient congestion when the additional motorist takes to the road) costs the inconveniences at the same sum as the additional motorist, the cost suffered in aggregate is a thousand and one times as

---

[1] To be sure, a 'London allowance' is generally offered to personnel working in the metropolis in recognition of the higher cost of living there (rents and travel costs being higher). But the other factors mentioned above, and they are not the only ones, do not enter into commercial costs.

great as the cost reckoned by the single motorist who makes the decision. If the additional motorist had to defray this increment of total cost – the *marginal* cost – he would desist from driving along that road. But, of course, he thinks only of his own inconvenience cost and therefore decides to drive along it.

As economists all know, an unregulated traffic flow tends to be too large whenever there is congestion. By one means or another it should be reduced to an optimal traffic flow – defined as one for which the *marginal* cost of congestion is equal to, or no greater than, the value placed by the marginal motorist on driving down that particular road (a value that will depend upon the costs of alternative routes and modes of travel).

The same principle extends also to the additional firm that settles in a crowded city, so adding personnel and traffic which further impede the movement of people and goods. Yet this firm takes into account only its own relatively negligible share of the additional inconvenience it inflicts on everyone. Again, each person who chooses to come and live in the metropolis gives no thought to the additional costs he necessarily imposes on others, and especially over the short period during which it is not possible to add to the existing accommodation, road space or public transport facilities. In the more crowded neighbourhoods of the metropolis, a few thousand newcomers are more than enough to destroy the standard of comfort and amenity of the original inhabitants.

It may be noted in passing, moreover, that if the immigrants to the city happen to arrive from other parts of the same country, or from other countries enjoying comparable living standards, the degree of discomfort to be endured by the original inhabitants – though below an optimal as calculated above – will remain within limits. For such immigration will not continue once living conditions in such neighbourhoods fall too far below the common standards prevailing within such countries. If, on the other hand, immigrants into the city come from countries with standards of living, hygiene and amenity well below those prevalent in the host country, the neighbourhood environment may have to decline drastically before it acts as a disincentive to further immigration.[2]

---

[2] Such immigrants may indeed be willing to tolerate worse conditions than those they were accustomed to, since (1) those who pioneer the way are often prepared to endure hardship for a year or two in the hope of bettering their lot later, and (2) some are resigned to dwell in quite squalid conditions for several years for the purpose, initially at least, of amassing a sum of money in order either to return to their native lands or to bring over their families. Finally (3) there is a time lag, measured in years, between the worsening of conditions in the neighbourhoods in which the new immigrants reside and the appreciation of this fact in the immigrants' homelands.

III

Consider, now, the spillover effects of urban construction. Today a commercial building is seldom regarded by its owners as more than a financial asset. To other citizens, however, it can be an asset or a liability. A stately building is a source of pleasure and of pride to citizens while a shoddy nondescript construction, of which there has been a proliferation since World War II, is a source of irritation and dejection. When one considers that the architecture of the city influences the humour and the character of its citizens, when one considers the civic pride and sense of community that may be inspired by architecture, it is a telling reflection on our kind of civilisation that we leave the initiative in the design of our cities, piecemeal, largely to commercial interests, subject only to the approval of revenue-seeking councils.[3]

Were amenity rights to be extended to the layout and the architecture of the city, presumably large sums of money would have to be paid in compensation to the citizens whose urban environment is marred by unsightly or incongruent buildings and by the additional traffic pollution generated. The inclusion of these economically-warranted social costs with the commercial costs would provide the incentive to promote an architecture that accords more closely with the public's taste. To be sure, any endeavour to implement amenity rights in respect of proposed or existing architecture would run into the practical problems of calculating the appropriate compensatory sums. But the problem arises as the unavoidable consequences of the attempt to bring into the economic calculus those social costs that, under the existing legal framework, are systematically ignored – to the all too visible detriment of the urban environment.

In view of the rampant postwar development not only in London and other cities but also in the innumerable seaside resorts and small

---

[3] Pre-twentieth-century architecture and the use of traditional materials apparently afford far greater pleasure to ordinary people than do modern buildings that follow the principle of unadorned functionalism. We still find delight in the remaining examples of Georgian or Regency architecture. The Crescent at Regent's Park and Somerset House are prized not so much because of their historic associations but for their inherent beauty and humanity. Much of the public architecture of the eighteenth and nineteenth centuries is suggestive of the more enlightened aspirations of those times, of spaciousness, proportion and leisure. It is with relief that the eye picks them out from the dreary uniformity of modern city blocks. Certainly if we cannot do better than the present assortment of engineering monstrosities – from which, for monumental folly, the palm must be handed to the designers of the Elephant and Castle centre – we had best call a halt to further building and redirect our energies to removing the postwar crop of eyesores that have so promiscuously uglified our towns and cities.

towns of Britain which before World War II had still some remnants of local character, there is a particular urgency about the public's recognition of these social costs. Intimate local architecture is everywhere being swamped by hostile and overbearing concrete edifices – tower blocks, egg-crates and barefaced slabs – bereft either of warmth or majesty, devoid of any artistic grace, and today spreading over the world like a malign fungus, equally prominent in London and Chicago, in Berlin and Buenos Aires, in Bangkok and Tokyo.

8 Traffic Blight

I

Let us pause at this juncture to contemplate modern society's greatest nightmare, motorised traffic. The city as a centre point of civilisation, as a place of human concourse, of life and gaiety, has become a thing of the past. Hoarse beneath the fumes emitted by an endless swarm of crawling vehicles, the city today bears resemblance to some gigantic and clamorous arsenal. None of the piecemeal attacks on the sorest affliction of twentieth-century society since World War II has produced any noticeable improvement. The transport economist's solution does not take one far. He can estimate the congestion costs borne by the traffic itself and calculate some optimal traffic flow, though only by ignoring the so-called 'intangibles' – which happen to be a far greater part of the social costs, inasmuch as the provision made to accommodate the ever-expanding flow of traffic over the half century has all but crucified the urban environment and has had the most far-reaching repercussions on the lifestyle of the modern world. The same blind eye is in evidence when estimating optimal parking charges, or rates of return on highway building or road-widening, or when employing the technique of cost-benefit analysis.[1]

The piecemeal methods of engineers in facing the same problems differ from those of the economist only in being cruder. They turn on the location of 'growing points' and on a variety of formulae, based on a traffic growth relative to road capacity, which yield critical ratios purporting to justify increased road investment. And ad hoc decisions are made to build by-passes, circuses, 'fly-overs' and 'fly-unders', a bridge here and an extension there, whenever it seems that something just has to be done. If such methods had anything to offer, we should

---

[1] The economics student interested in the concepts and analysis relevant to the calculation of social costs associated with traffic may wish to consult my *Cost-Benefit Analysis* (4th edn), especially Parts II, III and VI. (Appendix C, below, on the interpretation of the benefits of transport, may also be of interest.)

have had evidence of it a long time ago, especially from the United States where for many decades after World War II, state and municipal governments were bending backward in the futile endeavour to accommodate the motoring interest.

Yet the overall response of governments in Britain has been to continue to build roads and new highways in a feverish and foolish effort to meet the ever-growing demand of motorists for more road-space, apparently oblivious of a 'Parkinson's Law' of traffic which has it that the traffic expands to fill the road-space available. At the same time governments encourage the use of the nation's limited resources to install more plants to produce more automobiles, trucks, caravans, motorcycles, that continue to show a profit to their owners by steadfastly ignoring the mounting cost of traffic controls, of mutual frustration, and of the barely tolerable pressure of noise, stench, dirt and exasperation, to say nothing of the annual number killed and mutilated.

For the glad-eyed technocrat, impatient of tomorrow's cornucopia of innovations, the accumulation of the tribulations and vexations of modern living may be cheerfully dismissed as the inevitable cost of progress. To those living in the present, however, their cause has to be attributed to a growing tangle of spillovers that, partly by their nature and partly by historical accident, have escaped the price mechanism. Nor are there wanting those visionaries, convinced as they are that the automobile is 'a potentially highly beneficial invention',[2] who propose that our cities be redesigned and rebuilt so that we could have as much traffic as we want along with the amenity we seek. Such grandiose projects would draw upon various and novel principles such as the 'corridor system' which would intersperse 'environmental areas' within an interlacing network of highways. Particular emphasis is laid on the need for 'traffic architecture', envisaged as the integration of buildings and roads at different levels.

But before entertaining such futuristic visions we should pause to consider the full social costs of attempts to implement them, especially in this already overpacked island of ours. Such costs are properly to be compared, *not* with the existing traffic chaos (which, given our desperation, might seem tolerable) but with the costs of other radical alternatives. It may well be the case, of course, that the social costs and benefits of alternative schemes are too complex to measure. But the range of choices facing the public may be extended

---

[2] A phrase used by Sir Geoffrey Crowther in his introduction to the *Buchanan Report* of 1962.

by revealing to it a range of technologically feasible opportunities hitherto unconsidered. In view of the pervasive repercussions of transport on our way of life, the alternatives to be debated must go far beyond what has so far been thrown up by the existing market mechanisms and conventional government policies, even when modified by the humane but misguided aspirations of engineers.

II

The social significance of both the market and the engineering criteria involved, as well as that of the alternative solution proposed here, may be better understood if, for a while, we skirt direct controversy and approach these issues by a sort of parable. Thus, without straining his credulity perhaps, the reader may be able to picture to himself a region of some continent, say, on the other side of the Atlantic in which the traditional right to carry firearms is never questioned. Indeed, on the initiative of the manufacturers, who spend colossal sums in advertising their new wares, more than one pistol is to be seen in a man's belt. The young men in particular are anxious to be seen with the latest de luxe 'extra hard-hitting' model. Obviously the manufacture of holsters and other accessories flourishes as also does the manufacture of bullet-proof vests, leggings and helmets. These are not the only growth industries, however, for notwithstanding the purchase of bullet-proof items, the members of the undertakers' association do a flourishing trade. The windows of all but the poorer houses are fitted with shatter-proof glass, while the bullet-proofing of rooms and offices in the more dangerous districts is a matter of ordinary precautions. No family is foolish enough to neglect the training of their sons, and even their daughters, in the art of the quick draw. In any case, a number of hours each week is devoted to target practice and dodgery in all the best schools. Life insurance is, of course, big business despite the exorbitant premiums, and expenditure on medical attention continues to soar. For in addition to such normal ailments as bullets embedded in various parts of the anatomy, there is widespread suffering from a variety of chafed skin diseases, the result of wearing the unavoidably heavy bullet-proof apparel. Moreover, owing to nervous diseases and anxiety, about every other adult is addicted either to strong liquor or to tranquillising drugs. Taxes are burdensome for obvious reasons: a swollen police force employed mainly in trying to keep down the number of victims of the perennial feuds, extensive prisons and prison hospitals, to say nothing of the public funds devoted to guarding offices, banks, schools, and to the construction of special vans for transporting the children to and from schools.

In such an environment the most peace-loving man would be foolish to venture abroad unarmed. And since it is observed by the *laisser-faire* economist that men freely choose to buy guns, it would be regarded as an infringement of liberty to attempt to curb their manufacture. Moreover, since the market is working smoothly, the supply of firearms being such that no one need wait if he is able to pay the market price, no government intervention to match industrial supplies to rising demand is called for. Provided there is enough competition in the production of firearms so that, over the long period, prices just cover costs (and tend also to equal marginal costs of production), the allocation economist is well satisfied. Looking at the promising signs of growth in the chief industries, firearms and accessories, the business economist pronounces the economy 'sound'. If, however, for any reason the government begins to have misgivings about some of the more blatant social repercussions, it consults with the pistol economist, a highly paid and highly regarded expert. The pistol economist constructs models and, with the help of high-powered statisticians, amasses pistological data of all kinds, from which he calculates the optimal set of taxes on the sale of pistols and ammunition in recognition of those external diseconomies, such as occasional corpse-congestion on the better streets, whose monetary costs can, he believes, be estimated.

Notwithstanding all his scientific advice, matters eventually come to a head, and amid much government fanfare a committee of inquiry is set up under the chairmanship of a highly competent engineer, Mr B. If there ever was a realist, Mr B is one, and he soon satisfies himself that the economy is heavily dependent upon pistol production, and all the auxiliary industries and services connected therewith. Besides, the evidence is incontrovertible: the demand for guns continues to grow year by year. It must, therefore, be accepted as a datum. Undaunted, Mr B faces 'the challenge' by proposing a radical remodelling of the chief towns and cities, at an unmentionable cost, in the endeavour to create an environment in which people can have both their guns and a peaceful life as well. The chief features of his plan are based on what he aptly calls 'pistol architecture', and includes provision for no-shooting precincts fenced high with steel, the construction of circular and wavy road design to increase the difficulties of gun-duelling, the erection of high shatter-proof glass screens running down the centres of roads to prevent effective cross-firing, and the setting up of heavily protected television cameras at all strategic positions in the towns in order to relay information twenty-four hours a day to a vast new centralised police force equipped with fleets of helicopters. Every progressive journalist pays tribute to the foresight and realism of the B-plan and makes much of the virtues of 'pistol architecture', the architecture of the future. Alas, the government begins to realise that any attempt to raise the taxes necessary to implement the B-plan would start a revolution. So the plan is quietly shelved, new committees of inquiry are formed, masses of agenda are produced, and things continue much as before.

III

We need not continue save to press home a few parallels. Over the last seventy or eighty years a transposition of ends and means has taken place. Originally, the vehicle was designed for the roads. Today the roads are designed for the vehicles. Originally, the automobile was to be fitted to the pace of life. Today the pace of life is to be adapted to the speed of the vehicle.

The dominance exerted over our civilisation by this one invention is without precedent in history. So pervasive is its influence, and so inextricably has it woven itself into our way of life and habits of thought that the extent of its obtrusion and its intrusion into every facet of modern living is no longer perceived. To insist, therefore, on seeing the automobile as no more than 'a potentially beneficial' means of travel, and to propose an economic assessment of its benefits and costs to society, smacks of the quixotic.

Imagine the writer H. G. Wells journeying back in time on his invented time-machine to about 1780 and accosting Dr Samuel Johnson with the following conundrum. What gift to mankind is of such worth as to warrant the sacrifice each year of the lives of two hundred thousand of the earth's inhabitants, the maiming for life of over a million, the transformation of the cities of the world into concrete wastelands made hideous by noise, filth and danger; and along with this, the desolation of the countryside, and slow poisoning of the air in town and suburb, the impairment of health and the corruption of the character of people[3] and, to boot, the creation of

---

[3] 'As aggression is one of the primary instincts of man, it is not surprising that many drivers under stress become dangerously aggressive, cursing, racing, and "carving up" other drivers. Unfortunately the motorist's environment is accurately calculated to provoke just this sort of conduct. Anonymity and lack of social contact – the joy of the driver as he speeds along in his sealed tin box – are strongly conducive to aggression.' Adam Raphael, *The Guardian*, 17 November 1967.

conditions favourable to the growth of crimes of robbery and violence?[4] What reply could the sage give, but that it must be of a nature, sir, that is beyond the bounds of man's imagination?

And what in fact are we to count as benefits? Whatever the claims for the automobile, they are certainly not to be found in the more ubiquitous features that have developed in response to its popularity. These features include (1) the creation of a motorised environment in which, while the time spent in commuting grows, the automobile seems to become increasingly indispensable. The outcome is a revealing instance of a solution that creates a need for itself. For the automobile was hailed as the solution to the problems of travelling distances speedily and comfortably. Today, the claim is that we cannot do without the automobile because of the increase in distances which, of course, has been created by the automobile. The continuing growth in automobile ownership promotes the geographical dispersion over the country of housing, shopping, entertainment, restaurants, and consumer services generally, along with the decentralisation of industry and commerce in favour of locations in 'industrial parks' in the country. The distinction between suburb and countryside is becoming blurred as the population begins to spread everywhere in an ultimately foredoomed bid to 'get away from it all' – which development further increases the need for the automobile.

Accompanying this depressing social trend is (2) the growth of an economic environment that is closely dependent upon the continued popularity of the automobile. So large a part of modern industry is geared into, and has ramifications with, automobile production that the annual figure for automobile sales is officially recognised as a barometer of the country's economic performance. Worse still, the complex of industries involved in the production and servicing of automobiles, to say nothing of a militant army of car-owners, has given rise to entrenched interests that bar the way to serious consideration of radical proposals for cleaner, safer and more efficient forms of transport. In tandem with the economic environment is the psychological environment, which is one of almost abject dependence. For millions of motorists, the automobile has become an extension of their personality, an index of status, a totem of power, a sex symbol.[5]

---

[4] Without the means of a fast get-away in high-powered automobiles, crimes of robbery and violence would have a much smaller chance of success.

[5] With respect to makers' appeals to power and aggression, there has been no change over the years. Over twenty years ago Adam Raphael writing in *The Guardian* (17 November 1967) remarked: 'The point has not been missed by the car manufacturers. Few car advertisements ever made so blatant an appeal to masculine aggression as that for the high-powered German Audi Saloon

There is left then only the illusory benefit, the alleged 'freedom to go where one likes, at any time and in privacy and comfort'. As though our roads were uncongested, our streets and avenues unlined with cars, and miles-long crawling 'tail-backs' on our highways a thing of the past. As though driving through the city were a known specific for sweetening the temper and improving the digestion. As though the locust hordes of private automobiles moving along roads all over the country do not destroy the very pleasure, variety and amenity that motorists are seeking. And when all of us, knowing this, can do no more than shrug in resignation, one cannot but wonder whether the belief in free will is not, after all, an illusion.

IV

Be that as it may, the lesson from the parable is plain enough. If there is left in modern man an occasional glimmer of rationality, then occasionally he will dare to think about the possibility of abandoning all extravagant schemes for *accommodating* the mounting road traffic and instead think about schemes for *containing* it and, indeed, diminishing it. The one radical alternative he might be induced to look at before contemplating the range of compromise solutions is that of a plan for the gradual and systematic abolition of all privately owned automobiles.

For a fraction of the money the nation spends on the maintenance of its private cars and on public outlays necessary to keep the traffic moving – not to mention the costs of the multifarious spillovers already described – we could simultaneously achieve three objectives: (1) to provide a comfortable, reliable and efficient public transport service – bus, tram, train or tube – in all the major population areas and, in the interests of quiet and clean air, electrically powered;[6] (2) through public control of public transport, to restrain and gradually reverse the dispersion of the population that has followed in the wake of postwar highway construction and of speculative building which is currently transforming the South-East into a built-up suburban area;

– "Power like this tests a man . . . blazing take-off . . . frontal assault" which was withdrawn after a protest from Mrs Castle. Yet much car advertising is still firmly directed towards the gods of virility and violence: for example: "The Hot New Humber Mark II", "the Great '68 Symbol", "the Sleek, Scorchy new Victor", and of course the most famous of all, Esso's "Put a Tiger in Your Tank".'

[6] Provision for a taxi service in the cities should be conceded (on condition that taxis were either electrically powered or fitted with anti-fume devices or catalytic converters) simply in order to prevent abuses arising from exemptions being made in favour of privileged groups such as doctors or ministers of the Crown.

and (3) to restore amenity and dignity to our cities, indeed, by vast extensions of pedestrian precincts to enable people to wander unconfined and undisturbed by any kind of road traffic and to savour the pleasures of strolling about squares, parks and city centres.

Radical changes would have to be made also in the organisation of freight deliveries if we are to avoid growing commercial traffic as the variety of consumer goods expands. The movement of freight may be minimised by (a) substituting as far as possible existing rail links in the built-up areas during off-peak hours, in particular by adapting and extending London's Underground to carry freight, initially during the small hours of the morning, and (b) removing freight deliveries from the present multitude of small and large firms and placing them instead under a single authority, public or private, in order to avail ourselves of the economies of coordination. Finally (c) in order to protect the urban environment, the opportunities for organising shop deliveries at times when most people are off the streets – say, between the hours of two and six in the mornings – have to be exploited.[7]

At all events, if we are to have a comprehensive transport plan for the country at large, this is one toward which we could advance over time. It is radical enough, to be sure. But it is technically quite feasible, and it holds out the prospect of a far more civilised pattern of living than that to which we are currently bound.

It is not a solution that will ever be presented to us by the market operating under the existing legal framework, however, and it is not one that will ever be proposed by traffic engineers. But it is one that deserves careful consideration by a nation that prides itself on its social awareness and political maturity. In the meantime, local plans to prohibit automobile traffic (during certain hours at least) from designated areas in resorts, historic towns and city centres will enable people to recapture the sense of human concourse, community and gaiety, and in other ways make a modest contribution to the nation's welfare.

V

Before ending, let us briefly consider a wider spectrum of possibilities having affinities with a separate-facilities solution which invariably involves two interrelated kinds of decision.

---

[7] An outright prohibition against freight deliveries outside these hours need not be introduced during the transitional period: a levy on the size of the van or truck could be imposed instead, though with concessions that would favour electric-powered vehicles.

First, and *within* any area, decisions have to be taken about some particular features of traffic-containment. (1) At one end of the spectrum, the decision will be to exclude motorised transport of any description. (2) Alternatively, public transport alone is permitted, possibly supplemented by a restricted taxi service. (3) A prohibition is introduced against the use of commercial vehicles, except between the hours of two and six in the morning, within towns and suburbs. (4) A limited number of commercial vehicles are admitted at any time into the towns or suburbs, provided they are electrically powered – the number being regulated by the size of the vehicle tax. (5) All permitted traffic within towns is to be subject to speed limits not exceeding, say, fifteen miles an hour. (6) A public authority is to take over and coordinate all freight deliveries.

Secondly, the *size* of the area itself will be the subject of political decision. (a) The minimal traffic-free area can be no smaller than the conventional pedestrian precinct occasionally found within some towns or suburbs. (b) In addition, ancient, winding and narrow streets, secluded squares and open-air markets are to be set aside for the sole convenience of pedestrians. (c) The central parts of cities and towns, along with their historic areas, and their theatre and cafe quarters, could be cleared of all traffic. (d) Suburbs or cities themselves are to be free of all private motoring. (e) Selected regions, comprising a part or the whole of a county, are to be reserved for citizens who wish to live in an environment far removed from motorised and air traffic.

Whatever the decisions made, however, one thing is clear. Within the city itself there can be no long-term solution compatible with any vision of the good life that turns on schemes designed to accommodate the automobile. A continuation of the present policy of attempting to do so by piecemeal alterations leads ultimately to the crucifixion of the city by its traffic – a metaphor that aptly describes what has happened over the last four decades to cities the world over, from Madrid to São Paulo, from Tokyo to Mexico City.

PART IV

....

The Myth of Consumer Sovereignty

9 How Free Are We to Choose?

I

The social and economic implications of spillovers examined in Part II were restricted to those arising entirely within a framework of basic assumptions familiar to economists. Within such a framework it can be concluded that *only in the absence* of all unresolved spillovers does the operation of competitive markets tend to realise an optimal allocation of economic resources – in other words, to bring scarce resources into relation with people's expressed wants. I shall now argue that once this framework of familiar assumptions is revised so as to accord more closely with the facts of economic life, we shall have to conclude that, even in the absence of all spillovers, the operation of highly competitive markets does not in fact tend to bring the allocation of resources into relation with people's choices. And if this is so, the rationale of the competitive enterprise system, and therefore also the social justification of economic growth, begin to look very shaky.

An assumption frequently invoked to vindicate economic growth is that any extension of the *effective* range of choice facing a person – whether presented to him by the market or by the state – adds to his welfare. (The word *effective* here indicates that the additional opportunities presented to him, such as a fall in the prices of consumer goods, will induce him to select a *new* combination of goods notwithstanding that the original combination of goods is still available to him.) It will be contended soon that this assumption is far from being plausible. In the meantime it can be shown that consumer innovation need not result in any valid extension of choice.

Needless to remark, a person can only choose from the range of items that are offered to him by the market or the state. And a choice of alternative physical environments is not the only thing that the market and the state have so far failed to provide, though it is one of the most important. Less important, though worthy of attention, is the fact that the appearance of new goods, or new models of existing goods, on the market is more often than not an occasion also for the subsequent withdrawal of older goods or models. Whatever the economic explanation offered for this common phenomenon, it follows that economic growth is not necessarily accompanied by an expansion of the effective range of choice.

It is when we turn from the individual's demand for goods to his supply of services to the economy, however, that restrictions on his choice arising from technology become more evident. The older classical economist might argue that just as the individual chooses to buy various amounts of the goods offered by the market, so also, as a supplier of productive services, he is guided by the market prices of these productive services to provide them in different amounts. There is, of course, a professional interest in assuming symmetry in individual choice, qua consumer and qua worker, if only because of theoretical elegance and mathematical convenience. And one may exercise imagination in conceiving an economy wherein a person could spread his work among a variety of different occupations guided by the familiar equimarginal principle exactly in the same way that he is deemed to spread his income among the goods offered to him by the market.[1] Alas, the modern economy is not so accommodating, and for the apparently good reason that if a person were allowed to choose in this way – choosing each week to put in an hour or two each in a score or so of different occupations – the productivity of labour could not be mantained. The employee has therefore to choose his work subject to the condition that he accept the hours and other terms of employment offered by the firm.

In the narrow economic sense, that in which welfare is held to vary with output, the constraints on working hours may be vindicated. But if the economist is primarily interested in social welfare he is not at liberty to follow this custom. He has to address himself to the welfare effect of this restriction on the worker's choice. He is not to take the easy way out so popular among pro-market economists who seek to justify the private enterprise system by reference only to consumer satisfaction. The fact is that the citizen does have patterns of preference about different occupations though they cannot surface in conditions that afford him little choice but to adapt himself to current

[1] The economics student will find this assumption formalised in an early paper of mine, 'Rent as a Measure of Welfare Change', *American Economic Review*, 1959.

industrial techniques. Again, the economist does not address himself to the difficult task of calculating the changes in welfare that result from the continual change-over from one method of production to another.

Yet some reflections may be hazarded. The tedium of repetitive work in modern industry, including that from pressing computer keys each day, gazing intently at the endless flicker on the small screen, twiddling dials, pulling levers, and all such routine operations characteristic of a 'high tech' economy, is easy to overlook simply because no physical strain is involved. But if one bears in mind the expenditures and efforts of large numbers of people today in combating monotony, in taking up hobbies which recapture a sense of creativity or craftsmanship, one cannot doubt that social welfare could be augmented by extending opportunities for worker satisfaction. Nor need one contemplate a clear choice between the existing highly organised system of production and the extreme alternative of uninhabited choice in respect of hours, variety and degrees of craftsmanship. One need only admit the scope for greater social satisfaction – after allowance is made for consequent reductions in physical output – from extending to citizens of all ages a much wider choice of hours of work, a wider geographical choice in the location of smaller units of industry and, above all, a wider choice in methods of production.

Experiment on such lines is obviously inconsistent with any conventional criterion of technical efficiency. For certainly some material output would have to be sacrificed in the conscious pursuit of ways and means of deriving more positive enjoyment, stimulation and companionship in one's daily occupation. While it is unlikely that everyone would want to avail himself of the opportunity to sacrifice some of his earnings in exchange for a more congenial occupation, there are surely enough people capable of enriching their lives by such arrangements to justify the experiment.

Measured by the conventional index of finished goods, the implementation of such a proposal – which is properly regarded as yet another instance of the separate-facilities solution to situations of potential conflict – may appear to involve negative economic growth (as conventionally measured). And the mere possibility that an increase in social welfare – arising from a significant increase in the range of effective job choices – may result in a measurable reduction of output is enough to provoke committed growth-men. But that is because they are interested primarily in material growth, in productivity, in 'keeping up in the race', and only secondarily and coincidentally in social welfare. Should there be a conflict between them, they will stand firm under the banner of economic growth.

II

Again, economists engaged in calculating changes in welfare tend, not surprisingly, to disregard the institutional constraints under which choices are made. Insofar as they change over time, there can be substantial changes for better or for worse in the welfare of society at large.

Over the decision that is most relevant to his well-being, the epoch and the society and family into which he is born, the individual can exercise no choice whatever. As he is born at a certain point in time, into a particular social and physical milieu, into a particular family, much of the pattern of his life tends to follow as a matter of course. Many of the consequences arising from nature and nurture, from genetic endowments and from the influence of family and community, he cannot evade. Within limits determined by such consequences he chooses a career but, having adopted it, the subsequent range of choices is narrower. If, for example, he becomes a stockbroker or a bank manager, his choices of clothes, residence and life-style generally will not differ materially from those of his colleagues. The coventions and expectations of his associates, friends and customers must weigh with him at all times if he is not to forgo their good opinion of his character upon which his prospects depend.

Such mundane observations take on significance as the cost of keeping in fashion increases over time. Women's fashions are only a more notorious case in point. Popular columns in women's journals assert that women positively enjoy being in fashion – though such pleasure may be alloyed by a dread of being seen out of fashion. The choice of the pace of fashion, however, is not one that is open to the individual. At present it is left entirely to commercial interests to exploit fashion to the limit of public tolerance. Yet if we cannot escape fashion it would surely be less costly and less exacting to be subject to fashions that changed less frequently.

The fashion industry, conceived as a predatory institution, is a prime example of an uneconomic activity, dedicated as it is to using up resources not to create satisfaction but continually to destroy satisfaction with what people already possess – in effect to create obsolescence in otherwise perfectly serviceable goods. Although it may be said that it has been doing this for ages, it is the unconscionable frequency today of fashion changes and their extension to a growing variety of articles that is so patently wasteful. What pass each year for innovations or advanced models in automobiles, furniture, refrigerators, stereophonics, hardware and electrical goods generally, are little more than fashion changes in disguise. Any practical proposal to regulate the rate of change in fashion might therefore attract a great deal of public support. Our would-be pace-setters would, of course, be deprived of approved opportunities for self-display, but the saving of resources should more than suffice to compensate the nation.

Turning to the range of goods itself, although producers also use up resources in creating a market for their goods, they are not legally permitted to produce any goods for which a market might be created. A variety of drugs, weapons, pornographic literature and entertainment, at present illegal and therefore costly, would be readily available at competitive prices in the absence of legal prohibitions. Again, men and women might agree to sell themselves or their children into virtual slavery for immediate and tangible benefits if the law countenanced the institution. And in a country having a conscript army there would be no difficulty, in the absence of legal impediment, in promoting a market in draft tickets – the richer young men buying their way out of national service to the ostensible benefit of both parties to the exchange.

Suppose, finally, that the penalty for killing a pedestrian in a motor accident were not, as it generally is at present, merely a fine[2] or temporary suspension of driving licence but, instead, that of being boiled in oil, I should predict with perfect confidence a vast changeover to public transport, a voluntary though drastic diminution of driving speeds, and a quite magical reduction of death on the roads. This outlandish proposal should help to persuade us that too much attention is being paid to the market's contribution in expanding consumer choice and too little to the power of legislation in altering, for better or worse, the sorts of choices that people make.

---

[2] At the time of writing, BBC radio reported the case of a motorist who, momentarily attending to his car radio while driving, accidentally killed a little girl who was with her mother. To the outrage of the mother, and the public, he was fined but £100 by the magistrate who claimed to be guided by the law in making his decision.

III

In order to evolve methods for calculating changes of welfare consequent upon changes in the economy, the assumption is made that people's tastes remain the same over time. Difficult as it is to defend such an assumption, it is basic to the economist's method of calculation. For if a man's given wants were being met over time by more goods or better goods, a *prima facie* case could be made for his being better off over time. But if his wants were changing over the same period of time – either because he were becoming greedier or because (with the same set of prices) he came to prefer a quite different assortment of goods – the condition necessary for making comparisons of his welfare over time would no longer exist. In general, the more rapidly people's tastes are changing the less confidence there can be in the belief that an increase in per capita output over time produces an increase in per capita welfare.

And in the advanced economies of the world, people's tastes do indeed change rapidly, if only because consumers' expressed wants can hardly be said to be independent of the activities of producers. It is this recognition of the sustained influence exerted on consumers' choices by producers which makes it so misleading to perceive the market today as a mechanism that is continuously acting to bring the resources of the economy into relation with material wants of society. In fact, not only do producers determine the kinds of goods from which consumers have to make their choice, they also seek to persuade consumers to choose that which they now wish to produce today and also to 'unchoose' that which was being produced yesterday. Therefore to continue regarding the market, at least a market within an affluent and growing economy, as a 'want-satisfying' mechanism – the classical view – is to close one's eyes to the important fact that it has also become a want-*creating* mechanism.

To be sure, the fact itself is hardly a revelation. Yet its implications are not wholly appreciated. An unchanging pattern of consumer wants over time would just not suffice to absorb the continuing growth in the flow of goods coming on to the domestic markets of the richer countries. The sustained rise in consumers' expenditure at all levels of income has come to depend upon the unflagging zeal and enterprise of the advertising industry,[3] a theme whose ramifications

---

[3] Admittedly it is difficult sometimes to separate the informative from the propaganda elements of an advertisement, to say nothing of gauging the accuracy or the relevance of the information provided. 'Smart people prefer to smoke Cancerettes!' is a claim which is not easy to test. If we could agree first on a definition of smart people we might well discover that, though only as a consequence

are more intensively explored in Part VII.

Some of the nation's resources, then, are used to create new wants. These new wants may be deemed imaginary or they may be alleged to be as valid as the original wants. What cannot be denied, however, is that in these circumstances the basic condition necessary to enable economists to calculate or even to presume any increase in social welfare as a result of economic growth no longer obtains. Indeed, one may reasonably conjecture that the unremitting efforts of modern business directed to stimulating material aspirations and to enlarging consumer appetites may cause people's wants to grow faster than their living standards, so increasing over time the margin of social discontent.

Whatever our judgement in this regard, it is abundantly evident that modern business strives to create an atmosphere which glorifies the 'pace-setter' and derides the fashion laggards. As productivity rises over time without a commensurate rise in leisure, the accent on boosting consumption becomes more brazen and more obviously directed toward maintaining production and employment. In truth, private enterprise in the affluent society is in effect engaged in the 'forced feeding' of an increasingly indiscriminate buying public, and of incidentally inverting the traditional rationale of the economic system. Thus instead of allocating and expanding scarce economic resources in order to bring them into relation with the given pattern of people's wants, a stage has been reached in which the pattern of people's wants has to be altered and expanded in a sustained endeavour to bring it into relation with the increasing resources of an expanding industrial capacity.

---

of the prolonged advertising campaign, a large proportion of the class of smart people have indeed taken to smoking 'Cancerette' cigarettes. Yet we might also find that they could not distinguish them from other brands once the labels were removed.

A picture of the product, or the printing without comment of the name of the brand, can be expected to induce people to buy more of the product in question. And if claims are made for a product or service, it is not unusual for some of the claims to be true, some false, and some simply untestable. But whatever the assertions made for the informative content of modern advertising as against its persuasive content, the case for or against advertising does not turn on such a distinction. The simple argument can be made that everything which is relevant in enabling the public to make a rational choice from the range of goods provided may be more economically conveyed by an impartial consumer agency concerned to report the results of controlled tests. The economic case in favour of this proposal is the saving in resources, both those expanded by commerce either in advertising or 'counter-advertising' and those wasted by the public as a result of choices induced by misleading advertisements they have since come to regret. (For a more thorough treatment, see my *Twenty-One Popular Economic Fallacies*, London, 1969.)

Under these novel conditions growth-men may take the linguistic liberty of equating economic growth with 'enrichment' or with more of 'the good things in life'. But it is no longer possible for the economist to establish a positive link between economic growth and social welfare.

10 The Weak Link Between Choice and Welfare

I

In order to establish a criterion for comparing alternative economic arrangements, the economist has to accept the liberal dictum that each man must be assumed to know his own interest best. The dictum may be regarded as a maxim of political prudence only, formulated in the belief that it is better to act as if each man did indeed know better what was good for him than could any other person or authority. Yet only if it were a fact that each person, in choosing among alternatives, really knew what he wanted or, more strictly speaking, what would give him satisfaction, would the economist's criterion have validity. Moreover, only under this condition could the economist equate an increase in the area of choice with an increase of welfare.

Now insofar as a person is choosing between carrots at 30 pence a pound and green peas at 40 pence, the maxim that he, the consumer or citizen, knows best what is good for him is a reasonable one. But it is supect for larger and more complex choices such as those involved in allocating his time between different activities, or in allocating his income between broad categories of goods entailed by his currently adopted life-style. Indeed, whereas for the economist the individual's choices between various activities and broad categories of goods have to be accepted as the expression of his wants, for the psychotherapist they are wont to be interpreted as an expression of his problems. For the former, then, welfare is said to be increased according as the individual satisfies his expressed wants. For the latter, it is more often his opinion that the individual's welfare can be increased only according as such expressed wants can be altered in the interests of greater harmony between his basic human urges and the external world.

Be that as it may, this assumption about the authenticity of choice is the singular characteristic of the economist engaged in welfare comparisons. Vulnerable though it is, the assumption need not, as indicated, impugn the relevance of the economist's analysis when restricted to relatively minor choices. But since few of us go through life without some regrets, without spending some time unwishing decisions we had made years ago, this assumption cannot be extended to many choices having far-reaching consequences, nor to choices of social policy where the issues bearing, say, on foreign trade, industrial disputes or fiscal controls are complex. We may also conclude that in the modern economy, where new goods are continually appearing on the market and existing ones are being withdrawn, the consumer has little opportunity to gain the experience necessary to guide his choices which, therefore, cannot reasonably be accepted by the economist as indicative of changes in his welfare.

This last proposition can bear elaboration. One of the chief manifestations of the affluent economy is the relentless growth in the number of brands and models of already popular goods. Car buyers in the United States now face 572 different models; up 50 per cent from 1980. It is not surprising that stress has become one of the afflictions of the affluent citizen. The task of choosing in a rational way, on each occasion, a particular brand or model from an ever-changing and ever-growing array of goods – that is, to weigh up the relative merits of quality, taste, appearance, performance, longevity, health hazard, and other characteristics, and to consider them all in relation to the range of prices for each of some several score or several hundreds of alternative items all purporting to serve the same need – is more conducive to bewilderment and exhaustion than it is to raising the consumer's welfare. The entire staff of a consumers' advisory board could be placed at the disposal of the hopeful buyer without making the burden of choice much less wearing. In the event there are many things a person buys from habit and much else that is bought on impulse. Even for purchases that involve fairly large outlays, the process of choosing judiciously is so time-consuming a business that nearly all consumers reach a decision on limited information, on impressions from advertisements, on personal recommendation, or on advice from a salesman or shop assistant.

Touching on this question of the strain of choosing as the range of alternatives expands, it has been argued that no person in fact need inconvenience himself if he does not wish to: he can always reach out and take the first thing that catches his eye or else he can adhere to his customary brand or model – provided it remains available over the years, which is doubtful. One may legitimately call this possible reaction to the problem rational. But rational or not, the possibility affords little consolation.

As the pace of fashion accelerates, as goods become more technically complex, and as their variety increases, the plain fact is that ordinary people do become apprehensive about the likelihood of their making a bad choice.[1] If, therefore, an independent panel were charged with the task of radically reducing the existing variety of different brands or models of consumer goods to a few clearly differentiated kinds of each good, and of maintaining their availability for some years, much time would be saved and anxiety eliminated – not to mention some decline in manufacturing costs arising from the resulting standardisation.

The observation that the range of consumer choice has in many cases expanded to unmanageable dimensions, and has therefore become productive more of exhaustion than of pleasure, finds a parallel in the range of choice that today faces the citizen as producer or worker. After all, a necessary condition for the continued advance of knowledge and the progress of industry is yet further specialisation. Since World War II, the range of specialisms in every field of knowledge has multiplied exceedingly and, along with it, the spectrum of career opportunities. Compared with earlier times, the ordinary man or woman, contemplating the staggering variety of educational courses at the universities or other institutes of higher education, can hardly be free of some anxiety. Later on, again, he is painfully aware that it is all too easy to make the wrong choice from the range of career opportunities that face him. For that matter, the choice today of a short holiday at home or abroad is not an easy one to make. Bearing in mind the countless number of resorts or package tours on offer from numerous travel agencies operating in fifty different countries, choosing how to and where to spend a vacation has become for many quite a time-consuming and excruciating experience.

In an age bursting with 'exciting new opportunities' the pre-industrial tradition of a son following his father's occupation or craft,

---

[1] If, beginning with a situation in which but one kind of shirt were available, a man were transposed to another in which twelve different kinds of shirt were on offer, he could of course continue to buy the original shirt. But it does not follow that if he does so he will be no worse off than he was. For he is now aware that in staying with the original shirt he is rejecting eleven others, a decision that carries with it an 'opportunity cost' – knowledge, that is, that he is forgoing opportunities for choosing a better shirt. He will feel less comfortable also since some of the eleven new shirts may be more fashionable than his original shirt. Rather than feel uneasy, he may be tempted to spend more time in the hope of finding a more suitable shirt.

Once it is acknowledged that fashions change apace, that the shirt he originally favoured is no longer produced, and that he is therefore compelled to choose among a changing variety, it has to be conceded that he cannot escape having continually to make such decisions.

learning to become a farmer, a tanner, a silversmith, or potter, and of the daughter learning domestic skills in the home, may well seem dull and restrictive. But at least people were spared the searching anxieties, the perpetual misgivings, the sore regrets, and the occasional despondencies that assail so many today.

II

The link between free choice and welfare can be further attenuated by considering how unwelcome events and political restrictions can operate to increase people's satisfaction with life. Thus, according to the economist's calculation, turning as it does on the individual's own valuations, the man who chooses at current prices to smoke two packets of cigarettes a day is distinctly, indeed measurably, better off than he would be if, instead, he were rationed to one packet. Yet if there were a tobacco famine, or if he were conscripted into some task force and sent to a place where no tobacco was available, the man might live to bless the event. He would continue his life in better health and pocket and roundly declare that his well-being had been improved by the initially frustrating circumstances.

Such possibilities may be discussed with great political sophistication, but whatever is concluded it cannot be denied that there are ample opportunities for raising social welfare by initial departures from people's expressed choices. If, for example, television or cinema audiences were deprived for a longish period of the sort of entertainment they had succumbed to, after a period of vexation or tedium many might be expected to develop a taste for the more sophisticated fare being made available, so increasing the range and intensity of their aesthetic and emotional sensibilities.

There is much to be said in favour of wealth, competition, enterprise and free institutions – and, indeed, much has been said in favour by radical conservatives in the West – but it is also abundantly evident that they provide no safeguards against the prevalence of appalling standards, not only of the urban environment but also in journalism and entertainment, in art and literature, and in popular taste generally. Without political intervention, the opportunities for increasing society's welfare through raising standards of taste and appreciation are not likely to be tapped in a highly commercial society. In the entertainment business in particular, the competition to arrest and capture the attention of a mass audience or a mass viewing public has led inevitably to visual sensationalism and to repeated scenes of sexual voyeurism, sadism and violence.

Such observations do not necessarily strengthen the argument for the institution of philosopher kings or weaken the argument for political liberty. But they do serve to reveal the unavoidable bias of the pro-market economist who accepts as ultimate data the expressed choices of people at any moment of time. If, therefore, the conventional wisdom insists that private enterprise should continue to have the freedom to spend all it wishes in influencing the tastes of the public in the interests of profit, and if for the most part it has been successful in influencing them for the worse, there can surely be no objection to the endeavours of non-commercial agencies – even where state-supported – to influence them for the better.

To put the matter more formally, subsidies to agencies dedicated to supporting the arts (beyond the support given by the market) may be economically justified by the net social benefits generated. And the opportunity of such net benefits exists whenever private or state organisations can encourage people to form those habits of good taste and discrimination that enlarge the capacity for aesthetic enjoyment. A prolonged campaign designed to raise standards of taste in this country would be a far more efficacious way of promoting social welfare than the government's policy of building more highways.

III

A critical weakness of attempts to link choice to welfare is to be found in what, in economists' slang, is called 'the Joneses Effect' – the thesis that what matters to a person living in a high-consumption society is not simply his absolute real income, or his command over material goods, but also his income relative to others. In its extreme form, the thesis would assert that, given the choice, a man would choose, say, a 5 per cent increase only in his own real income rather than a 25 per cent increase in real income along with a 25 per cent increase in the income of everyone else. There can be no evidence to support the thesis in this extreme form, but in a more modified form the thesis is incontrovertible.

After all, the satisfaction we derive from some of our possessions depends upon their general recognised scarcity irrespective of their utility. It is not difficult to imagine the gratification experienced by a person living in an economically primitive country in which all the neighbouring inhabitants are aware of his being the sole possessor of a transistor radio, hi-fi recorder, washing machine, and other labour-saving durables. To be envied by all we meet is surely a great source of satisfaction. Nor is it difficult to imagine his pride and joy melting away as such appurtenances become common possessions or, indeed, his mortification as his neighbours come to possess more modern and sophisticated models.

We need not labour the point with further examples or instances, however, to conclude that the prevalent and the more significant is this 'Joneses Effect' – and one can hardly deny the increasing emphasis on status and income-position in the modern economy – the more futile as a means of increasing society's welfare is the official policy of promoting economic growth.

To conclude, facile generalisation about the connection between choice and satisfaction, whether of consumer or worker, which has led to an implicit translation of expanding output into expanding welfare, has served also to quieten doubts about the near single-minded pursuit of economic growth. The fact that what is coming to matter more to the citizen of the affluent society is less the growth of his purchasing power *per se* than its growth *relative* to that of others is a fact that robs the standard policy of economic growth of much of its conventional rationale – even in the absence of spillovers and other deficiencies.

In sum, rapid economic growth in the West since World War II has failed to provide men with those choices that are really significant in raising welfare. Indeed, as indicated, there can be no presumption whatever that welfare has been rising over the past four decades or so, and more than a possibility that it has been declining.

IV

The factors mentioned in this chapter, in addition to those discussed earlier, are among those which escape the price system and are sometimes omitted also from sophisticated though conventional economic calculation. An unavoidable consequence is that significant sources of human welfare are being eroded directly and indirectly by continued economic and technological growth in already prosperous countries: being more directly eroded by the multiplication of spillovers on a scale we can hardly expect to be able to cope with for reasons to be adduced in Part VI, and indirectly eroded in numerous ways to be mentioned in Part V, which touches upon some of the more telling defects and omissions in the conventional economic measure of real income.

More generally, however, the range of consequences of economic growth on the less tangible but more potent aspects of human well-being are reserved for treatment in Part VII.

PART V

....

Measuring Real Income – an Economic Delusion

11 Growth of GNP: Conventional Adjustments and Reservations

I

Implicit in any reasoned critique of economic growth is a critique also of the conventional index of the growth of goods over time. As we have seen, not all goods are really good, and not enough allowance is made for the subtraction of bads, or adverse spillovers.

The most popular measure of the nation's aggregate of goods in any year is known as Gross National Product, or GNP for short.[1] And the annual changes in GNP continue to be used as an indicator of the annual changes in the output of finished goods or in real income. It is as well therefore that the reader become familiar with some of the broad principles underlying the computation of GNP, along with its limitations, reservations and irremediable defects, if only because of the hypnotic effect it appears to exert on our material aspirations. Certainly departments of economists in all the industrial nations find remunerative employment in forecasting the GNP, in calculating it, and in analysing in tortuous detail the economic implications of the annual, quarterly and monthly changes in its components. So just what significance can be attributed in particular to those year-to-year changes in GNP?

II

When expressed in 'real' terms – when the aggregate money sum is

---

[1] A few years ago, a new measure, Gross Domestic Product, GDP, became popular in Britain. For the purposes in hand, however, the difference between the GDP measure and the GNP measure is of no consequence. Since the GNP measure has been established much longer than GDP, and since it is still used in North America, I prefer to illustrate my arguments by reference to the older measure.

76

corrected for the rise in the cost of living[2] – the figure for GNP has long been regarded by the business world as an overall index of the nation's economic performance during the year. The intelligent citizen who casually follows the reported movements in GNP cannot, however, be assumed entirely innocent. He does not expect the coverage to be complete or the calculation exact. He is not surprised when informed by experts that estimated GNP could be in error by as much as 5 per cent or more compared with some 'true' or ideal GNP calculation. He can readily understand that the costs of services provided by the government, which costs enter into the GNP calculation as the value or price of these services, will tend to overstate the 'true' GNP, whereas transactions taking place in the so-called black economy (where services are exchanged directly, or for cash, in order to evade taxes) constitute an omission which therefore acts to understate the 'true' GNP – unless speculative estimates of the magnitudes are made, as they frequently are.

But these concessions to possible inaccuracies in the computation tend rather to incline the citizen to think of GNP as an imperfect estimate of what is, at base, a strictly definable magnitude: a hard figure indicative of the nation's economic activity over the year. If this belief is a delusion, he can hardly be blamed for being gullible. After all, the nominal, or money, figure for GNP is indeed defined as the gross aggregate expenditure on finished goods during the year. And this gross expenditure is known to bear a close relation to the aggregate of personal incomes over the same period.

Actually, the more relevant measure of aggregate economic activity is not GNP but *net* national expenditure, the latter being equal by definitional accounting conventions to net national income, NNI, or the sum of all personal incomes.[3] In fact GNP exceeds the more relevant measure, NNI, by a sum equal to aggregate amortisation costs – notwithstanding which, since economists are interested mainly in *changes* over time, we may follow convention and accept the view

[2] As the student of economics knows, in order to express the nominal or money figure for GNP in 'real' terms requires, first, that all goods be valued at their factor prices (or prices net of any taxes in them), the resulting sum then being 'deflated' by the cost-of-living index.

[3] GNP is the aggregate expenditure over the year on both consumer goods and *gross* investment, as a result of which some double-counting is involved. This is because the nominal value of the aggregate of finished goods produced during the year will also include an imputation for capital amortisation. And the aggregate of the amortisation contributions is *roughly* equal to the annual expenditure on 'replacement capital'. But this replacement-capital figure is also a component again of the *gross* investment (the other component being new additions to the capital stock).

Thus GNP counts replacement capital twice: once in the value of finished goods and again in the value of gross investment.

that *differences* in GNP are a good proxy for *differences* in NNI.

Among the standard adjustments is that of reducing the nominal value of GNP to real GNP for the purpose, say, of comparing it with the real GNP of preceding years. As indicated, this requires that we divide nominal GNP by an index of the price-changes that have taken place between the years being compared. Since in general not all prices change in the same proportion, even when they change in the same direction, the price index that is calculated will vary according to the relative weight attributed to the price change of each class of goods in the index.[4]

After having decided, somewhat arbitrarily, to deal with this index number problem in estimating the change in GNP between two or more years, the economist has recourse to a number of fairly obvious adjustments. If, say, the calculated growth in GNP happens to equal the growth in the nation's population over the same period, there is no cause for rejoicing since real GNP per capita has remained the same. Should the economist be interested in technical progress, however, he will divide GNP by aggregate working hours to obtain GNP per man hour, or output per man hour (OPMH) as it is called. Thus even though the economy is not performing well as a result, say, of large-scale involuntary unemployment, OPMH could be rising and, therefore, we may conclude that technical progress is taking place.[5]

III

Primary concern with the growth of real GNP, or the growth of per capita real GNP, as an index of material improvement in the standard of living requires the economist to make allowances for some of the current trends in the economy. If, for example, the average number of hours worked per week is being voluntarily reduced over time,

---

[4] As every economics student knows, by using weights that are proportional to expenditures on each class of goods during the *original* year (or using 'base-date' weights) and then, again, using weights that are proportional to such expenditures during the *current*, or later, year (or using 'reference-date' weights), quite different figures for the change in GNP can be contrived.

In cases where some prices rise and others fall, it is possible to calculate a GNP for year 2 that is higher than GNP for year 1 when using base-date weights, the reverse being true when reference-date weights are used.

An idea of the logic of this seeming paradox and its implications are broached in my paper, 'Welfare Criteria: Resolution of a Paradox', *Economic Journal*, 1973.

[5] OPMH as an index of technical progress is not always dependable. For example, the OPMH index calculated for women in the workforce may be increasing. It may also be increasing for men in the workforce. But if the proportion of women to men in the workforce grew substantially, the overall index could in fact decline. This would be because the output per hour of women, although rising, is so far below that of men in the workforce that it 'drags down' the overall average.

allowance has to be made for the value of the increased leisure being enjoyed by the working population. Some further adjustment is called for inasmuch as in a dynamic economy the nature of the tasks being performed by workers is itself altering in many occupations. Such changes can be more congenial or less congenial to the worker, but, as indicated, they are difficult to measure.

It is no less difficult to measure the welfare contribution of differences in the quality of consumer goods. For a particular class of goods, say radio sets, performance may have improved radically over the last three decades along with a fall in their prices relative to all other goods. The relative fall in their prices will enter the price index in the usual way. But the attribution by economists of some addition to GNP in virtue of the improved performance involves arbitrary, and possibly controversial, assumptions. The contrary tendency, a decline over time in the quality or flavour of fruits and vegetables resulting from modern methods of production, storage and transportation associated with large-scale agribusiness, will pose a similar problem. Needless to remark, the frequent introduction in the modern economy of novel consumer goods, and the withdrawal of other goods, also exercises the ingenuity of the economist while, at the same time, extending the penumbra of doubt about the validity of the adjusted GNP estimates.

Proper valuation of the services provided by the government or public sector adds to the problems that beset the conscientious economist. For whereas there is a *prima facie* case for the assumption that – at the moment of purchase, at least – a willingness to pay £20 for an item on sale is evidence that the item cannot be worth less than £20 to the buyer, there can be no such assurance that when a man is obliged to pay an additional £20 in taxes he believes he is getting his money's worth. For in the latter case he is not free to choose. As a citizen he may well appreciate the range of services being provided by the government, but he himself may not use all or any of them. And if he did use any, he would use them in different amounts from those which he would use were he, instead, obliged to pay for them at prices that covered their costs.

Again, a common belief is that government agencies tend to become overstaffed and their efficiency low whenever their output can be compared with that of private industry. Yet the resulting higher cost of the government's output enters into the initial estimate of GNP on a par with the value of goods that the public buys from the private sector of the economy.

Further reservations arise from the fact that many useful services are performed for the nation other than those produced by the private and public sectors of the economy, such as household repairs and gardening performed by the family itself or the many services performed by voluntary organisations. The most blatant omission, however, is of services rendered by housewives in the home. It is possible, nevertheless, to make some crude estimate for the aggregate of these unpriced services by reference to the average hourly market rates for domestic services, and this is sometimes done. The best excuse for excluding such estimates from the official GNP figure has been that they do not change much over short periods and, therefore, that their inclusion would not make much difference to the year-to-year *changes* in GNP. This conventional pretext is, however, at variance with the facts. Over the last two decades the proportion of women entering the workforce has been rising sharply. In the West this proportion is approaching 50 per cent. Consequently, their service in the home has been declining over the same period, at least when measured in hours. This is a subject to which we shall return in the following chapter.

12 Why Estimates of Secular Growth in Real Income are Untenable

I

Notwithstanding these acknowledged sources of error in computing GNP for any particular year, most economists engaged in the task believe that, when used as an index of the year-to-year changes that are taking place, the resulting trend provides a fair idea – or at least not a misleading idea – of economic performance over time. Now over short periods of, say, two or three years, such errors or biases that cannot be corrected with any confidence are, in any case, not likely to vary wildly; not enough, at any rate, to vitiate the propriety of comparing GNP for two or three successive years.

But this plausible belief cannot be extended to long periods of 10, 20 or 50 years. For those who are interested in the larger question – whether the affluent societies of the West are better off in some significant welfare sense than they were 20, 40 or 100 years ago – close attention has to be paid not only to the sources of error or bias already mentioned but to other more potent sources of error and to more criticial omissions.

It should by now be evident that the ultimate ingredient of GNP or real income is not some compound of tangible goods, such as shoes and ships and sealing wax. As economists who write elementary texts are at pains to point out, although it is the price of shoes and the price of ships and the prices of all other finished goods that enter into the calculation of GNP or real income, it is the value of the *services* provided over the year by all these goods that are really to count as consumption over the year. And what is more important yet, the consumers themselves are held to be able to decide whether or not a particular item (produced in the private sector of the economy) has value, and if so what value. In other words, the value of goods produced in the private sector of the economy – the sector in which the consumer has choice – is *subjectively* determined by people according to the amount of satisfaction they anticipate from its use or possession.

Thus the aggregate of real incomes, or real consumption, over the year is, in the final analysis, an aggregate of the value of the *satisfactions* anticipated over the year by the buying public. And an index of changes in GNP, or else of changes in aggregate real income, over time is to be regarded as an index of changing satisfactions anticipated over time by the buying public.

In the event, rather than follow an older economic tradition that draws a distinction between 'economic goods' and 'non-economic goods', it is more accurate to talk of the *contribution* that economic activity can make to society's overall satisfaction or overall well-being. The goods produced by economic activity are then to be thought of only as a component of the sum of satisfactions accruing to members of society, or only a part of the total well-being or welfare enjoyed by society. But the aggregate value of these goods produced is not, as it happens, a separable and additive component. Irrespective of the trend of real income, aggregate or per capita, the changing methods of production and the flow of consumer innovations interact with and permeate people's attitudes, values, behaviour and style of living, making life for ordinary people either more or less wholesome and more or less enjoyable. The

Therefore to conclude from the upward trend in per capita real income over the last half century that our welfare has grown over time may be natural enough for those born into a quantomaniac establishment. But it is more likely that they are victims of a statistical hallucination. At all events, there are grounds enough for entertaining legitimate doubts about whether, by reference to more searching considerations, overall well-being has been rising over the last fifty years or so.

II

First, a minor observation, though worthy of attention when comparisons cover a span of some fifty years: the growing size of the government sector acts always to overstate the growth in real incomes. Inasmuch as productivity in the public sector, however measured, tends to lag behind the productivity of labour in the private sector, and does so without any commensurate lag in the salaries of public service employees, the cost of government services rises over time compared with the cost of services in the private sector. And since over a period of about fifty years the public sector in most Western economies has grown from about 10 per cent to between 40 and 50 per cent, the overestimate of real income could be significant.

Military expenditure is the largest single item in public expenditure today and is, of course, subject to the tendency mentioned above. But the expansion of military expenditure raises a more fundamental question, and one which has ramifications that we shall follow later. The question is: should economic accounting include it as an increasing component over time of per capita real income? Is the increasing expenditure on the military a contribution to welfare on a par, say, with the increasing expenditure on consumer goods?

Some competent economists have answered in the affirmative. The nation, they argue, has collectively chosen to use an increasing portion of its total resources on defence rather than on other goods. It should therefore be inferred that an additional $100 billion spent, say, by the United States on defence is worth more to the nation than any alternative collection of goods that could have been produced with this expenditure of $100 billion.

Let us concede that the nation, in its political capacity, has agreed that there is no better way of spending this $100 billion than on military defence. But is such a concession to the purpose when what concern us are the implications for welfare? If the potential enemies of the United States had not increased their military strength, the country would have chosen to spend the $100 billion on civilian goods. It follows that the nation judged it necessary to make this sacrifice of $100 billion of civilian goods that it might otherwise have enjoyed simply in order to restore military parity. It certainly does not follow that the people of the United States are made any more secure by this £100 billion of military expenditure than they were *before* the potential enemy had increased his strength.

Additional military expenditures in the endeavour to maintain the level of security are properly speaking *regrettable* expenditures. For in the absence of the perceived increase in threat from abroad, the material standard would indeed have been higher. Regrettable also are the additional expenditures being made over time in the attempt to maintain given standards of internal security. And if, notwithstanding the substantial increase in expenditures either on external or on internal security, apprehension of increased vulnerability continued to grow over the period, the economic calculation of real income would also require a further deduction from aggregate real income of a sum in addition to the deduction of the extra expenditure on security. Extension of the argument to public and private expenditures incurred in order to curb the spread of drug abuse or any other untoward postwar development is, of course, equally valid and equally indicative of the need for deductions from the original estimates of real income.

These corrections are far from being minor. When it comes to crime, which has burgeoned at an alarming rate over the last forty years, regrettable expenditures should include not only the additional ones on police, security agents and private detectives, but also expenditures by the public on more elaborate locks, on defence weapons and defence training, on security systems, and on insurance premiums. More important yet, these vastly increased outlays fall far short of the additional cost of crime to the nation for the simple reason that they have signally failed to maintain the level of security which prevailed during the years immediately following World War II. Thus, as stated above, an additional subtraction from real income has to be made in virtue of the far greater level of anxiety and occasional suffering. Although practical difficulties would attend efforts to calculate it, in principle the required sum should equal the aggregate of the minimum sums that would reconcile each member of the community to the growth in crime over the period in question. And it is not impossible that this sum, if it could be accurately calculated, would exceed the current figure for GNP itself.

The basic argument is applicable to expenditure on pollution reduction, although we have to be a little more careful since – as distinct from the trend in crime – some sorts of pollution have indeed been reduced over time. For example, public expenditure on a reduction in water pollution in year 2 is to be regarded as a good, a benefit, when compared with year 1, a year in which that much more water pollution was in existence. But expenditure in this year 2 is *not* to be regarded as a good, or benefit, when compared with a much earlier year, say year zero, when there was no water pollution whatever. For this latter comparison, the expenditure on water purification in year 2 must be regarded simply as a *regrettable*.

Thus, provided that in the movement from year zero to year 1 we do make a subtraction from GNP in consequence of the increase in water pollution, which is clearly a bad, we are entitled in moving from year 1 to year 2 to conceive the expenditure on water purification to be a good, and therefore a contribution to GNP. In our example, however, we shall still be worse off in year 2 than we were in year zero since, despite the expenditure on water purification in year 2, some water pollution remains.

What is particularly to be borne in mind from the above simple example is that the economist's choice of the base year, whether year zero or year 1, can make a decisive difference in determining whether we are being made better off or worse off with respect to one or many effects. We may, for example, conclude that we are better off in some respects compared with 10 or 20 years ago, but we may be far less certain that we are better off if we place the base year farther back in historical time.

III

Now if the arguments in the preceding section are valid, we cannot stop there. For the logic employed in questioning the propriety of regarding additional expenditures on external and internal defence, or on anti-pollution devices, as real contributions to welfare can be extended to cover all too many components of real income. On inspection, that is, and if we take our bearing from an earlier period of time, such components that enter the grand computation begin to look less like contributions to finished goods themselves and more like regrettables or intermediate goods. Put otherwise, such components of GNP can be conceived more realistically as additional *input costs* in maintaining (or attempting to maintain) a given output, or a given level of satisfaction, rather than an addition to output.

By a small stretch of the imagination much of the output currently produced by women in the workforce can be fitted into this category. The essential point can be brought out by envisaging a somewhat ironic situation in which all wives sally forth each day from their homes in order to work in local factories that specialise entirely in producing domestic labour-saving appliances. With their take-home pay they are just able to install in their home the latest microcomputer appliances so that nothing remains to do in the home but set the switches. Thus the erstwhile housewives now work exactly the same hours in the factory as they used to work in the home with the old-fashioned household implements. No less work is done in the new situation compared with the old, and no more household services are produced – the women's work in the factories being, in effect, an input of labour that is directed, ultimately, to producing exactly the same household services. Yet, as compared with the old situation, GNP will be calculated to have risen by the annual (pre-tax) incomes that these women have earned.[1]

[1] Even in so simple an example in which directly-provided household services are omitted from the original calculation of GNP, there will be some loose ends. On the one hand, there is initially a preference for factory work rather than housework. On the other, there may be some diminution in the care of home and family.

More obviously, a large part of the expenditures of modern governments, which, as noted, have grown enormously as a proportion of GNP since the turn of the century, can properly be rejected as a contribution to the value of finished goods, being instead additional costs of administration that are necessary to control and monitor a modern and more complex economy. For example, the growth in government expenditures on regulatory agencies, rate-setting agencies, conciliatory agencies and the like are clearly a part of the increased costs of running industry; as also are the additional costs incurred in order to revise standards of purity, safety and quality in the light of scientific advances, and costs incurred in order to analyse and classify scores of thousands of products and by-products coming on to the market and to disseminate the findings; as, again are the greater expenditures on tax collecting (and, of course, on tax-evasion by private corporations), and on diplomacy, on espionage, and so on.

But why stop at public expenditures? Looked at in historic perspectives, many of the services provided in the private sector of the economy – provided, for instance, by private banks, labour unions, employment agencies, travel agencies, lawyers, accountants, welfare agencies, marriage bureaus, family-counselling concerns, computer-dating firms, race-relations organisations, sex-advice clinics, and so forth – were not needed in a more traditional society of small towns and villages. They come into being and grow in importance as population grows, as it becomes more mobile, as urban areas take on metropolitan dimensions, and as the economy and the mode of living become more complex. All these agencies and institutions which spring up in response to the resulting growth in individual bewilderment and in the need for information, advice, comfort, guidance and expertise in the industrial and post-industrial milieu may be thought of as costly institutional lubricants needed for smoothing the operation of the increasingly complex machinery of society – this complexity being an unavoidable by-product of technological progress.

To be included also with intermediate goods, or with input costs, is the large and growing proportion of GNP contributed by expenditures on travel and commuting that is not enjoyed for its own sake – that, indeed may be disliked – but has to be incurred as a means of reaching a destination. And in a civilisation where stress diseases have become commonplace, a good proportion of the rising expenditure on medical care and also on vacations may be included as input costs inasmuch as they are necessary for, or at least conducive to, the continued functioning of the modern economy.

IV

We can go further. Much the larger proportion of the costs of education, in particular higher education, is a form of current expenditure that – with its predominantly vocational nature in mind – is analogous to the annual expenditures on maintaining the stock of physical capital which enter as costs in the production of finished goods. For this annual investment in higher education is likewise incurred as an input in order to maintain (and sometimes to increase) the stock of skilled human capital without which the running of a modern economy is impossible.

What has been said of education can be extended to the information media. A large part of the nation's expenditure on books, professional and popular journals, on newspapers, radio and televisions is today needed not only for direct vocational education but also for coping with the mass of accumulating information necessary for effective participation in the economic, social and political activities of a high technology civilisation. To that extent, such expenditures are, again, not so much contributions to GNP as a part of the inescapable cost of living in such a civilisation.

If these and other deficiencies in the conventional methods of estimating changes in GNP over time were recognised, and allowance made for them, the comparisons frequently made between living standards in the West and those of less industrialised nations would look much less impressive. Nor is it any less certain that if such allowances were made in calculating per capita real income in Western countries over, say, the last hundred years, the resulting growth would look significantly smaller, possibly negligible.

Taking a longer look into the past only adds to one's scepticism. With the collapse of a social life that in Britain once centred about the villages and small towns, the search for new forms of mass diversion and solace produced the music halls, the carnivals and the brass bands of the Victorian and Edwardian eras. These were followed after the turn of the century by the cinema and radio, and in the postwar era by stereophonics, television and computer games, supplemented by fantasy-sex in erotic magazines, in 'adult' theatre, in videos and 'phone-ins'. It all costs a lot more. But whether we are more amused, entertained or fulfilled it is hard to say.

The affluent society is now liberally sprinkled with private and public agencies designed to cope with the rising incidence of distress and breakdown which result from a life-style fashioned by an unrelenting technological progress. Emergency services proliferate. 'Hot-Line' facilities cater for everything from drug-abuse to post-abortion depression, from suicidal impulses to homosexual loneliness.

It is difficult to call a halt to the train of instances of technical and social innovations, of new services and institutions, that appear at first blush like contributions to a better standard of living but which turn out on reflection to be more like contributions to a higher cost of living. For although many do appear to meet a need, more often than not the need itself has been created by the process of modernisation.

The more one thinks about it the more one is compelled to recognise that much of the nation's effort and ingenuity is currently being spent producing sophisticated products and specialised services which cater ultimately to those basic biological and psychological needs that, it could be argued, were more easily and more naturally met in some of the pre-industrial civilisations.

PART VI

....

Institutional Obstacles to Environmental Sanity

13 Can 'The Tragedy of the Commons' be Averted?

I

In order to place the more vexatious features commonly associated with the modern economy we have, in Parts II and III, employed a popular framework of economic enquiry that turns on the implications of spillovers – using that term in the broadest sense. In the process the exposition has been extended to include a number of proposals and recommendations for alleviating the more conspicuous disamenities suffered by peoples in the West, in particular those inflicted by motorised traffic.

In the twenty-five years that have passed since the first edition of this book was written new instances of environmental and ecological devastation have come to the fore. Some of them, of global dimensions, are mentioned in the section below: prior to a systematic appraisal of the economic and political difficulties of effectively curbing them. Before this appraisal, however, it will be necessary to uncover another dimension of the economic approach to the spillover problem, an approach suggestive of a resolution of the problem. As we shall discover, the application of such a solution is restricted; and in a more chastened spirit we move on to consider the implications of modern aspirations and modern institutions that, in spite of our growing awareness, alarm and resolve, continue to hamper endeavours to design and implement radical environmental programmes.

II

Although popular interest in environmental issues was sparked off in the 1960s, it is only during the last decade that the media have been active in spreading environmental concern among the population at large. Today there cannot be many people so isolated from news about events that they are unaware of such phenomena as population pressure in Third World countries, or of the destruction of rain forests, marshlands, everglades and wilderness areas, or of the threatened extinction of the whale, the elephant, the rhinoceros, the tiger and other species. And only a person cut off from all sources of information can plead ignorance of the current alarm about the so-called 'greenhouse effect' on global temperatures and sea levels, about the dissipation of the planet's protective ozone mantle, and about the mounting pollution of seas, lakes and rivers.

In addition to these global perils, environmental problems have become prominent enough within the economically advanced countries. Public attention is repeatedly drawn to the damage suffered by forests and lakes from acid rain and also to the matters touched upon in earlier chapters – the traffic nightmare in the cities, the suburbanisation of the country, the fouling of beaches, and so on.

All this and more have now become part of the daily bread of our affliction that goes to feed the vague but persistent sense of guilt so much in vogue in the West. The sense of disquiet, however, is tempered by gathering expectations or hopes, that at last something is about to be done to 'stop the rot'. After all, something has just got to be done, and to be done soon. *Ergo* something surely will be done.

Such hopes can draw sustenance from the fact that in the past two years governments and politicians have become articulate about threats to the domestic and global environment. Indeed, each of the three main political parties in Britain can be seen today self-consciously daubing bits of green along the edges of their political platform. Hopes are also incited by the fact that organisations such as Greenpeace, Friends of the Earth, English Heritage, the National Trust and conservation societies generally are growing in popularity and resources; that the number of concerned scientists is increasing; that economic and ecological expertise is more sophisticated; and that the potential for meeting the challenge – in terms of information, communication, wealth and new technology – has never been greater.[1]

To be sure, for those actively engaged in exposing or combating specific environmental disorders, and for those immersed in the

---

[1] Optimism has also been fostered by the eagerness of corporations to clamber aboard the bandwagon by claiming commitment to 'environment-friendly' products and processes. Simply 'talking green' has become profitable.

planning of new controls, it is natural enough to feel optimistic or at least hopeful. Yet, once we distance ourselves from these front-line pressures and from issues of immediate concern in order to gain perspective, we shall find it hard to avoid the conclusion that the economic and political imperatives which underlie the dynamism of the modern age have not only been instrumental in moving us toward global disaster; they have also operated to resist withdrawal from it.

III

It is instructive to begin our investigation of the economic difficulties of safeguarding the environment, or more broadly speaking the biosphere, by following the economic approach to a particular kind of spillover – that which is internal to the activity itself. This approach is well illustrated by Garrett Hardin's celebrated parable of 'The Tragedy of the Commons', in which an area of land is initially available to all cattle farmers within the vicinity. Since use of the land is free, farmers continue to bring their cattle to graze there until, eventually, the numbers grazing there are unable to eat their fill, and the average weight of the cattle starts to decline. None the less, so long as each farmer can make some profit by bringing additional beasts to graze on the common land, the total number continues to rise until a point is reached at which no farmer makes a profit above his bare subsistence. Competition under these conditions clearly leads to disaster.

This homely example, which has obvious affinities with the Malthusian theory of population, is easily recognisable by the economics undergraduate as a simple example of the law of (eventually) diminishing returns, a law that is operative whenever a finite resource is involved – in this case, land, which limits the number of cattle that would otherwise expand indefinitely. And, as we shall see, in one form or another, this economic proposition has relevance to quite a range of problems in today's overcrowded planet.

In order to complete the picture, however, and to carry the argument further, it has first to be juxtaposed with Adam Smith's 'Invisible Hand' which, in seeming contradiction to the tragedy of the commons, ensures that each person pursuing only his own interest unwittingly promotes the interest of society also. And it is the logic of this providential mechanism described by Smith that underwrites the economists' presumption in favour of the competitive market.

An initial synthesis may now be effected. As Hardin himself points out, there is a simple way of avoiding the tragedy: by collective action. This can take the form of a prohibition against increasing the size of the herd on the common land beyond some predetermined size. Alternatively, the number of cattle each farmer may be permitted to bring to the commons can be rationed. In either case, the total number of cattle permitted on the land can be set at that which maximises the collective profit to the community. Again, this resulting 'optimal' number of cattle can also be brought about by levying the appropriate tax on each beast admitted on the common land.

Yet another solution is to hand over the common land to a monopolist, albeit one who has to accept the price of beef as a datum, and let him choose the number of cattle that maximises his profit. On further reflection, however, it should be apparent that exactly the same result obtains by dividing the land (not necessarily equally) among a number of farmers and conferring the same exclusive rights on each one of them.

This last case is, as indicated, of particular interest to the economist. For by removing land from common ownership and placing it instead under private ownership, the number of cattle is necessarily restricted because of the incentive for each private land-owner to exact the maximum yield from each acre of land in his possession. No state intervention is necessary.

It is not surprising then that the device of conferring property rights in the ownership of any finite natural resource – regarded as a wonderfully simple means of ensuring its optimal use – is so much favoured by economists. And it is particularly favoured for competitive markets where firms are deemed to be unable to influence the prices either of goods or of resources.

Before moving on, however, it is important for the reader to understand that this optimal, or ideal, use of a scarce resource does not afford much solace in a world where aggregate consumption itself is not limited. Where aggregate consumption is being continuously increased by the growth in aggregate income and population, the global supplies of irreplaceable natural resources will continue to diminish. The concept and the operation of 'optimality' in these circumstances amount only to continuously making the best of a steadily worsening situation.[2]

---

[2] The pro-market economist can be counted on to retort that as resources become scarcer the rise in their prices provides incentives both to discover new sources of supply and to use substitute materials or synthetics – in support of which argument he will cull a few examples over the last 200 years of industrial progress, the change-over from wood, to coal, to oil, and more recently to nuclear power, being a particular favourite. Nobody would seriously deny that for some materials and over some periods of time, the working of the market will suffice to overcome, or at least to postpone, a potential shortage. But there is no warrant for deducing from this limited experience, or from theory alone, that the economy will be able over the future to avoid all material depletions. There can be, and there have been, diminishing returns also to substitution opportunities and to investment in research.

IV

In other respects, also, the real world is less accommodating than the economists would wish. Extending property rights to arable land or to pasture land, to mineral land and to marsh land, and possibly also to the smaller lakes and to stretches of river, may work well enough, though not always well enough to prevent damage occurring on a significant scale. In other cases, however, property rights in a scarce resource are quite impracticable.

Property rights in forest lands do not work well – not unless timber companies are restricted to areas sufficiently small that, over the long term, their profits depend closely upon selective logging and reafforestation. Unfortunately, nearly all tropical rain forests, even when they are officially under government control, are treated by logging companies virtually as a commons. Thus they are being rapidly and irrevocably destroyed both by large tractor-using companies in search of quick fortunes from the export of hard woods to the industrial countries, and also by migrant peasants who use 'slash and burn' methods in levelling the forests to clear more space for farming. In the bid for quick profits or in the struggle for survival, no account is taken of the losses to be borne by future generations nor, for that matter, of the cumulative effect on the global atmosphere or climate.[3]

Deep sea fishing is another instance where, although property rights are conceivable, they would be difficult to enforce. Systems of rationing the fish catch, with the aim of preserving the fish population, may seem a bit more practical. But they are unpopular in the industry and they are costly to monitor.

In other cases, the economist's favoured solution is a non-starter. There is no way in which the earth's atmosphere can be parcelled out to corporations or private persons so as to make them responsible for its maintenance.[4] And since this is impossible, the air will continue to be used – as it always has been used in the absence of prohibitions or controls on emissions – as a common sewer.

[3] Only if all governments in the industrial countries agreed to ban imports of all tropical woods that did not originate in forest lands so controlled that reafforestation ensured maintenance of the number of trees could the global rate of deforestation be substantially reduced. In view of our political institutions and aspirations the hope of such an agreement being reached is not great.

[4] We are to conceive of each corporation not only making economic use of its own particular portion of the atmosphere allotted to it but also – since the spillovers it generates include the damage its activity inflicts on others – having to cover the costs or losses borne by all inhabitants in the area affected.

Nor is anti-pollution legislation that effective. The installation, say, of tall smoke-stacks can indeed reduce the amount of smoke suffered by the local populations but, as we now know, the wind-borne gases produced by burning fossil fuels move across national boundaries and descend on other countries as acid depositions, so damaging soil, lakes and forests.[5]

And not only does the planet's finite atmosphere continue to be used as a common sewer, its seas and oceans have long been used for dumping waste and, especially in the last few decades, extremely toxic chemical and radioactive wastes.

Aside from a few familiar instances, then, the property-rights solution has very limited application to the more serious environmental problems.

---

[5] In southern Sweden, for example, soil acidity is estimated to have multiplied ten-fold over the last 60 years. In West Germany also, where acid rain is held to be the prime cause, the number of dying trees rose from 8 per cent in 1982 to 50 per cent in 1985.

As for the contribution of carbon dioxide to the so-called greenhouse effect, for the earth as a whole, the level of this gas has increased by 40 per cent since 1860. Climate modellers warn us that as the concentration of the gas approaches a level twice that which prevailed in 1860 it will produce dramatic and irreversible changes in world climate. Yet despite the reports and the recommendations of international bodies, virtually nothing is being done to control the emissions of carbon dioxide and other gases. And in the absence of such controls, the volume of such gases will increase by about 50 per cent over the next 10 years as a result of the growth in world demand for energy.

14 Self-Sustaining Economic Predicaments

I

As conceived by economists, the standard environmental problem is simply the consequence of uncorrected spillovers. Such spillovers are marked by a disjuncture between the beneficiaries of an economic activity and the incidental losses that this same activity imposes on others either concurrently or at a later date.[1] These spillovers are the source of what economists are pleased to call 'market failure' – inasmuch as the market or price-system fails to include all the losses (or gains), present and future, that are generated by the community's economic activity. The resulting market prices, then, are 'distorted': they no longer reflect the true (marginal) costs. And since, as we know, market prices act as signals in directing the flow of economic resources, the resultant pattern of production and consumption is necessarily distorted also. There will be too much of some things on the market, and too little of others, as compared with an ideal economy in which there is no market failure.

It is not surprising therefore that a device for correcting spillover effects popular among economists is the effluent tax (or emissions tax) which is a tax on the delinquent item in question set to equal the marginal cost of the damage inflicted on society.[2] The resulting price of this item will then be one that – in this particular at least – corrects the market failure. Clearly, if all offending economic activities were corrected by such taxes, all environmental problems would be eliminated.

There is not much comfort, however, to be gleaned from this

---

[1] Since the adverse spillover is properly regarded as a collective bad, symmetrical reasoning discovers a disjuncture arising from the production of a collective good whose costs of production are borne by people today but whose benefits are enjoyed only by others at a later date.

[2] Such a tax is in fact recommended in the *Pearce Report* which came out in August 1989. In essentials, the same tax was proposed by A. C. Pigou in his *Economics of Welfare*, 1932. Since then it has been the subject of continued discussion and development in the economic literature.

reflection. Even if attention is confined to local and single spillovers, with which economists are most familiar, it is entirely possible that the costs of monitoring the effluent or pollution and the costs of collecting the tax can together exceed the calculated benefit anticipated from its imposition. This means that although the *status quo ante* – that which existed *before* the introduction of the spillover-generating activity – was better for society than is the *status quo* (with the uncorrected spillover), it is now in fact uneconomical to return to the *status quo ante*. Or to use the terminology introduced in Chapter 4, the transactions costs of correcting the spillover exceed the benefits from doing so.[3]

More serious doubts assail us when we turn to the more complex spillovers arising from our massive intervention in the biosphere. First, the range of consequences flowing from modern industrial techniques and their products is not fully known, and what is known is only partially understood. It was only in the seventies, for instance, that we began to be aware of a connection between the volume of carbon dioxide and the 'greenhouse effect', and also between the use of fluorocarbon and other gases and the erosion of the ozone layer. And the exact relations are as yet uncertain. Other equally insidious consequences of modern industrial activity may well remain hidden from us for years or decades, possibly creating irreversible damage until such time as they are identified, or not even then. In the meantime, significant and possibly critical evaluations of perils are perforce omitted from the economist's cost-benefit calculations.[4]

Secondly, even where the nature and the dimensions of some of the injurious consequences on the biosphere of specific economic activities are eventually realised or become highly suspect, the belief that years must elapse before the cumulative effect is seen to be critical encourages governments to defer taking radical measures that would impose restrictions on industry.

Thirdly, even where drastic measures are eventually being contemplated, the knowledge that years must pass before the economic sacrifice entailed will yield dividends to the community – in the form, say, of restoring an environmental amenity or of curbing the trend towards some ecological calamity – also tends to discourage thorough-going remedial action by governments.

Thus time enters in three distinct but cumulative ways to militate

[3] This important proposition is explained and illustrated in my 'Postwar Literature on Externalities: An Interpretative Essay', *Journal of Economic Literature*, 1971.

[4] A short chapter (23) of my *Cost-Benefit Analysis* (4th edition) illustrates the scope for error.

against timely reaction by peoples and governments in dealing firmly with the range of environmental consequences of industrial and agricultural activity.

Finally, insofar as the environmental and ecological consequences are transnational or global, any one government acting alone will have a limited or negligible influence in curtailing untoward trends. At the same time its initiative, which raises its export prices, will put it at some disadvantage in international trade.

So much in general is common both to the countries of the Third World and to those more affluent ones of the 'First World'. The socio-economic contexts in each of these two types of country are not altogether identical, however. Each deserves further comment.

II

In contrast to the situation in the West, the peoples of the Third World, struggling to survive in the face of relentless population pressures, are collectively more tempted, impelled almost, to ignore the clear signals of what looks like impending economic disaster. They continue to mine the soil, to level the forests, to pollute rivers and lakes, and in other ways to undermine their ecological-support system. It used to be said that disasters from this reckless despoliation would fall upon the future generation. But the day of reckoning is today all too close. Already, famine and disease stalk the land in various parts of Africa and Asia.

Thus, given an outsize population and mass poverty, ecological disaster appears to be built into the economy. The growing awareness of the impending disaster cannot, of itself, halt the process. Each and every peasant may be entirely convinced that the existing rate of population growth must, if sustained, cause widespread starvation, economic chaos, civic collapse, or internecine conflict, revolution and war, within his own lifetime. But he realises also that self-restraint on his part will do nothing to delay their occurrence. Whatever the existing or anticipated scarcity of food, whatever the ecological catastrophe predicted, it is patently in his own best interests to continue practising those incidentally ecologically-destructive methods of farming and of obtaining heat and energy that best help to support him and his family. And however unsustainable the population growth, it is equally in his own best interests to have many children in order to make provision for his later years, notwithstanding the availability of contraceptives.

97

The hope, commonly expressed, that a significant rise in living standards from increased economic involvement by the West may lift such people out of the so-called demographic trap is wholly unrealistic.[5] No aid that the government of the West could conceivably provide over the next few decades could so raise living standards among the multitudes living in Africa, Asia and South America that, as in the West, the rearing of children becomes a net cost rather than a net material benefit – a luxury rather than a form of economic insurance.[6]

Let us turn now to the countries of the First World. So impressed have they become with the need to keep abreast of new technologies and hold their position in the 'economic race' that they too are under temptation to discount the future and to shirk the collective effort necessary for a rational response to mounting environmental perils. The reluctance of governments to respond even to the most appalling spillovers is evident in their attitude to the year-by-year expansion of urban traffic, air travel, and mass tourism – an attitude of complacency if not of satisfaction at the growth of these thriving sectors of the economy. Yet, as economists know, unless the expansion of such activity is somehow curtailed, the associated disamenities will continue to accumulate until the time is reached at which the most insensitive travellers finally desist from adding to levels of traffic or to the numbers of tourists. And, of course, the closer we approach this absolute saturation point, the greater must be the resource-cost and the time-cost involved in any attempt to undo the resulting damage or, guided by optimality concepts, to reduce and contain the traffic. As indicated earlier, however, the sheer magnitude of the economic effort that would be entailed by effective remedial action in such cases acts as a deterrent.

The point can bear emphasis. Although it has been said of the modern metropolis that experts today 'know virtually everything about it . . . except how to make it clean, beautiful, and safe', the exempting clause is not literally true. We do know that, say, by

[5] Even if an economic miracle were somehow to occur within a decade or two as a result of which living standards in Third World countries became comparable with those currently enjoyed in the affluent West, the multiple increase in global consumption would devour such quantities of raw materials and dispose of such amounts of industrial and domestic waste as to wreck the global ecosystem within a few years.

[6] Nor can mass emigration from these poor countries be contemplated as a solution to their expanding populations. Given that the 3 billion people living in Asia, Africa and South America are adding annually to their numbers by over 70 million, any attempt to absorb such numbers each year by the West would cause economic and social havoc.

prohibiting all private automobiles and replacing them by electric-powered public transport, traffic clamour, fumes and congestion would disappear and lives would be saved. We know that by increased vigilance and harsher penalties, litter and vandalism could be effectively controlled. We also know that by removing postwar architectural eyesores, and by favouring more traditional architecture with greater space between buildings, the city could be made to look more attractive. And by gradually relocating much of its commerce and population, the city would assume a more human scale.

We know this. But we also know that, because of the time that would be involved in so massive a transformation, the full benefits of so ambitious an urban project would be enjoyed more by our children and our children's children, whereas the enormous costs and the prolonged incommodation would fall on us. One should not be surprised therefore at the reluctance of governments – especially democratic governments having an eye to the next election – to undertake nothing more than cosmetic and traffic-diverting schemes.

III

The world we now live in is becoming permeated with examples of the sort of daunting spillovers into which time enters in this way, and in other ways to be described.[7] And such examples are sure to multiply as our technology advances, if only because of the rapidity of innovation and of the discovery of new synthetic materials, these being a necessary consequence of modern industry's growing dependence on applied science.

Chemical fertilisers are prime examples. For decades now the dependence of agriculture in the West on nitrates has been increasing. It has taken time to recognise, as we do today, that among other environmentally injurious effects is their gradual poisoning of lakes and rivers. As for the cumulative effect in destroying the natural powers of the soil, although opinions are divided, no informed person can dismiss the potential danger. We must remind ourselves, however, that whatever the methods proposed for their control, the costs of their implementation would be considerable. Certainly attempts to control their use have so far proved ineffectual.

Pesticides are even more of an ecological threat. Currently there are

---

[7] In general, the range of spillovers grows according to (1) the density of the population, (2) the mobility of the population, (3) the prevailing material standards, (4) the variety of goods available, (5) the level of technical sophistication, and (6) the rapidity of technological change.

about 1500 varieties in common use, the number having grown ten-fold in the last twenty-five years. We learned from Rachel Carson a long time ago[8] of the expanding spiral of use and dependence that results chiefly from the increasing resistance of pests to new pesticides, and also from the circumstantial destruction by pesticides of the pests' natural enemies – to say nothing of the widespread ecological devastation wrought by these powerful chemicals. And the more persistent is their use by modern agribusiness, the more resistant become the surviving pest populations, which in turn leads to the creation and application of yet more powerful pesticides, and so on.[9]

This resulting 'pesticide addiction' by agribusiness may be regarded as another example of the disjuncture between the interests of the individual or business and those of society as a whole which, as illustrated above in Section II, is also at the heart of the population problem in the Third World. For, again, no matter how well known are the mechanics of the spiral of disaster, no matter how great is the alarm about an approaching agricultural doomsday, each individual pesticide-dependent farmer – faced as he often is with an immediate threat from new strains of pest – clearly finds it in his own economic interest to use some new and more powerful variety of pesticide.

The design and implementation of an effective solution to this current predicament are not going to be easy. Proposals to prohibit the use of pesticides would meet with strong resistance, and not only from the farm lobby. The magnitude of the costs of monitoring and enforcing controls, and of the costs of compensation, along with the time needed to move the economy to an ecologically sustainable agriculture inevitably entail higher food costs and are enough to deter governments from introducing radical anti-pesticide legislation.

IV

To conclude, the unfortunate developments we have been describing can be traced in the main to two closely related phenomena in which the common link is the driving force of technology.

---

[8] Rachel Carson, *Silent Spring*, New York, 1962.

[9] The more recent new strains of biogenetically created pest-destroying organisms are no more able to escape the same vicious spiral. Initial success will again – through the processes of natural selection – beget more resistant strains of the targeted pests, the biogenetic-engineering response to which will be the creation of powerful new predator organisms, and so on, ending possibly with some super-pest resistant alike to chemical and organic pesticides.

First, there is the mutual reinforcement of population and technology. The expansion of population can activate technology while technological advance tends to foster population growth. This process which has in varying degrees been operating for millennia has culminated today in a global population that, expanding at an exponential rate, can no longer be comfortably accommodated by the planet's finite space and finite natural resources. Although the average rate of population increase for the world as a whole is about 2 per cent per annum, it is close to zero in a number of Western countries (if we exclude illegal immigration) while being closer to 3 per cent in some of those Third World countries that are currently courting ecological breakdown.

The second phenomenon is active even in the absence of population pressures, encompassing as it does the expanding range of spillovers inevitably generated by technological progress. Thus, while there can be a defensible presumption in favour of the *laisser-faire* doctrine for the earlier and more stable economy, once technology advances beyond a certain level of complexity – a level reached by the British economy round about the second half of the eighteenth century – these spillover effects, arising initially from the new productive methods and subsequently from the sorts of consumer goods created, begin to increase rapidly and also to become more complex, far-reaching and unpredictable.

Indeed, the resulting 'market failure' is far too mild a term to denote the almost hopeless inadequacy of the price system today in directing our economic resources so as to prevent injurious environmental effects on a scale that could be moving us toward global disaster. Nor, in view of the preceding remarks on the economist's difficulty in coping with modern spillovers, and the remarks to follow on the political difficulties of introducing controls, can we suppose that growing public awareness of the nature and magnitude of the problem will, of itself, be much help.

15 Political Obstacles to Environmental Accountability

I

One can readily appreciate the political difficulties in Third World countries of implementing controls on family size or on the rampant destruction of tropical rain forests. For such controls could be seen as in fact attenuating the already meagre prospects of hundreds of millions of people clinging on to survival in various parts of Africa, Asia and South America. Within the prosperous countries of the West, on the other hand, where environmental concern, if not alarm, is everywhere apparent, the decline in urban amenity and the rise of ecological vandalism has little to do with population pressure. It has more to do with those increasingly powerful and complex side-effects that are so prevalent a feature of the modern economy.

None the less, one might have thought that the dawning realisation of the perils we run in our unflagging endeavours to extend our mastery over the planet would have begot caution if not humility among technocrats and growth-men. True, efforts are currently under way – in Britain, often enough by local councils – to combat urban decay, to reduce litter, remove unsightly hoardings, improve street lighting, widen pavements, plant trees, install more benches and bottle banks, introduce or extend pedestrian precincts or facilities, and invest in environmentally acceptable sewage plants. We may also anticipate, though with less certainty, legislation requiring the fitting of catalytic converters to automobiles, or of silencers to motorcycles and perhaps even to garden implements. Neither is it wholly impossible that emission taxes on the more toxic industrial wastes may be widely enforced, and the standards of safety and food purity raised.

Yet beyond the introduction of a limited number of schemes that are not too costly or politically controversial, there cannot be much warrant for optimism. Proposals for a radical programme of urban rehabilitation, or for enforcement of a comprehensive system of controls on all the chief sources of pollution, are likely to be costly, disruptive and time-consuming. What is more, and what is now to be emphasised, the very characteristics of the age we live in, as reflected in its basic aspirations and institutions, make it difficult for the peoples of the West – in their capacity as citizens, consumers and producers – consistently to rank environmental commitment before material considerations. To illustrate:

First, the overwhelming majority of citizens, and almost all those at the helm of policy, are deeply imbued with the concept of sustained, if not accelerating, economic growth, which they generally regard as a self-evident economic imperative. And this universal policy objective is supported by common myths that serve, respectively, in the capacity of carrot and stick.

Within the carrot category are those populist and egalitarian sentiments repeatedly echoed by the spokesmen of all credible political parties, the emphasis being on 'the good things of life' for the ordinary person – even when, as it happens, he is already immersed in an environment that is half choked with the noxious by-products of all too many of those 'good things'. This politically unexceptionable rhetoric is frequently accompanied by exhortation to greater economic effort, seen as the necessary precondition of yet more of those 'good things of life' and also as the sure means of removing residual pockets of material hardship within an otherwise prosperous community.

The stick is no less in evidence than the carrot in muting environmentalist protest about the malignant overspills of industry. For are we not perpetually being lectured by successive chancellors about the vital importance of a 'sound', and more 'dynamic' and more efficient economy if the country is to survive, or to hold its own, in this new and more competitive world? Some environmental improvements there must be, they concede. But, as always, 'economic viability' is the more immediate and the prime consideration, a consideration reinforced by recognition of the manifest competitive disadvantages suffered by any country that pioneers effective environmental legislation.

Fortifying the contemporary presumption in favour of faster economic growth is the argument that only thus can we provide the wherewithal to meet the scientific establishment's voracious demand for more resources – for more sophisticated laboratories, more powerful equipment, and more funds for research at all levels which, it is alleged, extends man's power over nature and so enriches our lives.

The economic growth imperative, then, is deeply embedded in the ethos of the modern age. Well-oiled rationalisations in its support roll calmly over all doubts and protests. Whenever they are faced with disturbing evidence of environmental degradation or hazard, politicians resort to the rhetoric of environmental commitment while unrepentant growth-men are apt to take refuge in vacuous phrases about not abandoning economic growth but giving it 'a new direction'. The sum of all, according to the authorised version, is that although we should give ear to all green proposals, in the end we have to be 'realists'. Only limited resources can be diverted to environmental improvements if our economy is to survive in an increasingly competitive world.

II

The *second* characteristic of the age that enters into an explanation of why, even within the more affluent economies, the scale of environmental progress will continue to be limited is the uneven distribution of political power in the community. Irrespective of the extent of public protest, each environment-offending industry – for example, the nuclear industry, the chemical industry, the automobile industry, the oil industry, the farming industry, the travel industry – eventually creates a well-organised and highly motivated lobby having articulate press officers and with ample means for advertising and for wooing the support of political representatives. They also tend to have ready access to government departments where their views are often sought and their recommendations carefully deliberated.

In contrast, the ordinary citizens whose health or amenity is under threat from the operations of, or the items produced by, an industrial plant located, or to be located, within the vicinity are, initially at least, unorganised, unequally informed, unequally articulate, and dispersed over a large area. Even though they may all be deeply concerned, in the absence of specific legislation it is both costly and time-consuming to bring into being an organisation durable and effective enough to persuade local or central authorities to take their views seriously.

All the same, and notwithstanding these obstacles, a number of well-informed and resourceful organisations have come into being since World War II, outstanding among which are those dedicated to environmental protection. Their limited personnel and funding, however, enables them to focus at any one time only on a limited number of issues, and although such organisations are usually represented at major inquiries, their views and recommendations carry little weight whenever they conflict with the broad tenor of government economic policy.[1] To illustrate, despite the protection accorded to National Trust land and despite vociferous public protest, successive British governments have succeeded in appropriating thousands of acres of natural beauty in 'the national interest' – for the armed forces, for motor highways, or for 'vital new' industries that create employment opportunities.

The organised opposition of industry to systematic controls, including emission taxes, has been recently strengthened by the resurgence of faith in the economic virtues of private enterprise.[2] Opposition to government intervention in industry is rationalised by the difficulty of measuring and monitoring the flow of waste emissions, by the considerable costs of enforcing emission taxes or other controls, and by the access of power conferred on government departments along with the unavoidable opportunities for corruption. These arguments are by no means ill-founded. Indeed, there is mention in Section I of the preceding chapter of cases in which, although the pre-pollution state of affairs was economically preferable, unchecked pollution could well expand beyond the point at which it would then be too costly to correct – which, of course, is one more reason why hopes for a restoration of environmental amenity will recede before economic realpolitik.

III

A *third* factor militating against proposals to restrict the operations of the private sector of the economy is the time-honoured presumption in favour of industry; there is a tradition of court rulings, reinforced by local authority decisions, in support of the maxim that some public inconvenience is to be borne with in the interests of economic progress. The maxim, however, is less convincing in an affluent 'high tech' economy that looks to be pressing the bulk of the consuming public ever closer to the margin of surfeit while simul-

---

[1] To be sure, there are now ministers of environmental affairs in Western governments. But much of their expertise is directed toward defending government policies against criticism by environmentalists.

[2] Among the torch-bearers of the private-enterprise culture, honourable mention should be made of the Institute of Economic Affairs, in London, and the Fraser Institute in Vancouver, Canada. Both organisations pay ritual homage to the writings of Milton Friedman and Friedrich Hayek and assiduously ignore criticisms of their arguments.

taneously exposing it to an expanding horizon of environmental hazard.

Yet no matter how high our material standards of living, no matter how much we are now getting in each other's way, the hard-line establishment continues to find in favour of economic expansion whenever it conflicts seriously with environmental preservation. Notwithstanding official inquiries, and continued opposition by local populations and conservation societies, choice areas of Britain's countryside, including those areas of outstanding natural beauty ostensibly protected against encroachment by industry, are destined to dwindle over time.

Sooner or later, and probably sooner, the pressure of a more nomadic motoring population, whose mobility is being augmented by massive highway developments that are so popular with the motoring public, and whose spending power is growing over time, comes to inflate the demand for tourist accommodation, and also the demand for second or third homes in once remote villages, near the sea, or in the countryside. Suburbanisation will therefore continue to spread outward and to invade hitherto protected areas, woodlands, coastlands, so-called green belts – a process that will end only when every market town, fishing village and country retreat is sucked into the swirl of motorised motion that is engulfing the country.[3]

Add to this pressure the current trend toward decentralisation of industry and commerce, the siting of industrial parks in rural surroundings, the development of new and existing holiday resorts (supplemented by coastal marinas and conference hotels) with the declared aim of attracting greater numbers of domestic and foreign visitors – investment that is not only activated by expectations of high returns by businesses and local councils but is also officially sanctioned by the prospect of increased reserves of foreign exchange and inevitably, of course, by the creation of 'employment opportunities' – and this time-honoured presumption in favour of industry can be depended upon to diffuse the area of environmental degradation and to destroy irrevocably ever more of Britain's dwindling heritage of natural beauty.

[3] A report published by the Council for the Protection of Rural England in May 1989 states that since 1986 there has been a dramatic shift from farmland to housing sites. Conservation experts believe that within a few years once-rural Sussex will complete its transmogrification into a sprawl of yuppy houses, business parks and by-passes. The situation will be worse still if the government implements its plan to link Dover to Southampton by a super highway.

IV

This presumption in favour of industry is, moreover, buttressed by an unwritten convention, one possibly inspired by common law, to the effect that, as with any accused person or body, an economic activity also is to be presumed innocent unless proved to be guilty beyond any reasonable doubt. In consequence, whatever the injury or peril to society that is attributed to an industry or its product, there is a conventional predilection in favour of freedom of the industry to continue its operations until evidence of serious damage to the public interest has been established beyond reasonable doubt.

This implicit methodological rule, that industrial activity be regarded as beneficial to society unless the contrary has been clearly demonstrated, might be justified if its products were vital to the survival of the community or if, at least, it made a critical contribution to the material welfare of a population in which most people live close to subsistence levels. But in the post-industrial economy, where physical subsistence has long been passed and where a growing proportion of the goods consumed are far from being necessary,[4] this methodological rule is an anachronism. And there are instances where adherence to it is sheer folly.

The continued dumping of radioactive wastes into the sea, there being as yet no clear evidence of large-scale radioactive contamination of fish, is a topical example. Another can be found in our response to the annual emission of some 5 billion tons of carbon dioxide from the burning of trees, coal, oils and natural gas which, it is believed, is gradually raising global temperatures, therefore raising sea levels, and otherwise globally affecting climate. Since a reliable relationship between the volume of gas and the global rise in temperature has not yet been determined, no radical controls are currently being planned.

Sparks of hope may have been ignited by the international agreements of 1988 and 1990 by which a number of industrialised and Third World countries bound themselves to phase out the use of

---

[4] Working housewives, both in America and Britain, are often quoted as saying that they need to find work outside the home in order 'to make ends meet'. This strikes the economist as strange since, according to conventional indices, living standards are estimated to be more than twice those prevailing in the late thirties – at a time, that is, when most housewives remained at home, the husband being the sole provider.

The explanation, however, is not that elusive. Rising material expectations, encouraged as they are by politicians, act to transform one-time luxuries into ordinary necessities. Automobiles, videos, labour-saving gadgetry, extensive wardrobes, foreign travel, frequent dining out, are among the goods that were unavailable even to middle-class families before World War II and are today commonplace goods for all but the poorer families.

chlorofluorocarbons and other suspect gases by the end of the century. This future self-denying ordinance has not been universally adopted by a long chalk, even though complying with it would not in fact place much strain on either industry or consumer. More pertinently, no one can say at present whether the global volume of these gases is currently rising or falling, or even whether it is more likely to rise or fall over the next decade.

Given the record of persistent reluctance of governments to introduce draconian legislation to enforce controls over industry, we continue to run the risk that the kind of indisputable evidence that will alarm governments and impel them toward immediate and drastic action will begin to surface only when disaster, possibly global disaster, can no longer be averted.

Certainly this anachronistic burden-of-proof convention should be reversed, at least for already affluent countries. A prudent concern for our own and our children's survival should suffice to countenance a presumption *against* industrial innovation. Translated into policy, such a presumption would lay it down that no innovation be adopted, or placed on the market, until exhaustive tests over a long period had established beyond all reasonable doubt that its production or use carried with it no uncontainable risk to human health or human survival. To be sure, strict implementation of this policy would tend to provoke resentment in 'the enterprise culture' even though the resulting delays would cause no real hardship to the already pros-perous countries of the West.

It is unlikely, however, that sanity will prevail in this respect. For the adoption of this more prudent procedure, one which puts the burden of proof squarely on the shoulders of the innovators and commercial sponsors, would assuredly weaken the incentive to enterprise and innovation: it would slow down the pace of economic expansion and delay opportunities for consumer gratification.

V

It is hard to avoid the conclusion that hopes currently entertained of a brighter environmental future are unlikely to be realised. Admittedly, we may confidently anticipate some local improvements of the sort mentioned in Section I: more provision for pedestrians and cycles, more park benches and tree-planting, more bottle-banks and more recycling of paper and other materials, better methods of garbage disposal and a reduction of litter. Again, and possibly under the conspicuous guidance of benevolent Eurocrats in Brussels, some progress may be made in the control of noise levels and pollution levels of inland and coastal waters. Legislation requiring catalytic converters to be fitted on automobiles cannot be ruled out. And it seems likely that standards of food and water purity will continue to rise. All such modest though worthwhile measures can count on broad public support. They are not too costly and they are unlikely to incite strong opposition from industry or trade unions. Finally, and within a global context, one may anticipate more determined measures to protect endangered species of fauna and flora.

There is, in contrast, practically no hope of saving the countryside from continued suburbanisation in view of the growing demand, foreign and domestic, for second and third homes in the country arising from the increasing wealth and mobility (soon to be augmented by the Channel Tunnel), and in view also of the expansion of industrial parks and caravan sites, and of the efforts being made by national and local tourist boards to attract business people and foreign and domestic holiday makers. Nor can there be much hope – in the absence of alarm among travellers about the growth of crime in foreign resorts – of arresting the spread of 'tourist blight' in the Mediterranean region and beyond, even though governments are aware of the economic and social instability that can be imported along with a massive annual influx of foreign visitors. The short-term interests of governments, commerce and the travelling public all coincide, and their power completely swamps that of the environmental lobby. Indeed, the knowledge that areas of rare natural beauty, hitherto untouched, are now to be built over by developers only makes us all the more anxious to fly there and enjoy what remains before it is too late.

Finally, one cannot feel optimistic about the future of the global environment. While it is not entirely impossible that the poisoning of the oceans with chemicals, with oil, and with radioactive wastes will diminish with advances in monitoring techniques and other innovations, international accord will be hard to reach so long as the danger is not clear and imminent. Much the same remarks apply to the pollution of water and soil with landfills of toxic industrial wastes and of the atmosphere with carbon and nitrous gases from the burning of fossil fuels and of forests. Even if the industrialised countries somehow managed to agree to limit ground and air traffic and also to place tighter controls on factory emissions, such agreements are unlikely to have more than a temporary and limited impact in delaying the greenhouse and other effects that could lead to global disaster. For one thing, the major Third World countries, desperate to expand their industrial base, will soon draw upon the immense reserves of coal in China and India and will not be too fastidious about the resulting pollution.[5] And between the operations of giant corporations and the land needs of migrant farmers, their forests will continue to dwindle. Finally, so long as populations continue to increase in Africa, Asia and South America so, over the next decade at least, will the extent of deforestation and 'desertification'.

One has to be inordinately optimistic not to be a neo-Malthusian. As Third World populations continue to expand, so will regional disaster increase in frequency and scale. The wealthier countries of the West will be continually called upon for supplies of food, medicines, clothing, equipment and assistance of many kinds, all of which will place a growing strain on their resources and, inevitably alas, also on their patience and goodwill.

Pessimism, warranted pessimism, does not end there, however. As the pressure of population builds up in various parts of Africa, Asia and South America, there will be more determined efforts to escape the engulfing poverty or internecine conflicts by migrating to the industrialised countries of the West. And as such people infiltrate (legally and illegally) into Western countries in increasing numbers, one may anticipate ethnic antagonisms which will act to strain existing political institutions and to undermine the traditions of the culture of the once-nation states. Within the resulting more divisive pluralist societies, the maintenance of law and order will entail more restrictive legislation and readier intervention by a more powerful police establishment.

VI

Yet even before the Malthusian nightmare engulfs the greater part of the globe our attention will be engrossed by a particular facet of the population problem – the number of overswollen cities that will have

---

[5] The notion, occasionally broached by Western politicians, of annual tribute to poorer countries in order to encourage them to finance ambitious programmes of reafforestation, and of changeover to less toxic technologies, cannot be taken seriously. The astronomical cost of attempting so grandiose a global economic strategy takes it out of range of the politically feasible. And even if a contract of this sort could be drawn up between the West and the major Third World countries, we should be faced with the problems, both technical and political, of continually monitoring and, where necessary, enforcing the economic policies and industrial technologies agreed upon – possibly in the face of popular resentment and of political instability among the recipients of economic aid.

become increasingly vulnerable and ungovernable. The greater number of monstrously distended metropolitan cities are located within the Third World: Mexico City with a population of 18 million and still expanding, to say nothing of Cairo currently approaching 14 million, or Calcutta, São Paulo, Buenos Aires, Bangkok, to mention only the more familiar. Each is teeming with traffic, forested with high-rise hotels and luxury apartments, and girdled about with slums, the whole being surrounded by a vast expanse of improvised shacks, the so-called shanty towns, home to hundreds of thousands of half-starved families struggling each day to keep body and soul together amid wretchedly primitive and often insanitary conditions. Bearing in mind that about fifty per cent of the peoples of most Third World countries are below the age of twenty, and that the young continue to pour into the cities, for the most part hungry, desperate for employment, easily disoriented by the endless clamour and concrete, easy prey for upstart demagogues and crime gangs, it is not far-fetched to regard these outsize conurbations as living near the brink of urban disaster.

A breakdown of the electricity or the water supply, an acute shortage of fuel, a crop failure, an outbreak of food poisoning, an epidemic, a sudden influx of migrants into the city or one of its neighbourhoods, a spell of oppressive weather, some chance event releasing alarm or fury – any one or other of such contingencies could act as a catalyst and transform pockets of disaffection into blind rebellion, with incensed mobs rampaging through the streets, looting and burning. It could end with bands of desperados roaming the countryside, scavenging, stealing, and murdering for food.

So far this combustible material has not exploded. But as pressure on limited space and resources grows apace, as the economic struggle for the vast 'underclass' becomes more precarious, civic control becomes weaker until a critical point is reached at which any of the catalytic events mentioned overwhelms the attenuated forces of law and order, so plunging the city into chaos and, possibly also, the country into civil war.

It is admittedly possible to take action to avoid such catastrophes. The implementation of by now familiar recommendations in official reports – effectively to dismantle the new urban jungles, to disperse their industries and office buildings, and to resettle most of their populations in new areas – might prove effective were such pro-grammes to be completed within a few years. But because of political obstacles, because of internal feuding and frequent border skirmishes, because of the time and financial strain involved in implementing the necessary radical programme, whatever steps are taken by governments are generally irresolute, tardy and ultimately ineffectual. The plain fact is that the problem is becoming more acute and the danger drawing closer – although, in our human frailty, we go on hoping that what looks as if it must almost certainly happen can somehow be averted.

BOOK TWO

....

The Social Consequences

PART VII

....

Towards an Admass Future

16 Reflections on the Good Life

I

Few phrases can sound more impressive to the layman than 'the free and unchecked spirit of enquiry' or, more poetic perhaps, 'the questing spirit of man' – phrases by which the diverse, fitful and narrowly specialised research efforts of thousands of scientists are blithely sanctified regardless of the social consequences they eventually produce. When one speaks of *man* in these rhetorical phrases, it is generally understood that it is the scientific fraternity which is being envisaged. The joys of 'free enquiry' are, in any case, the preserve only of the few. It may be suspected that they are treading the Faustian path to perdition. But their fate, alas, will be shared by the rest of mankind.

Looked at in historical perspective, the scientific way of life is a new way of life, one shaped by the specialised techniques that the scientist has to master and employ. In truth, problem-solving has become the opiate of the scientist, and too often also his refuge from the brawling world. His research and his published articles are the sources not only of his livelihood but also of his self-esteem. The kudos includes travel to conferences in exotic places, public orations, press notices, professional recognition, a secure place in the pecking order, media interviews, political consultation, and the prospect of public honours. Vested interests could hardly be more compelling and, accordingly, the propensity of the scientist to rationalise the fruit of his labours in terms of potential benefit to mankind is all but irresistible. What is more, few scientists will openly object to a research project simply because no apparent purpose could be attributed to it (how can we know?) or because the research could result in discoveries which may be used to expose humanity to new perils.

Certainly there are increasing dangers in continuing the efforts to push forward the frontiers of science when once the process has come to depend on a yet more minute fragmentation of the existing branches and sub-branches of science. And there are dangers also in the growing complexity of the products being created and the substances being discovered. The former, the multiplication of the already specialised divisions within a branch of science, is evidently an unavoidable trend in view of the sheer accumulation of knowledge and its pace of advance. But it acts to diminish the aptness and reliability of the advice that the scientist tenders to officials. For no matter how narrowly the issue is defined, there can be consequences or risks of consequences that lie outside his field of competence. Indeed, there can be a range of consequences that are unforeseen and unforeseeable at the time by any scientists.

As for the latter trend, that of the complexity of new substances and products, the ecological and health hazards are by no means evident at the time of discovery. In spite of legal requirements for extensive testing of new chemicals, it is easy enough to recall instances of harmful chemicals that were widely marketed in recent years, such as DDT and other pesticides, or Thalidomide and other sedatives.[1]

Bearing in mind the reluctance to abandon expensive projects even when they are known to be both uneconomic and dangerous, and the equal reluctance to withdraw suspect drugs from the market until the case against them is established beyond reasonable doubt,[2] one has to be exceptionally sanguine to believe that we shall be able over the future to escape man-made disasters, local and global.

But are the risks worth it? Even if we were able to run the gauntlet of potential disaster without grave mishap, can there be any reasonable presumption that we are moving toward a better life, a more harmonious civilisation? Before giving reasons for doubt at

[1] It is far from improbable that there are a number of thalidomide drugs in current use that have deleterious genetic effects which operate more slowly over time, making them difficult to detect. Some fifteen years ago an article in *The Sunday Times* (25 May 1975) estimated that about 100,000 women each year in Britain had been taking pregnancy tests with drugs currently suspected of giving rise to birth deformities.

[2] Not all readers may be aware that at the turn of the century, German scientists working in the Bayer Company succeeded in synthesising a crystallised compound from morphine which was marketed under the trade name of 'Heroin'. It was stated to be non-addictive and was recommended in the medical journals as a means of treating morphine addiction. Ten years had to pass before heroin was recognised by the medical profession as highly addictive and dangerous.

If it were not so grim a tale it would be amusing to discover how, in this instance, history repeated itself. Methadone, a synthetic drug developed during World War II, again by German scientists, had been widely used as a substitute drug in the treatment of heroin addicts. After encouraging reports of success for many years, investigations undertaken by the US Drug Enforcement Administration in 1974 revealed that the deaths from illicit use of Methadone surpassed those from heroin, and that Methadone constituted a substantial share of the illegal traffic in drugs.

For further details the reader is referred to E. J. Epstein's article, 'Methadone: the Forlorn Hope', *The Public Interest*, Summer 1974.

greater length, it may be laid down as a judgement of fact that sustained economic growth, the spread of democratic institutions, progress in reducing levels of pollution and global hazards, and success in preserving areas of natural beauty, are all compatible with a manifest deterioration in the quality of life – at least they are so whenever that term is less restrictively interpreted and therefore more realistically extended to encompass those less tangible and more psychological dimensions of life more readily evoked by such words as 'the good life'.

To be sure, every innovation, whether of some appliance or service, whether of some chemical or wonder material or method of production, initially promises some saving or some novelty of sensation or experience. A minor question is whether a sequence of innovations, insofar as they are passed on to the consuming public, does more than punctuate the tedium that threatens the affluent society; whether, after the first twinges of exhilaration, or after the novelty has worn off and it becomes but another bit of trivia, there remains any residue of enduring satisfaction.

The major question, however, is that of the continuing effect over time of this unending succession of innovations on the shape of our civilisation and therefore on our capacity to enjoy life. And it is in an endeavour to answer this larger question that we have now to consider the main tendencies operating on what is commonly referred to as the quality of life. The term is a rather loose one, however, having a penumbra of connotations. But since the ongoing transformation of the quality of life is the central issue – the issue about which our final judgement has to turn – it behoves us to be as explicit as possible.

II

Expressing the matter in the most general terms,[3] we may conceive the good life to be one that manages to bring man into harmony with himself: one establishing an external order that does no violence to his internal order, so that his basic instincts and his aspirations may range without hurt to himself or others. More specifically, however, we take the bold step of listing the chief constituents of the good life, or a good life, that are likely to command support among those who have given serious thought to it. Acknowledging some overlap among them, we

---

[3] With the West in mind, I am ignoring the material prerequisites: adequate food, clothing and shelter. What residual pockets of poverty and deprivation remain in the West arise from institutional and political causes, not from any shortage of productive capacity.

may label them as follows: amenity, leisure, self-esteem, culture, community, family, love, trust, faith and freedom. A word about each:

Amenity is a broad category including, as it does, the sense of space and ease and, therefore, a well-designed urban area, clean air, protection against noise, and easy access to meadow and woodland.

Leisure regarded as part of the good life has to be distinguished from time spent on travel, recreation and vacations, insofar as they involve tight schedules, haste or anxiety, or are otherwise chiefly a means to realising self-appointed objectives. The leisure in question is that unpre-empted carefree leisure that imparts margin and gladness to life.

Self-esteem arises from successful achievement, from mastery of a craft or skill, or at least from assurance that one's work is valued by the community. It may be strengthened by familiarity with modern knowledge and culture.

Culture is used here as a shorthand for civilised standards of taste, in manners and the arts, as maintained perhaps by an elite but also generally recognised by the mass of the populace. The coexistence of high culture and low-life vulgarity is all too common in history. Yet concern is warranted only when vulgarity comes to dominate everyday discourse, when obscenity struts brazenly in the market-place, and when the nation no longer has the desire or the will to curb or arrest either.

The *community* that is relevant is not that of an association of scholars or artists, or of professionals of any sort, valuable though these may be; nor yet that of trade unions, business associations, or of societies or clubs where dues are paid for the use of facilities. In connection with any vision of the good life, the community is to be understood as a community of families living within a locality, say a village, or the neighbourhood of a town or suburb. Within it, the families regularly enjoy the hospitality of each other's homes: they 'drop in' without appointment. And they come to depend upon one another for solace and support, for gossip and entertainment.

The *family*, whether nuclear or extended, is still conceived as the primal cell upon which all social organisations from the tribe to the nation state are built. The psychological importance of a good and dependable family relationship, both for its abiding source of comfort and support for the individual and for the formation of his character – which impart stability and cohesiveness to society – can hardly be overestimated.

Love: a life without love, or one without even the hope of love, is an arid, dreary and painful fate. Indeed, the belief that one has been cheated of love can lead to bitterness, vindictiveness, ruthlessness and even crime. The term encompasses not only romantic love but also filial love, fraternal love, and those abiding friendships that evolve slowly and are therefore more likely to be formed within stable communities.

Trust is essential to any good life inasmuch as without it there can be no real communion, no mutual unburdening of the soul. It is, of course, also essential in day-to-day affairs and the world of business since, without some minimal confidence in the integrity of those we have to deal with, the country's economy would hardly be viable.

Faith: no matter how enlightened the age, men yet crave belief in the existence of a supreme being – or father figure, as psychologists would have it – but certainly a divine overseer and protector who is deemed to be an infallible source of understanding and compassion. Apparently there is a deep-rooted need to discover such a being if only because it opens the heart and in doing so brings people into closer communion through a shared spiritual conviction and common worship.

III

Freedom is a word that can be extended to cover any conceivable aim simply by appending to it the operative preposition 'to' or 'from'. Familiar examples are 'freedom from hunger', 'freedom to travel', 'freedom from unemployment', 'freedom from disease', 'freedom from police molestation', 'freedom from barking dogs', and so on. Important though such contrived freedoms may be to some people, the freedom that is to be included among the components of the good life is confined to the classical conception in which three elements are variously emphasised: (1) freedom from state repression, (2) freedom of speech and action, and (3) freedom from intimidation by others.

The first, (1), tends to receive the greatest attention, at least within the Western democracies and within those nations which aspire to become liberal democracies, since it is commonly (though mistakenly) associated with democratic government. Among political philosophers, ancient and modern, however, freedom from state oppression – in effect, the rule of law – is ranked well above democracy which, until recently, was often more feared than any other form of government. Certainly in Britain, freedom from state oppression preceded democracy. Centuries before the spread of enfranchisement in the nineteenth century the liberties of Englishmen were protected by the Common Law, by *habeas corpus*, by the independence of the judges, and trial by jury.

The second element, (2), comprising freedom both of expression and activity, can be separated. Both John Milton in the seventeenth century and Lord Acton in the nineteenth passionately defended freedom of utterance in the name of conscience, chiefly of religious conscience. In John Stuart Mill's famous treatise on liberty, however, freedom of expression was regarded not only as a means of sifting truth from falsehood but also, and as a corollary, a precondition for social progress. As for freedom of individual action, it was to be curbed only where it abridged the freedom of others. This proviso is more liberally interpreted as applying to the limiting of those activities that are a nuisance to others or, in other ways, to the direct reducing of their welfare. And it is often extended to activities that are deemed to interfere with the duty of the state to protect society.

As for the third element of freedom, (3), it may no longer be guaranteed even within the most powerful state. Yet without freedom from the threat of violence by others the capacity to enjoy life is seriously impaired.

The most pertinent observation to be made with respect to each of these elements of the classical conception of freedom is that the greater the degree of moral consensus – which consensus encompasses norms of propriety – the less likely is any man's speech or writing or behaviour to offend others. In consequence, there is less need for state regulation and intervention. Moreover, the more enduring the consensus, the more enduring is the resulting libertarian establishment. Once this consensus erodes, however, the social conflicts that emerge may be contained only by increasing state regulation and control.

IV

I shall not trouble myself at this stage to persuade the reader that, with respect to each and every feature of the good life mentioned above, the trend since World War II has been downward. On the criteria proposed, therefore, the quality of life has undoubtedly been declining. Certainly in any comparison with the generation before World War II, the peoples of the West have become more impatient for more of everything (as evidenced in such phrases as 'the revolution of rising expectations', the widespread insistence on 'rights' and 'entitlements', and the frequency of wage-claims); more unruly (as exemplified by recurrent demonstrations, confrontation with the police, and occasional revolts against legislative acts); more violent (as universally acknowledged, and confirmed by burgeoning crime statistics over the last four decades); more morally perplexed (as revealed by 'modernistic' rejection of the concept of sin or evil, by the trend toward acceptance of the idea of 'moral relativism', and by popular recourse to the adjective 'judgmental' as a form of censure); and increasingly vulgar and shameless (as can be confirmed by the growing popularity among all age groups of four-letter words in ordinary conversation, and by the tolerance of the promiscuous, the obscene and the near-pornographic, in the media and the theatre).

The question that should engross us is whether these unfortunate trends are a fortuitous outcome or whether, instead, there are clearly discernible tendencies operating within modern civilisations which necessarily act in this and other ways to diminish the quality of life and, therefore, its enjoyment. If we conclude that the latter is the case, we must also conclude that such trends will continue.

In as brief a space as is consistent with coherent argument, reasons will now be given to substantiate my belief that there are, indeed, tendencies inseparable from the ethos, activities and aspirations of modern societies that necessarily act to depress the quality of life. These tendencies themselves, however, have been given shape and direction by the primary forces of science and technology, on the one hand, and, on the other, and more particular to the West, by the institutions of liberal democracy and the market economy.

V

Pure science seeks to uncover the physical laws governing the universe, and from these laws or constructs *applied* science, directed toward more specific research, exerts an increasing mastery over nature. Technology translates this control over nature into innovations that both transform the methods of production and contrive new artefacts for the greater convenience and pleasure of the citizen.

Contributing also to the emergent life-style common to the Western nations are the institutions mentioned. On the one hand, there is popular democracy, being formally the process by which the collective will of the nation is directed toward efforts to promote social justice and security. On the other hand, there is the free market operating within a private enterprise system and regarded today as a powerful mechanism in the creation and diffusion of material prosperity.

To these primal and institutional forces may be attributed the economic and political achievements of the Western nations, and impressive they certainly are. Yet, as we shall see, each alone or in combination is also coming to exact a fearful toll on the quality of our lives.

We may mention in passing that among those who have begun to perceive that there is indeed 'something rotten in the state of Denmark', either of two explanations finds favour. The first, and more general and philosophical, explanation turns on the hubris of men who, blind to their fallibility, are driven into error or excess. Condemned in particular is the scientists' thirst for glory, the greed for profits, the zeal of technocrats, the craving for office. The second explanation is more specific and more familiar among economists. Practically all the untoward trends arising from a misallocation of resources are attributable to that vexatious phenomenon we have referred to in Parts II and III as 'spillovers'. Such as they are, they are seen to hamper the otherwise providential action of Adam Smith's 'Invisible Hand'. Thus it is, according to the economist, that the individual's pursuit of self-interest within the legal framework can also promote social friction, disharmony and occasional disaster.

Both explanations are valuable, and the second, in addition, has already been shown to be far-ranging. Yet neither goes far enough, not nearly. I intend, therefore, in the remaining pages to exhibit in more detail the crucial connections between, on the one hand, the aforementioned primal and institutional forces and, on the other hand, the many developments that, particularly since World War II, have come to afflict modern societies.

VI

Consider first some of the social implications of the unquestioned ascendancy of science in the West. I say 'unquestioned' simply because in the recognised accommodation between science and religion, whatever concession has been made since the eighteenth century has invariably been made by the church, though more particularly by the Protestant churches. The fact is that no educated person living in the West, including churchmen, would ever think of upholding any religious dogma that is seen to conflict with the historical or scientific evidence. In this critical respect, then, our civilisation is patently a secular civilisation.

To be sure, the passing of the age of faith also precludes further opportunities for directing people's religious fervour into crusades against the infidel or for engendering internecine persecutions. Yet it is no less evident that citizens of the godless society are more exposed to despair, anguish, and tormenting doubts about life's purpose and destiny. The unshakeable belief in an omnipotent and benevolent divine creator has, in ages past, been a source of joy and hope to ordinary people; a source also of support and comfort whenever they were overtaken by misfortune or bereavement. Secular societies are also prone to other infirmities, in particular to gnawing doubts, forebodings and moral disorientation. Insofar as man has an innate desire to open his heart to a higher being, the spiritual vacuum created by a secular establishment eventually fills with a desperate assortment of new cults: commercialised evangelism, totalitarian ideologies, and other fanatical movements.

The resulting pandemonium is often referred to as 'religious pluralism', pluralism being the favoured term to convey the impression of an establishment of greater tolerance and choice. Yet the postwar multiplication of religious sects, factions and breakaway bodies in the West appears to have bred the notion of a religion as an instrumental entity, a purpose-built construct of beliefs and rituals assembled from the components displayed in a do-it-yourself religious emporium, the aim of any parvenu religion being to impart a measure of sanctification – and perhaps legal protection also – to new social or political activities, to fashionable ideologies and aberrant movements.[4] Even within the larger loose-knit denominations remaining – such as the Church of England – what were once perceived as spiritual doctrines and injunctions are reinterpreted to carry political implications and to serve secular objectives.[5]

[4] It is true that religions have evolved over time or, rather, changed over time with the rise and fall of civilisations. It is also true that there have been periods of acute conflict between competing religions, often enough when they were being used for worldly purposes. But it does not follow from such historical facts that the mass of people living in any age were aware of the connection between economic and political conditions and the prevailing forms of worship. All past religions were deemed to be of divine origin at the time. They have all centred on personal gods who were believed to be closely involved in the affairs of men. And whatever the religion adhered to, it was held to be true for all time.

[5] Surrendering to the exigencies of modernism, Protestant religions are active in demolishing their own credibility. Riven by dissent from within, the Church of England is creating disbelief from without. Apart from the vogue among bishops to air their theological doubts in public, there are those controversial but persistent attempts by many churchmen to be seen 'moving with the times'. Having 'colloquialised' the English translation of the Bible for the benefit of a fringe of apathetic and

Clearly such 'pluralistic' developments have no affinity whatever with that serene faith in the ultimate benevolence and wisdom of a supreme being and, among Christians at least, with the acceptance of the Bible as a sacred trust, as a narrative of both revelation and mystery, and as a unique source of divine precepts to guide the conduct of the children of God. So far as the West is concerned, then, the spell has been broken. Ceremonial lingers on. But people behave as if God is not. And with the erosion of a sustaining faith there begins that descent into superstition which often involves a return to pagan rites, or else to an immersion into the occult in a fevered search for new sources of power and mystery. In general, the 'liberated' individual who has jettisoned his moral ballast is the more likely to be swept along by some all-embracing political or ideological movement; more likely to acclaim a new Messiah, one promising to give new purpose to his otherwise vacuous existence.

Again, a secular society is more prone to disintegrative pressures. For a viable and cohesive society rests ultimately on an ethical consensus – upon a common set of values, themselves arising from precepts that transcend intellectual enquiry inasmuch as they are held to emanate from a divine source. Thus, once faith in the divinity has been undermined by science so also is the moral consensus which holds society together. The resulting vulnerability of society is revealed today in the eruption of moral and social issues that are productive of discord and conflict.

semi-literate citizens, they now give anxious thought to revamping church services with an eye to entertaining the young. A vessel without a rudder, the church now drifts with any tide. Spiritual doctrine has given way to feminist doctrine with its insistence on ordination of women. And it is currently being borne along also by homosexual liberationism officially countenancing homosexual prelates and mooting the sanctification of homosexual marriages. With a church such as this, Lucifer is expendable.

17 When Goods Cease to be Good

I

Three aspects of modern consumerism deserve emphasis. The first is our evolving attitude to man-made goods in a high-technology economy, an attitude aptly summarised by the expression 'the throwaway society'.

Contrary to expectations, the plethora of material goods has not made people any less materialistic: a decline in material greed has not been one of the more salient characteristics of the affluent society. The desire to command more purchasing power, or more purchasing power relative to others – irrespective of the assortment of goods available on the market – is apparently quite consistent with the tendency to attach slight value to all goods in common use.

In the more traditional society, ordinary goods in common use were themselves a source of gratification, not only through appreciation of their individual workmanship but also by virtue of their relative scarcity. In consequence a person's possessions generally accompanied him through life and became a link with his past, a fond reminder of events, personages and places. When life was such that a little girl could not hope for more than one doll, she was overjoyed to receive it, and treated it with loving care. Today, she can expect about a dozen and will tend to treat them rather as items in a collection. Gifts lose their power as people come to have more of everything and when incomes are such that not much sacrifice is incurred in giving them. After all, the gifts themselves are items from that mass-consumption economy which necessarily emerges from a mass-*production* economy, an economy founded on thoroughgoing standardisation.

The 'Age of Abundance', it transpires, is abundant with pre-packaged and chemically processed foodstuffs, with plastic knick-knacks, with plug-in electric gadgets and stereo equipment. And a part of the price that people in the West pay for this unending procession of shiny assembly-line products is the concomitant loss of those now rarer things that once imparted zest and gratification – the loss of individuality, uniqueness and flavour; the loss of craftsmanship, local variety and richness; the loss of intimacy and atmosphere, of eccentricity and character.

Thus the coming of the age of universal plenty, which entails rapid obsolescence and rapid replacement, cannot but breed a throwaway attitude toward man-made manufactures irrespective of materials or quality. There is no time to become fond of anything, no matter how well it serves: in any case, it will soon be superseded by a new model. Everything bought, or received, soon comes to be regarded as potential garbage. In terms of human feeling, then, the 'more and better' that economic growth is said to offer us turns out to be 'more and worse'.

II

Moving on to consumer innovations, the more significant ones in moulding our lifestyles have been labour-saving appliances and auto-entertainment contrivances. Many of the latter become a nuisance to others, and nearly all tend over time to curtail human intercourse. Daily contact between persons has declined with the spread of supermarkets and vending machines, with automated lifts and turnstiles, with television and video, with teaching machines and language laboratories, with office and home computers, with closed-circuit television, with patient-monitoring machines in hospitals, with computer-controlled treatment and computer diagnosis, and also with the growing number of devices that are designed to enable us to dispense with the many personal services once performed by craftsmen, small businesses and others. Thanks to miniature computers, we are also able to dispense with partners in card games and games of chess. The trend toward self-catering innovations never falters.

Although we are prone to fall in with popular opinion and express wonder at the 'consumer revolution', or jubilation at the cosy imagery evoked by phrases such as 'the global village' or at the stirring vision of an evolving network of communications drawing us closer to mutual understanding and brotherhood, the sad fact is that since the turn of the century consumer innovations have continued to eliminate the incidence of direct human intermingling. They have therefore to be perceived also as the elegant instruments of our mutual estrangement since they necessarily diminish over time the flow of feeling and sympathy between people.

III

Another consequence of the irresistible flow of consumer innovation is no less deplorable and no more avoidable. The sheer accumulation of new technical all-sorts that clutter up the homes of today's affluent consumer comes to press ever harder against the ultimate economic resource – time itself. As economists now recognise, more goods necessarily use up more time. And this pressure on the limited time at our disposal is augmented by the greater amount of time devoted today to the maintenance and repair of our 'mod cons', to our daily commuting, to our self-ordained tasks such as keeping up with the relentless flow of international news and media events, and to having to select goods from an expanding variety of new brands, new models, and new ornaments and novelties.

Thus, economic progress in the West, far from increasing the leisure of its harried citizens as so often claimed by technocrats, continues to encroach further on their free time – a fact obscurely perceived when we complain of the hurry of modern life.

18 Friendship and Trust

I

Can anything be said of the economic and social conditions under which love and trust are more likely to blossom? In what sorts of civilisation should we expect love to flow more easily between people, whether romantic, fraternal or filial? Such questions provide a fascinating subject for debate among social historians, though one I do not propose to enter. More pertinent to our purpose is some rumination on the more limited question: is it reasonable to believe that personal ties will be formed more easily, and that love and trust will flow more easily, in a modern growth-bound society than in a more traditional and pre-industrial one?

It may be argued, and it has been argued, that in releasing the mass of people from 'drudgery' and providing them with opportunities to move about speedily at home and abroad, so enabling them to meet and get to know many other people, economic growth promotes personal contacts and widens the scope for friendship. Sad to record, otherwise able economists have reasoned thus. Indeed, much of the reasoning of pro-growth economists is singularly unworldly and engagingly innocent of observable social trends. Along with liberals and socialists, we can also find economists who continue to believe that poverty and inequality are the chief causes of crime – apparently undisturbed by the fact that the past four decades have been those of a historically unprecedented growth in material standards for the mass of people in all industrialised nations while, during the same period, crime has been rising at a phenomenal rate.

On the same unsophisticated logic we should be able to reason that, with the spread of material plenty, there would be a decline in bribery and corruption, financial fraud and political graft – again, quite contrary to the observable facts since World War II. Of course, the obsession with material wealth *should* be less important when there is so much more of it about. After all, that is what should be inferred from the economist's basic concept of diminishing marginal utility. This superficial reasoning, that is, would indeed suggest that in societies marked by material abundance, there *should* be a decline in acquisitiveness and a growth in ease and leisure, a decline in the friction of human relationships and an increase in good spirits, in good-heartedness, and in courtesy.

Such naive conclusions float around today as part of the unsinkable froth from the backwash of beliefs common to nineteenth-century reformers. They were superficial then. Today they are manifestly spurious. They not only ignore theoretical developments in orthodox economics, but give no thought to the actual direction being taken by industrial and consumer innovation. Four characteristics of modern economic growth will suffice to illustrate this criticism.

II

First, the pace of modern life does not lend itself easily to the cultivation and nurture of friendships. It is not only that the tight scheduling of a life directed in so many cases by considerations of efficiency makes one edgy and impatient, or that the deluge of news and views spewed forth by mass media sponges up too much of our spare time. It is also the case that the cornucopia of goods produced by the economic system tends to rob us of the sense of ease and spaciousness. As indicated earlier, the citizens of the wealthier countries begin to find themselves under strain trying to cram the services of a growing assortment of new goods – including, ironically enough, 'leisure goods' and 'recreational goods' – into an unexpandable week. There is, then, a sharpening awareness of the pressure of time; a perpetual feeling of lagging behind, of things left undone, and of so much to be fitted in.

Moreover, with the continued flow of innovation, with the discovery of new chemicals, new machines and novel productive processes, comes the need for new standards, new regulations and controls; hence, the growth of detailed legislation, government bureaucracy and enforcement agencies. In the circumstances, the computer may be regarded as a providential instrument enabling us to cope with the ensuing and changing complexity of economic and social life. But with the revolution in its capacity for storage and retrieval of detailed information, it also acts to encourage the trend toward growth of government control. More information came to be demanded by government agencies, and also by private agencies, and more information was disseminated. Inevitably, then, communication became increasingly depersonalised and mechanised.

Such developments serve to compound the pressure on our time and, indeed, on our tempers. A larger portion of our lives will, in consequence, be spent filling in forms, standing in queues, arguing with the computer, listening to recorded messages, talking into answering machines, sorting out junk mail, and fretting with indecision at the mounting number of appeals launched by charities, by innumerable good causes, and by political or environmental campaigns. There will be less ease and time left for the cultivation and enjoyment of friendships.

Again, if long familiarity with personages and places is itself a source of gratification, and if only through long association can the bonds of trust and friendship be formed, we cannot but conclude that the prospects for this form of fulfilment in the modern world are bleaker than they were. The trend in mobility which shows more people moving more frequently year by year from one city to another, from one country to another, does of course enable them to extend the number of their acquaintances by the score. But clearly this is not the answer. A week spent in a mountain hotel, a package tour in Turkey, a jet bargain that enables us to visit 'seven countries in ten days', and to meet other 'beautiful people', may well offer moments of elation or at least some pangs of anticipation to help us bear the routine disillusions of life. Yet in truth there is only time enough to assume postures, to go through the conventional motions of revelry, to grasp at some visceral excitements and, for the rest, to hope that something or somebody will turn up. For the very young there is, of course, the flush of animation, the breathless exchange of personal data and confidences, the stylised infatuation, and not much more.

Indeed, the sheer numbers of people we meet, the crowds we have to jostle our way through, induce a reaction similar to that produced by the proliferation of man-made goods. Masses of people, that is, begin to seem expendable too: items in a throwaway society. Thus as the numbers of people we see and move through, and as the amounts of goods about us, continue to grow, the quickness of our response to them diminishes. A subliminal sense of oppression or irritation underlies our humour.

III

Another characteristic of modern life that weakens the formation of affective ties springs from the faith in the power of scientific techniques to solve all problems, industrial, medical, social, and now personal also. This faith in the power of technology is perhaps the distinctive feature *par excellence* of modern society. For whether success or failure meets the application of a particular technique, the response is the same – more research. The defects of technology are to be remedied by technology.

Broadly defined as a form of systemisation of all activity, technique has begun to edge itself into every niche of what used to be a person's private life and private feelings. Popular techniques for expanding a person's capacity for love, passion, potency, surrender, repartee, laughter and fantasy are putatively imparted to the buyer of the booklet or cassette, or to the enroller in the course. For the would-be lover – which, in this age, invariably means sexual lover – the precise movements, the breathing and rhythm, the timing of a variety of caresses, pinches, sighs, grunts and bites, are now elaborated in films and illustrated in booklets.

No personal problem is so intimate that a technique cannot be fashioned to deal with it. Social science 'experts', for instance, have begun to introduce a range of 'life-adjustment' courses as part of the student services of American universities. Almost twenty years ago, the American University Community Center, Washington, D.C., offered its students a variety of therapeutic services which included:

> Encountertape Groups – These are personal groups designed as structured encounter experiences focussing on themes of trust building, giving and receiving feedback, direct communication, and sensory awareness. They will serve as an introduction . . . for well-functioning groups.

> Interpersonal Skill-Building Groups – In these ten-session skill-focussed groups, students will be taught to monitor and master anxiety, using . . . . improved social skills by learning to be appropriately assertive, and more direct empathetic communication.

Such pathetic exhibitions of inept jargon are themselves a corollary of the sanctification of a techniques approach which views the hapless human as an operationally defective machine in need of a routine overhaul. The very acceptance of the idea that emotions of trust and affection, which should come to humans as naturally as breathing and sleeping, are necessary 'skills' to be acquired by a course of instruction is itself indicative of the sorry state of mind induced by our faith in technique. Well may we marvel at the state of mind of a person who expects that by taking a course or two and diligently practising the exercises he will quickly learn to 'control and direct aggression' and to 'convey and receive empathy'. But a rapid growth in the enrolment of such courses is a fact, though a fact that is indicative more of the gullibility or despair of students than of the success of the instruction.

IV

An increasingly individualist ethic, associated as it is with the universal trend toward formal contracts, is a third characteristic of modern economic growth. The consequent replacement of market services for personal ones in an economically more complex society – which, as observed in Chapter 12, also acts to inflate estimates of real income and its growth – can be, and has been, described as 'the commercialisation effect'. It is more illuminating, however, to interpret this historical transition as an extension of the individualist ethic, while remarking its operation not only in a market economy but in any modern economy. For the term 'individualist ethic' comprehends not only the dependence of the modern economy on detailed calculation and forward planning, but also the self-regarding search by individuals to procure more of their satisfaction in life from the finished goods and services produced by the economic system. It is therefore a feature also of any collectivist economy that seeks to increase output by offering material incentives and, in the process, replacing personal services with economic goods.

The dominance of the individualist ethic has been promoted by the growth of mass affluence, mass urbanisation, mass mobility, and by those labour-saving innovations mentioned in Chapter 17. Together they have been active in undermining local communities and personal interdependence and therefore also the virtues of mutual obligation and mutual trust that were so essential to the day-to-day operation of the pre-industrial economy, dependent as it was on immemorial custom, unwritten conventions and informal understandings. In their stead, and as mutual trust between today's citizens – between buyer and seller, employer and employee, landlord and tenant, and more recently, alas, between teacher and student, and doctor and patient – has faded, we observe the unimpeded proliferation of formal contracts with increasingly detailed provisions.

Ironically, it is this universal diffusion of the individualist ethic, cherished by pro-market conservatives and liberals, and its success in transforming a man into a self-contained independent decision-making unit, that has brought into being the expansion of the collective countervailing power which they deplore. For as a man is cut off from the traditional sources of assurance and comfort provided by a real community and realises his individual helplessness in a world of powerful economic and political forces – one that is subject today to rapid changes that increasingly threaten his livelihood, material standards, or peace of mind – his search for some dependable form of security impels him to make common cause with others. There come into being the instruments of countervailing power which are familiar to us in the form of labour unions, tenant associations, consumer organisations, citizens' advisory councils, and business federations.

No personal friendship or care or respect is involved, however. We are now far removed from this little world of obligations and privileges, of custom and mutual understanding. The individual simply pays his dues, his fees, or his taxes, and obtains the services of the organisation, in particular its expertise and its forms of insurance and protection.

To regret at the transformation involved we may add economic concern. For the decline in mutual trust in a world of increasing material fixation is apt to produce a decline also in standards of personal integrity and public trust – qualities that are necessary for the efficient operation even of an impersonal economic system. Indeed, casual observation suggests that corruption and irresponsibility among people in positions of power have already gone some way to impair the operation of the post-industrial economy.

V

We turn finally to those optimistic spirits among us who are credulous enough to discover in the rise of the welfare state the emergence of what they are moved to call 'the compassionate society'. Reference instead to 'the compassionate state' provides a more revealing and more accurate terminology.

In order to appreciate the origin and the *raison d'être* of 'the compassionate state' we need not go far back in history: in Britain, to the collapse of the self-sufficient village community in the wake of the agricultural revolution in the latter half of the eighteenth century, followed as it was by 'the industrial revolution'. About a century later, urban and suburban communities began to fold up. For in an increasingly mobile and anonymous society – each family equipped with its own set of electric labour-saving appliances, its stereophonic equipment, television and private automobile – people became too hurried, too stretched, too 'motivated', too worried about 'slipping behind' or 'missing out', to find the time to know or care about their transient and equally mobile neighbours. Indeed, over the last three decades the media have reported innumerable instances of people being victimised in public – that is, of being visibly assaulted, robbed, raped and even murdered – while passers-by and lookers-on, not wishing to get 'involved', did nothing at all; did not even trouble to telephone the police.

At all events, it is just because in our new atomistic, self-regarding, supermobile mass civilisation, ordinary people who respond well enough to charitable appeals and other good causes find themselves uncomfortable in dealing with individual casualties or misfortunes; find less time available; find themselves less willing, less trusting, and – possibly because so many are driving their automobiles – less able to take a genuine interest in the plight of other people they pass on the streets; less willing and able, then, to listen to the petitions of strangers, to tend the old or infirm, to raise the fallen, to help the human casualties, and generally too self-absorbed to care much about what is happening to others in the immediate vicinity. It is just because of these untoward developments that the state has perforce to expand the umbrella of its welfare, rescue and protection services. In sum, since direct interpersonal compassion can no longer be depended upon in the new rootless metropolitan society we are busily forging, compassion has to be *institutionalised*, and in this form it has to be administered in part by large centralised voluntary organisations, but in the main by an army of state employees, local and central. Not surprisingly, this army of private and state-employed social workers come to have a strong vested interest in their vocation. As with all bureaucracies, the members seek to augment their powers – in this instance by seeking ways and means of increasing the number of their 'clients', the extent of their funding, the magnitude of their domain, and the range of services they provide.

It is important to understand, moreover, that the growth of this institutionalised compassion not only replaces the more personal compassion of the traditional community or neighbourhood, it also facilitates and fosters the spirit of individual irresponsibility – an individual irresponsibility that is an important component of the psychological underpinning of the so-called permissive society which is to be discussed in Chapter 22.

Indeed, society as a whole bears the earmarks of irresponsibility. It becomes habitually improvident, belatedly reacting to foreseeable developments. The Establishment, it seems, is not much troubled by the number of avoidable misfortunes and disasters that occur. And this seeming complexity can also be rationalised. After all, a hideous environment, a population increasingly prone to nervous diseases, a rising trend of family breakdown, disoriented adolescents, delinquency, an uninterrupted climb in the figures for teenage pregnancies and abortions, drug-taking and vandalism – all such facts and statistics that distinguish the age we live in also offer vast opportunities for workers in the social and medical services, and support their cry for more funds, for more staff, for more counselling centres, for more psychiatric clinics, and for more scientific research.

19 Travel – the Opiate of the Masses

I

Before turning our attention to the environmental devastation resulting from foreign travel, we may remind ourselves briefly of the related affliction wrought on our lives by this now-indispensable accessory to foreign travel, the automobile. The assertion that the invention of the automobile is one of the greatest calamities, possibly *the* greatest calamity, to have befallen the human race is no exaggeration. However, since its many disastrous effects on the urban environment have already been discussed in Chapter 8, we shall be brief in touching here on this particular aspect.

More than any other modern device, the automobile has succeeded in transforming us into a nation of strangers. In the process we have become inured to living, eating, working, sleeping, within a gaseous habitat besieged by endless traffic movement and clamour. Our towns and cities, already ravaged and contorted in the futile endeavour to accommodate the ever-growing flow of motorised vehicles, are becoming venues of perpetual transit; nodes in a dense and intricate network of roads, freeways, junctions, parking towers, and airports. Once leafy suburban lanes are now thick-lined with private cars, the overspill choking up alleyways, with increasing numbers on display in front gardens. This mass motorisation is transforming us into a nomadic society. Each year in Britain millions of families change their abode, never finding the time nor the inclination to get to know, much less to care about, their immediate neighbours.

And no relief is in sight. More goods in the shops, as there will be, means more commercial vans and lorries in our towns and cities. More tourism – relished and encouraged by governments, and soon to be promoted by cheaper air fares – will further thicken the traffic congestion as will the planned expansion of inter-city highways.

And the damage is not confined to towns and cities. Woodland areas, through which modern highways run, are beginning to rot and decay from the exhaust gases emitted by the increasing flow of traffic. For instance, in 1955 about half a million vehicles drove through the Brenner Pass in the Swiss Alps. Today the number is about 12 million. According to the Swiss Forest Agency more than half of the mountain forest is damaged or dying as a result of exhaust fumes and other man-made pollutants.

Although, technically speaking, the traffic problem is resolvable, the massive producer and consumer interests involved render it politically intractable, as indicated earlier. A few short years and we shall find ourselves constantly enmeshed in traffic chaos within the cities, and with yet longer 'tailbacks' along the highways.

II

The large numbers of people who today are alarmed at the rapid and irrevocable plundering of the natural habitat of flora and fauna, and the defacement of countless places of unique charm, are practically helpless before the commercial power exercised by tourist agencies, airlines, automobile interests, hoteliers, developers, to say nothing of the governments themselves eager to augment their reserves of foreign currencies.

Formally, the problem can be expressed in terms of uncontrolled spillover effects, the sheer magnitude of the number of tourists being a consequence of setting the price of travel equal only to its commercial costs, but far below its *marginal* social cost once all spillovers are included in the calculus. The price paid by an additional tourist, that is, takes no account of the additional congestion costs that his travel imposes on others, whether other tourists or inhabitants. Nor does it include, as it should, the additional loss of quiet, of fresh air, and of the scenic destruction suffered by everyone, present and future. These prodigious 'inter-marginal' social costs are difficult to calculate with confidence – which, again, is no reason why they should continue to be ignored.

The 'additional tourist', moreover, could be the most reverent nature-lover. For he is quite aware that any personal sacrifice he could make by cancelling his trip would have no practical effect in reducing the growth of mass tourism – any more than his discontinuing to drive his automobile would reverse the trend toward increasing congestion in the towns and cities. If anything, there is a strong incentive not to postpone the opportunity; to travel the sooner, and to travel more frequently, before the beauty and tranquillity of the resort in question is irredeemably ruined. What else should he do but heed the newspaper advertisement that bids him 'Go now!' so as to 'Enjoy it before the crowds get there'?

As things stand today, the tourist business is engaged in a competitive scramble to uncover all places of once-quiet repose, of wonder, beauty and historic or scenic interest, to the money-flushed multitude. In the process, it is, of course, literally and irrevocably destroying them. In spite of the international clean-up schemes, sewage continues to pollute Mediterranean beaches while increasing numbers of speedcraft roar over and churn up the coastal waters. Once lovely and alluring towns such as Andorra[1] and Biarritz have been smothered over with new hotels and submerged beneath the roar and dust of motorised traffic. The isles of Greece have become a sprinkling of tawdry lidos in the Aegean Sea. Delphi is hemmed in by high-rise hotels. In Italy the real estate man is responsible for atrocities exemplified by the skyscraper approach to Rome seen across the *campagna*, while the annual invasion of tourists has transformed once-famous resorts such as Rapallo, Capri, Alassio, and scores of others that were no less enchanting before World War II, into so many vulgar Coney Islands.

Much the same may be said of Britain. In 1978 Stonehenge had to be roped off to prevent the lower stones being worn away. In the Lake District the annual influx of visitors are wearing away the footpaths and other areas about the lakes.

None the less, tourist agencies continue to conjure up for the young and gullible visions of far-away places, mysterious, romantic, pristine, exotic, all to be enjoyed with 'mod cons' at a bargain price. And their enterprise and promotion are lauded by establishment figures who regard this gathering avalanche of tourists as a great democratic achievement, a unifying force in the world, and a growing oppor-

---

[1] As far back as August 1959, a correspondent for *The Economist* wrote a short piece on 'The Last Days of Andorra'. He observed that tourists still went to Andorra in search of the exotic and in order '. . . to see its medieval houses and bridges, fine Romanesque church towers and unsullied mountain vistas; to enjoy its eyrie-like calm and pure air. As a result of the tourist invasion, however, Andorra's air is at the moment a nicely balanced blend of exhaust fumes and cement dust, vibrant with the competing *chachachas* of Radio Andorra and Andorradio; parking is the same kind of problem as in London; and every other beauty-spot is pock-marked with hotels, bungalows and camping sites. One of the liveliest church towers in the country, that at Ordino, has been dwarfed by a graceless new block sited exactly six inches from it.'

'. . . Building sites are being snapped up in Andorra-la-Vella at £25 a square yard. At the present rate of development the whole of the central valley from Encamp to Santa Julia will soon be one unbroken ribbon of flamboyant façades.'

With slight alterations, these observations summarise the recent architectural history of hundreds of Mediterranean resorts.

tunity for the common man 'to see the world and to perceive its life and art'. But like extending the opportunity to motor into the centre of London to every car-owner in the country, the opportunity is a purely illusory one. Travel on this outlandish scale to any one country, to Spain, Italy, Greece, and more recently Turkey and Thailand, along with the developments necessary to accommodate each year between 10 and 40 million people, most of them eager to cram their week or fortnight with exciting experiences, necessarily disrupts the character of the region and necessarily corrupts the character of the indigenous population.[2]

As hordes of holidaymakers arrive by air, sea and land, by coach, train, and private car, cameras at the ready, hot in pursuit of pleasure, impatient to forage in the bazaars and restaurants, to swarm on to the beaches or into the squares, to motor along highways and by-ways in search of 'sights', quaint villages, bargains, ruins, anything, as concrete is poured over the earth, as new hotels, casinos, night clubs, blocks of sun-flats, chalets and caravan sites crowd into and about the area, local life and local industry shrivel, hospitality evaporates, and much of the host population drifts into a quasi-parasitic way of life catering with contemptuous servility to the promiscuous prodigality of the squandering multitudes.[3]

III

The issue is not – as it is often misrepresented to be – that of aristocratic privilege versus democratic freedom, nor is it that of the genuine connoisseur versus the philistine. Geographical space, the

[2] As one should expect, the nature and extent of corruption is worse in those Third World countries that have recently been included in the West's tourist itinerary. For instance, Pattaya in 1960 was a quiet coastal village of about 5,000. Despite its now having the worst polluted beaches in Thailand, it can boast close to 300 hotels and – according to a report in *The Observer* (19 August 1990) – in recognition of its 20,000 prostitutes and its hundreds of bars peddling sex of every description to foreign visitors it is sometimes referred to as 'Sodom and Gomorrah by the Sea'. Homosexual males are wooed in an area called 'Boys Town'. Child prostitution is rife, and paedophiles are openly catered for. Not surprisingly, venereal diseases are escalating. The Communicable Diseases Department in Bangkok believes that by the end of the century as many as two million Thais could have Aids.

[3] *Holiday Which* for March 1990 describes Naples as follows: 'Napoli, a large port and commercial centre, is afflicted by every kind of urban miasma there is. A sickly yellow haze hangs permanently over the city. Traffic throttles the central town and the noise is unholy: you're haunted by the cacophony of horns and engine revs even inside the hallowed halls of museums and churches. On the seafront "Danger – no swimming" notices front every patch of accessible pebbles. Buildings – monumental or humble – are uniformly grimy, their fronts cracked and their plaster crumbling. In a pizzeria, once your inflated bill is settled, the waiter will kindly tuck in your necklace and point to the camera – "they'll snatch it".'

choicest bits of it anyway, is one of the strictly limited resources of this now tiny planet. And, as in so many things, what the few may enjoy in freedom the crowd necessarily destroys for itself. Notwithstanding which, under existing institutions, and since there is still a lot more money to be made in promoting tourist travel, only international agreement to reduce and control the traffic will prevent our children from inheriting a world that is almost wholly bereft of places of undisturbed natural beauty.[4]

But is international agreement at all likely? True, interest is now being shown in what is fashionably called 'green tourism', or tourism that is restricted to particular areas or else directed to specially built holiday enclaves, or vast recreational centres, in an endeavour to protect wildlife and areas of outstanding natural beauty against further destruction. More generally, the principle at least of imposing stricter controls on tourist activity (such as game-shooting), on tourist locations and on tourist development has begun to be debated. And, indeed, it is not hard to advance technically feasible proposals for checking the spread of damage even at this late stage, proposals that draw their rationale from the separate-areas approach treated in Chapter 6.

It is perfectly feasible, for example, to ban air travel to a wide variety of mountain, lake and coastal resorts, and to a selection of some islands from the many scattered about the globe; and within such areas also to abolish all motorised traffic. Regions may be set aside for the true nature lover who is willing to make his pilgrimage by boat and willing leisurely to explore islands, valleys, bays, woodlands, on foot or on horseback.

Yet when one considers the extent of the irrevocable destruction already perpetrated over the past four decades, and when one bears in mind also the current projections of a doubling of the existing numbers of tourists within the next ten to twelve years, there is little room for optimism. For the powerful interests of travel agencies and local developers will almost certainly oppose, or at least dilute, future schemes designed to limit or control the spread of tourists. And, as we already know, in all public inquiries conducted by central or local authorities, the prospect of 'job opportunities', and the anticipated

---

[4] Up to the present, almost all foreign travel has originated in the more developed countries. If now sufficient economic progress is made over the next decade by the former Soviet Union, the countries of Eastern Europe, India, Pakistan and China, as a result of which just 5 per cent of their aggregate population join in the tourist spree, the addition to the tourist traffic generated by the developed countries at the turn of the century will be about 100 million a year.

increase in local trade and in government revenues, tend to exert a preponderant leverage in favour of development.

It is, then, far from impossible that a new generation of sensitive environmentalists will agitate in vain; will be destined to gaze in helpless anguish at the spectacle of an irrepressible tide of world tourism sweeping all before it. After all, within a few short decades we, the peoples of the West, have all but wrecked a heritage of unmarred natural beauty that had else endured the passage of centuries and millennia. With a complacency, nay a hubris, unmatched in history, and with a blindness peculiar to a consumer society, we have abandoned ourselves to a ransacking of the most precious and irreplaceable resources on our unique planet undeterred by the thought of the future desolation and deprivation of posterity.

PART VIII

....

Pluralism, Conflict and Repression

20 Science and the Seeds of Discord

I

In Part VIII, we shall uncover new connections between innovation and social turmoil. Two related issues have already been broached. In Chapter 18, some of the forces actuated by technological growth are to be seen operating against the continuance of enduring bonds of friendship and trust which are so vital a constituent of the good life. In Chapter 19, we remarked how the development of jet travel in the postwar period has led to wanton despoliation of the greater part of the earth's resources of natural beauty, so robbing future generations of one of the great sources of pleasure, wonder and solace.

In this chapter our curiosity will be directed to various ways in which advances in science and technology since the turn of the century, and more particularly since World War II, have – along with the collapse of the moral consensus (discussed in Chapter 16) and the rise of populism – given impetus to increasingly divisive and unruly democracies in the West currently characterised by internecine conflicts of interest and opinion and, on some issues, by seemingly irreconcilable antagonisms.

Subsequently and in the following two chapters, we shall trace, respectively, the influence of technology and mass affluence on two other infelicitous developments: the growth in the postwar period of a more vulgar and shameless populace, and the virtual explosion of crime and violence.

II

Let us turn our attention first to the technical progress made in industry. With the extension of mass production and the introduction of the combustion engine in the eighteenth century, there begins the slow decline of craftsmanship. Although pride in workmanship lingers on even with those new methods of production which pursue efficiency through standardisation, more specialised machinery and the division of labour, the sense of individual creativity has waned. This loss of personal pride in the mastery of industrial skills took a quantum fall after World War II with the widespread introduction of automation and computers. In Britain alone, several million workers now spend their working hours pressing keys in response to flickering symbols racing across the small screen. For the most part it is tedious work and, bearing in mind that there is little of the old shop-floor communication, somewhat dispiriting.

The very rapidity of technical innovation today, with its aim of replacing labour with more versatile and sophisticated machinery, is also active in increasing the level of worker anxiety. As the pace of innovation increases, so will the anxiety of both factory and clerical workers, of both technical and managerial personnel. Hard-earned skills and highly specialised training can become virtually obsolete overnight. In addition, work opportunities in different organisations and industries are tending to vary more frequently, expanding or contracting in response to consumer innovations and to the impulse-spending of an affluent buying public that is made all the more fickle by keen international competition and high-powered advertising campaigns.

It is not surprising then that there are continual conflicts between the interests of the consuming public, ably supported by pro-market economists, on the one hand, and those of workers and producers, on the other. The occasional and fierce resistance of labour unions to new and more efficient technologies that necessarily involve substantial reductions in now-obsolete skilled labour is understandable. And one can readily sympathise with the agitation of producers and workers, and their attempts to bring pressure on governments to support or to impose tariffs or trade controls, in the endeavour to protect themselves and their families from economic hardship.

Bearing in mind the consumer bias of the market, particularly in conditions of rapid changes in tastes and technology, the free trade versus protectionism controversy is likely to grow in importance.

Without drawing any firm conclusion about the respective merits of the opposing arguments, it is reasonable to believe that, inasmuch as the vicissitudes of consumer demand may be expected to grow along with affluence and innovation, the unavoidable 'trade-off' between consumer satisfaction and worker satisfaction will become less advantageous. For in high consumption societies, the increments to the existing area of consumer choice become less valuable whereas the consequent increase in worker unemployment and readjustment becomes more painful.

III

Let us now glance briefly at instances of the strife that has incidentally been generated by some scientific advances during the postwar period. Within this category may be included the methods of research and the progress of medical science which occasionally have given rise to quite fanatical animosities. For example, the progress made in relatively painless abortion techniques has led to prolonged struggles between the 'Pro-Choice' and 'Pro-Life' movements. In the United States, where the struggle has been most bitter, the more fanatical supporters of the latter movement have occasionally sabotaged or blown up abortion clinics. Physical confrontation between the opposing factions is not uncommon, especially outside abortion clinics. In the absence of a strong police presence such confrontations would certainly have resulted in savage violence.[1]

Another example is the growing hostility between 'animal rights' activists and anti-vivisectionists on the one hand and, on the other, animal hunters, factory farmers, and research personnel conducting animal experiments – experiments that are invariably rationalised as conferring benefits on mankind. Within the broad 'animal rights' movement there are, again, groups whose fury occasionally vents itself in sabotage and terrorism.

Even where disagreements are currently less antagonistic, as they have been so far in response to advances being made in genetic engineering, in research into cloning, in the prolongation of life for human 'vegetables', in experiments on human embryos, in the promotion of 'sperm banks' and 'test-tube babies', it is a fact that agonising moral problems arise which must eventually produce controversial legislation and its enforcement by new state agencies.

---

[1] Recent reports of the coming availability of an effective abortion pill are likely, if true, to reduce occasions for confrontation. But it will do nothing to abate the intensity of the moral conflict.

In addition, the past three decades have witnessed an unparalleled creation and expansion of organisations dedicated to opposing the spread or continuance of a variety of those economic activities, both private and public, that are now perceived to threaten the health and amenity of the citizen. Environmentalists frequently find themselves campaigning against the plans of industrialists or of government departments. Prominent in the news also are the several organisations established to protect our national heritage against the depredations of private developers and against the requisitioning of land for army manoeuvres or highway construction. Worth mentioning also in this connection is the scepticism and distrust of the farming and food industries by consumer associations, and the aversion to modern agribusiness by the ecological lobby and the green movement generally.

IV

An extension of the same concern returns us to the tragic and virtually irreversible environmental devastation caused by jet tourism and discussed in the preceding chapter. Every discerning traveller can bear witness to the fact that cheap package tourism has transmogrified hundreds of once-picturesque and tranquil resorts strung out along a thousand-mile coastline into an uninterrupted vista of tower blocks, parking lots and cement hotels, about which moves an interminable procession of automobiles. More immediately relevant to the thesis of this chapter, however, is the potential of modern tourism for dissonance and hostility.

On this massive scale, tourism fosters contempt, resentment and sometimes alarm also within the host countries, especially so during the summer months in the larger European cities and resorts when the indigenous populations have to bear with overcrowded stations, with thicker traffic jams, with congested parks, squares, galleries and museums, resulting from the endless throngs of pertinacious camera-clicking visitors.

Since host governments are still reluctant to discourage so profitable a source of foreign currency – and since each of us, aware, as he is, of the spreading destruction, becomes that much more eager to travel in order to enjoy what little remains – it looks as if mass travel can only continue to grow (unless perchance arrested by fears of criminal assault) encouraged as it will be by cheaper air fares and increasing affluence.

Certainly we face an alarming prospect. Having within the lifetime of a single generation irrevocably destroyed a unique heritage of natural beauty that would else have endured for millennia, we can lament but not desist. In the meantime, the dawning recognition of the desolation being wrought on the planet has begun to precipitate an agonising struggle within the post-industrial world about the moral obligation to control travel, a struggle that will be inflamed by conflicting sentiments and conflicting interests both within and between countries.

V

Let us turn now to the ethnic-minority problem in the West, yet another source of social friction that came with the postwar prosperity. Some of the economic and social consequences of this 'South-to-North movement' – the mass migration of (largely unskilled) people of different colour and culture into the towns and cities of Western countries – have been discussed elsewhere.[2]

Contrary to liberal expectations, there has been no marked diminution over time of racial discord in spite of – or, more likely, because of – the gratuitous introduction of race legislation and the unabating zeal of an official 'race relations industry' which has an obvious professional interest in reporting and highlighting instances of racial discrimination, overt and covert.

Although many of the postwar immigrants, or their children, have chosen to adopt the language, dress and manners of their host country, seeking to blend in with the mainstream culture, it has to be acknowledged also that this is far from being the universal practice. As with other Western countries, a significant proportion of the new immigrants into Britain continue to maintain a separate cultural and communal identity and have indeed been accused of forming a state within a state. Their primary allegiance to their adopted country, and their broad endorsement of its traditions and institutions, cannot be taken for granted. As has been observed, some of their cherished customs and religious practices are apt to disturb the public conscience or conflict with legislation.[3] And inasmuch as they can

[2] For a popular but fairly comprehensive exposition of the *economic* analysis of immigration taken from a number of technical papers written by a colleague and myself, see my essay, 'Does Immigration Confer Economic Benefits on the Host Country?' in the booklet, *Economic Issues in Immigration*, Institute of Economic Affairs, London, 1970. For conjectures on the social implications, see my article, 'What Future for a Multi-Racial Britain?', in the *Salisbury Review*, 1988.

[3] For instances in the case of the Asian communities, the reader is referred to recent articles in the popular press and in particular to those in *The Sunday Times* for 25 June 1989, 9 July 1989 and 12 January 1992. See also the pamphlet, 'State-Funded Muslim Schools' by Ray Honeyford, published in 1992 by *Majority Rights*.

count on the support of the media to impress the public with their dissimilarity and nonconformity in respect of language, apparel, customs, values and beliefs, they tend not only to provoke resentment among the xenophobic elements but to create unease among the population at large. Indeed, their tenacious attachment to their own customs and beliefs and their explicit rejection of Western values and culture have put a strain on the country's institutions, particularly its educational system, and have effectively diverted its political energy and resources from other pressing issues.

Moreover, owing both to the inter-factional intolerance and to the feuding that occasionally erupts within opposing segments of the various minority groups, a considerable burden is thrown on the machinery and the patience of the police.

In view of the growing difficulties faced by the Western democracies in maintaining their cohesiveness in an age of breathless change both of their physical infrastructures and of their morals, lifestyles and institutions, this massive inflow of Third World peoples could hardly have come at a worse time. Nor can the predicament be expected to abate over the near future if only because the numbers of these new ethnic grops are increasing disproportionately as a result of their higher birth rate and also of their continued illegal entry which becomes increasingly costly to monitor.[4]

How did it come about? The chief factor, obviously, was the revolution of communications and transport after World War II. Realisation of their poverty relative to the material standards current in the West began to spread among the masses in the Third World at the same time as lower travel costs were making the journey to Western Europe and the United States a feasible option for a growing number. Moreover, the initial influx was given a fillip by the realisation among those private and public enterprises in the West that were anxious to expand their personnel that it was cheaper to import relatively unskilled Asian or African or Caribbean labour than to compete for indigenous labour in the home market. Indeed, under the (fallacious) pretext of a 'labour shortage', the policy of importing 'cheap labour' was arrested in Western Europe only when governments finally awoke to the gathering groundswell of resentment within their countries and, belatedly, closed the doors to mass immigration.

---

[4] The ethnic problems within Western European countries are likely to be aggravated in the years following 1992 when all barriers to migration within the EC are to be removed.

VI

Consider, finally, the rise of the women's liberation movement regarded by its more enthusiastic devotees as heralding a new age of enlightenment, a view regarded with scepticism by other social thinkers who have been more impressed by the movement's ardent pursuit of power, its ritual taunts about 'male chauvinism', or its occasional flights into millennial fantasies.[5] Be that as it may, its achievements so far include specific legislation and agencies to enforce both 'equal opportunity' (translated generally as entailing equal representation of the sexes at all levels of organisation) and 'affirmative action' (better described as 'reverse discrimination' since it is overtly designed to expand the numbers of women – along with blacks and hispanics in the United States – in corporations, in the universities, and in the higher echelons of government, beyond those warranted by their professional competence or scholastic achievement). Needless to say, such legislation defeats its purpose, and the attempt to enforce it is costly and productive of tension and controversy.

Again, it may reasonably be argued that the feminist endeavour to create and diffuse a new image of womanhood; to condemn the housewife as an ignoble stereotype; to scorn motherhood as servile drudgery; to spurn the traditional complementary role of the sexes in favour of an equal sharing of all tasks; to propagate the notion of an 'open marriage' conceived as entailing only a limited liability partnership; to endorse the rise of the 'single-parent family' in the name of woman's independence and – among the broad lunatic fringe – to espouse the lesbian way of life as a legitimate option conferring a new dimension of sexual emancipation: all this has culminated in growing anxiety and perplexity among women today, the more so as their innate female instincts and maternal impulses come into conflict with the new image of modern womanhood purveyed by feminist doctrine.

Not surprisingly also, along with the change in the male perception of women which has been brought about, *inter alia*, by the unisex cult, and by the fashion among the young for cool and casual sexual affairs, much of the courtesy and, indeed, of the gallantry that was once accorded as of right to the 'fair sex' has faded out of our lives – and with it much of the romance too.

[5] For a cynical analysis of the feminist approach to history and an appraisal of feminist claims, see my article, 'Was the Women's Liberation Movement Really Necessary?', *Encounter*, 1986.

More portentous has been the feminist struggle for *sexual* emancipation, a struggle that was one of the more crucial factors in the transition to the permissive society (about which more anon) which was later to be encouraged by state recognition of the legal rights of unwed cohabiting couples. Once that Pandora's box was prised open, society became subject to unprecedented strains. Over the last three decades, the upward trends in divorce, in one-parent families, in children born out of wedlock, in teenage pregnancies, in abortion, in 'divorced children', have been truly staggering.[6] Indicative as such trends are of an appalling decline in personal responsibility and, in consequence, also of a concomitant increase in human distress, a more ominous portent lies in the threat they pose to the institution of the family, a threat to which no previous civilisation has been exposed.

There is, however, no prospect of any return to the *status quo ante*. The women's liberation movement was no fortuitous development. Rather it was the historical outcome of a conjuncture of occurrences, medical, technical and economic.

Its sexually emancipatory facet can be attributed to the discoveries, and ready availability in the West, of penicillin, of the contraceptive pill, and of the progress made in painless abortion. The technological contributions to 'economic emancipation' included, on the one hand, those domestic labour-saving appliances that, in the event, made women in the home increasingly expendable and, on the other hand, those industrial innovations in the postwar period that replaced muscular strength and traditional skills by easily controlled machines. Thus while women were becoming expendable in the home and, incidentally, being made increasingly restless by media visions of exotic opulence and romantic travel, new employment opportunities were sprouting in industry. The economic contribution to the movement can also bear emphasis, residing as it does in the concurrent achievement by the West of historically unprecedented material standards which put within reach of the mass of women the

---

[6] Half the marriages contracted today in the US are expected to end in divorce, and, as trends go, two out of every three children born there will spend their childhoods with only one of their original parents. Moreover, of the existing number of families, about 25 per cent are now single-parent ones.

Again, each year sees more than a million teenage pregnancies and a half million teenage abortions, while within the larger cities of America the estimates of the number of children from the age of ten selling sexual services on the streets have continued to rise.

One could go on citing comparable statistics for European countries. In what was popularly believed to be a conservative country, Switzerland, the number of children now born out of wedlock amounts to one third of total births. Figures for the USSR in 1988 reveal that 70 per cent of the marriages are dissolved within 10 years.

new domestic appliances and medical services necessary for their 'emancipation'.

In sum, the traditional role of the human female – her complementary role to that of the human male in rearing a family and creating a home – has inevitably been undermined by scientific and technical progress. The resulting social and political upheaval has begot increased legislation, state provision and bureaucratic control. And though feminists may evince exultation, women as a whole are today more tense, more uncertain, and more divided among themselves than they ever were.

The above illustrations serve to confirm the broad conclusion that as – in response to scientific and technical advance – moral consensus gives way to the so-called 'ethical pluralism', and as antagonisms and conflicts begin to emerge, internecine strife can be held within bounds only by enlarging the powers of the state, a thesis that will be further substantiated by consideration of the permissive society in Chapter 22.

21 The Erosion of Personal Freedom

I

The last component of the good life to be mentioned in Chapter 16 was that of personal freedom within which three elements were distinguished: (1) freedom from state repression, (2) freedom of speech and action, and (3) freedom from intimidation by others. Although we are concerned with all three, it is the first element, freedom from state repression, that receives more attention today since it is perceived as being under constant threat even within the liberal democracies. Certainly there has been a vast expansion of government power since the turn of the century and a concomitant diminution of personal freedom.

The explanation of this phenomenon has been various. Some scholars claim to have adduced evidence which suggests that the chief cause has been the state's mobilisation of the nation's resources necessary for the prosecution of the two world wars during the first half of the century, in pursuance of which virtually unlimited powers were conferred on the government for several years. By itself, the explanation is not entirely convincing. For following the cessation of hostilities, public sentiment in each case favoured a speedy return to 'normalcy', a policy that would have entailed a gradual dismantling of wartime controls, and the demobilisation of war-recruited office personnel. Another explanation, though one that is not inconsistent with the first, is the steady growth from the latter part of the nineteenth century of collectivist ideas which envisage a more active role for the state in tending the health, welfare and education of its citizens. A more pedestrian explanation, which may be viewed as supplementary to the preceding ones, resides in the undoubted temptation provided by any system of progressive taxation to expand the public sector since, in a growing economy, the revenue collected by the government becomes an increasing proportion of the nation's aggregate income. Whatever the causes and whether, in the event, the now more prominent role of the state is inspired by paternalistic or else socialist ideals, the economic implications are much the same: an expansion of state enterprise and control of industry in varying degrees.

The extent to which state control has increased in the West, especially since World War II, is difficult to measure. With respect to the existing magnitudes, current estimates of the economic activity of governments in Western countries range between 30 and 60 per cent of GNP. Compared with the former Soviet economy, of course, the control of industry in the West is limited. But it is prodigious when compared with the control exercised by the state at the turn of the century, and is still regarded as such by libertarian economists. More generally, public opinion currently tends to favour a reduction of government activity. And there is no doubt whatever that, at the time of writing, the consensus among mainstream economists is that a competitive capitalist system is economically far more efficient than a centrally planned system with respect to production, innovation and distribution. The libertarian is yet more emphatic in stressing the advantages of a decentralised private-enterprise system in offering citizens greater choice and also in acting to reinforce political freedom.

II

Among the libertarian economists who have been foremost in persuading the public of the political dangers involved in extending the economic power of the state, a unique position has to be accorded to Milton Friedman.[1] Declaring that economic freedom is best realised through the operation of competitive markets, Friedman goes on to observe that 'What the market does is to reduce greatly the range of issues that must be decided through political means, and thereby to minimise the extent to which government need participate directly in the game. The characteristic feature of action through political channels is that it tends to require or enforce substantial conformity. The great advantage of the market, on the other hand, is that it permits wide diversity.'

Yet this same competitive private-enterprise system that extends economic freedom acts also to promote political freedom. For by removing the organisation of economic activity from the control of

[1] His two most popular books in support of the market economy are *Capitalism and Freedom* (1962) and (with his wife Rose) *Free to Choose* (1980).

political authority, the market eliminates this source of coercive power. It enables economic strength to be a check to political power rather than a reinforcement.

Such in a nutshell is the thesis, and I confess that I am in sympathy with it. Like most of my colleagues in the economics profession, I am ready to concede a presumption in favour of decentralised enterprise and competitive markets unless plausible reasons to the contrary are produced – as, of course, they frequently are when it comes to the introduction of a public good or the curbing of a public bad. Although, as amply illustrated in this volume, free competitive markets cannot of themselves prevent a gradual degradation of the quality of life, they are at least more congenial to the exercise of economic and political freedom than is the concentration of economic power in the hands of giant corporations or, worse, in the hands of the state.

But my sympathy goes no further than this. For I do not subscribe to the libertarian view of the rationale of the trend toward state power. As the libertarian economist sees it, this trend is essentially a product of intellectual error, one that is perpetuated by socialist ideology – although he is also aware of the stream of impulse tending to the expansion of government which is fed by the enthusiasm of planners and engineers and by the empire-building propensities of bureaucrats. None the less, the libertarian economist is adamant in his recommendation that the excrescent apparatus of the state be dismantled and that through 'privatisation' large and vital industries including public utilities, which were appropriated by the state, be returned to the private sector of the economy.

By the lights of conventional economic criteria, the policy of privatisation as persistently recommended, and to some extent as being implemented, has genuine merit. But no matter how vigorously pursued, it will not avail. The actual size of the public sector in relation to the economy as a whole – whether measured in terms of employment, of revenue, of expenditure, or of the value of assets – may or may not be growing over the next few years. What will continue to grow, however, is the *power* of Western governments in the control and direction of the lives of their citizens. And this for the simple reason that there now arises a persistent demand and a need for new government powers in order to cope with the many threatening consequences generated by the pace and direction of modern economic growth.

Broadly speaking the powers appropriated by and ceded to the democratic governments of the West stem from the response of their peoples to two interrelated developments, each of which can be traced to the growth of science and technology: an awareness by the public of its increasing vulnerability, and a multiplication of its sources of conflict.

The increasing vulnerability of the public takes three forms: (1) the invasion of personal privacy, (2) anxieties engendered by the rapidity of innovation, and (3) exposure to hostile elements. We take them up in that order.

III

(1) We may begin with a glance at those techniques, based on either microfilm or computer technology, which have vastly facilitated the processing, storage and retrieval of information. Such innovations have provided corporations and government departments with inviting opportunities for extending the range of enquiries about their personnel, about their customers, and about the public in general.

As once observed by Jacques Ellul in his *Technological Society* (1965), if a thing is technologically feasible, a use for it will be discovered: invention is the mother of necessity. It is now technically possible, and not too costly either, for the government of an industrially advanced country to store detailed information on the locality, the movements, and the economic and political activities of all its citizens, and also to exchange such information with other governments.

Although any proposed scheme devised to extend the coverage of detailed information about the private lives of citizens would be viewed with alarm by the public, it would not be difficult to rationalise in the name of efficiency and even in the name of humanity – as, for example, enabling assistance to be forthcoming more expeditiously to any victim of accident or hardship, or again, as a powerful aid in the detection and obstruction of crime.

Apart from its existing uses by the police and the military, and its prospective uses just indicated, the need for more comprehensive dossier systems will grow with the high-technology economy's growing dependence on the sophisticated machinery used in controlling the operations of giant industrial plants. Computers, for example, perform such vital functions as guiding missiles and airliners, or controlling the sequence of operations in steel or chemical plants. They are becoming indispensable in telephone exchanges and in the provision of other public utilities such as those supplying gas, water and electricity. And since a single plant can be constructed to serve a vast metropolitan area, a breakdown is costly and could be disastrous.

Recognition of these new risks necessarily produces a system of closer checks and tighter controls on the personnel employed in the day-to-day management, repair and maintenance of such machines, a system which for its effective employment comes to depend, among other things, on the family histories and detailed psychological knowledge of the personnel in question. And the intimate knowledge required to implement these necessary precautions will be provided by specialised agencies, public and private, that have developed ingenious ways of eliciting confidential information about the private lives of citizens.

Despite the distaste with which such developments are currently regarded by libertarians, and despite legislation contrived to prevent abuses, such agencies will continue to grow and to become more resourceful. Indeed, the compilation of personal histories and other intimate information will be facilitated by the cooperation of those citizens whose employment opportunities come to depend upon the ready availability of such records.

IV

(2) Within this second category we can place innovations in methods of production – whether in agriculture, fishing, manufacturing or mining – which, although commercially more efficient, are known to be, or discovered to be, more hazardous both for the workers employed and for the inhabitants living in the surrounding area, to say nothing of their environmental damage. Since such innovations are being introduced into a wide range of different industries, new legislation designed to enforce safeguards, to monitor operations, to control location, to meter effluent, and to test the resulting products, will continue to proliferate along with the new agencies charged with ensuring implementation of its provisions.

More troublesome yet, the day-to-day application of science to industry, which results each year in hundreds of new synthetic materials, new drugs, new chemicals and food additives, exposes the consuming public to risks that are quite beyond its capacity to assess. Indeed, since the world simply has no experience of these new substances, scientists working in the field have difficulties in determining their efficacy and, more important, their safety. Although it is conceivable (though hardly likely) that the full range of adverse consequences, and the probability distribution of each of them, will come to light in the course of time for each new substance and for each possible combination of substances, the social problem is that of creating institutions capable of protecting the public from an expanding area of potential dangers.

The public does, of course, realise that new but as yet unknown dangers abound. Every so often – sometimes more by luck than by systematic research – some new material or drug or food additive comes under scientific or official suspicion and, after some preliminary enquiry, is withdrawn from the market. And, again, sometimes the damage already wrought is irrevocable.

Explicit forms of safety assurance are, of course, being demanded by the public, and nowhere more pertinaciously than in the US. Their recent Toxic Substance Control Act mandates that all chemicals (more than 3,000 at the time of writing) be tested for carcinogenicity, mutagenicity, teratogenicity and other effects. The difficulties are immense, if only because extension of results from animal experiments to humans introduces a high level of uncertainty.[2] In the meantime, the growing unease at this billowing but invisible cloud of hazards gathering about us tends to activate insistent public demand for more government control, and therefore, more detailed legislation, so confounding the hopes of those who labour and argue for a reduction in government power.

V

(3) At the beginning of Chapter 7, and in connection with the dereliction of the city, we had occasion to mention the economies of scale that can be reaped in metropolitan areas in the operation of such public utilities as those supplying water, gas, electricity and telephone services. On the other hand, the consequences of an accident or

---

[2] In some instances it is hardly a question of setting confidence intervals, for virtually nothing is known of the new substance or new technology save the fears of some scientists about the possibility of a variety of calamitous consequences. What, for example, is the risk that some malignant man-made bacterium may escape from its microgenetic engineering laboratory and spread an entirely new disease against which men have no natural defence and against which modern medicine – within the relevant time span – would be powerless? Perhaps not too great just now. But as the number of very small risks of precipitating an apocalyptic catastrophe continues to grow year by year – and not all the risks we run are negligible – one may legitimately conjecture that the passage of time brings us ever closer to a near-certainty of some such catastrophe.

breakdown are proportionally greater. More immediately relevant, however, is the fact that owing to the postwar revolution in communications, transport and small weapons technology, the public utilities serving the metropolis are now also exposed to sabotage or threat of sabotage by terrorists for the purpose of blackmail, and by fanatics, domestic and foreign, as retaliation for (imagined) grievances. An announcement by terrorists, or even a rumour, that, say, a pound of plutonium was to be dropped into the main reservoir, so poisoning the water, would be enough to create panic among the population.

Recognition of such potential dangers has resulted in closer scrutiny of the credentials and personal background of personnel, and the monitoring of activities and the movement of people within the vicinity.

There are today, however, yet more inviting targets for hostile agents. Nuclear power programmes may have received a setback after the Chernobyl accident, but it is unlikely that they will be discontinued. In any case there is already a large number of nuclear generating plants in North America, France and Britain producing enormous amounts of highly toxic materials which may fall into the hands of desperados. Most important of all is the continued scientific research to discover more complex missile systems and deadlier chemicals, gases, death-rays, bacterial bombs, and other fearful weapons of mass destruction, all assumed to be necessary in these volcanic times for the defence of the nation against fanatic and tyrannical regimes abroad. Scattered throughout the land, therefore, there will be highly guarded chemical laboratories, experimental centres, weapons factories, missile launching pads, arsenals, depots and underground control bunkers. Necessarily, then, there has to be an ever more elaborate security system.

Among other measures this will involve armed protection of the transport network along which move containers of chemical or atomic materials, a more comprehensive system of surveillance and, inevitably, the transfer to the police, or possibly to specially trained forces, of extraordinary powers of entry, arrest, detention and interrogation, if (as they will claim) they are to move fast enough to prevent highly organised criminals, fanatics or psychopaths from capturing positions from which they can effectively blackmail the nation or cause – inadvertently or deliberately – irreparable disaster.

And this extension of state control held to be necessary to defend the nation against foreign aggression is being augmented today by an increased police presence and increased police powers in the struggle to maintain law and order within the nation at a time when crime and violence is rising like a tidal wave. No more need be said here about this phenomenon, however, since Chapter 23 will be devoted to revealing its technological origins and its social implications.

VI

Some of the other ways in which the ascendancy of science and technology has generated internecine turmoil have already been illustrated in the preceding chapter with examples taken from medical science, from the diffusion of despoiling technology both by industry and citizens, and from the South-to-North migration responding to the revolution in communications and transport. In view, then, of the train of conflicts that follow in the wake of scientific progress, we are indeed fated to enter a more turbulent and apprehensive future. But, of course, the cheerless conclusion does not end there. For whether it acts in response to a growing public demand or else in anticipation of events, the government has no choice but to enter the arena of conflicts if only in a bid to hold the ring for the time being, to restrain animosities, and to prevent confrontations from flaring into physical combat. Eventually, however, the government is constrained to introduce legislation – usually controversial legislation – which tends to accord to new agencies the necessary powers to monitor, regulate and control the various activities in dispute, so further restricting individual freedom of choice.

It may be emphasised in passing that such legislation is indeed apt to be controversial since it has to strike an uneasy balance between the contending interests and the contending passions. Sometimes the opposing lobbies are inflamed by an inveterate hatred, each side being determined to continue the struggle by legal and other means should the decision go against it. Legislating in such circumstances would be trying enough even for a wise government addressing itself wholly to the long-term effects of its decisions on the welfare of society at large. The legislation actually resulting is likely to be less prudent and enduring in an age when governments are tempted to bow to political fashion and – goaded as they are by media comment and recurrent surveys of public opinion – are frequently influenced in their decisions by electoral considerations.

VII

It is legitimate to conclude, therefore, that modern economic growth, imposingly arrayed in its technological regalia, is inexorably impelling us along the road to repression: the power of the state will continue to grow and the freedom of the individual will continue to decline. This depressing thesis will now be reinforced by a close consideration of two other features unique to the postwar epoch. The first is the upsurge of crime already mentioned as a factor contributing to the growing vulnerability of the public. It will be treated at length in Chapter 23. The second is the so-called permissive society which, as we shall see, constitutes a critical milestone along the road to repression, and which we approach in the following chapter.

22 The Permissive Era – a Milestone on the Road to Repression

I

The most far-reaching transformation of the character of the peoples of the Western world – and that by which the quality of their civilisation will be assessed – came with the advent of the 'New Permissiveness' of the sixties, and is marked by three intertwined features: (1) an erosion of the customary norms of propriety and restraint, clearly evident in the licence usurped by popular media to revel in the depiction of scenes of sexuality, sadism and violence; (2) a decline in respect for long-standing political procedures upon which all self-governing societies are founded; and (3) a fragmentation of the moral consensus already mentioned. They are inauspicious developments inasmuch as an absence of prevailing norms and shared beliefs makes it increasingly difficult to resolve political differences and to avoid social strife. And this at a time when, as argued earlier, new conflicts are emerging in response to new techniques of life-control opened by advances being made in applied science. Democracy may well be entering a pathological state, riven by entrenched dissensions and smouldering hostilities.

II

What, we may ask, are the historical factors that ushered us into the Permissive Era? Certainly they overlap with some of the factors contributing to the genesis of the Women's Liberation Movement. Indeed, that Movement may be regarded as a powerful current within the larger tidal flow of Permissiveness, both impelling it forward and being borne along by it. Thus, central to the opportunity for a permissive life-style are the medical advances referred to (penicillin, the contraceptive pill, easy abortion) along with those domestic innovations that made women expendable to the home and those industrial innovations that attracted them into the workforce. And, again, there already existed in the West those two ancillary but potent factors: first, the mass affluence necessary for the spread of the resulting opportunities and, second, the more populist forms of democracy that were readier to sanction the new hedonism. Last, but no less powerful, were the dynamic commercial forces generated by private enterprise.

These commercial forces, operating through the 'free competitive market' on which so many today repose their hopes for a better future, deserve special mention in this connection. For the prospect it holds out, as seen through conventional lenses, is an exhilarating one: a consumer cornucopia spilling over with fabulous new gadgets, entertainments, thrills and travel opportunities. But let us note also that this emergent amoral society – the triumphant product of sustained material progress, which is so joyously rejecting 'Victorian guilt', indeed, rejecting any restraint on appetite – is a wondrously providential development by means of which the modern technically sophisticated economy, continuously under institutional compulsion to expand, can be kept growing.

Put more explicitly, the persistent expansion of modern industry depends today on its success in perpetually whetting and enlarging the appetite of the consuming public so as to enable it to engorge the sheer volume and burgeoning variety of goods provided. Clearly a discriminating public will not serve; nor yet a public whose demand for goods is restrained by considerations of seemliness and good taste, or by ideas of right and wrong. What is required, and therefore what is commercially fostered, is rampant promiscuity.

The ideal public for the modern growth economy, that is, is one uprooted from traditional restraints, liberated from the sense of shame, morally disoriented, insatiable, indefatigable in hedonistic pursuit – or, as seen through the keen eyes of the advertising barons, a buying public that is excitable, volatile, free-floating and malleable. And this indiscriminate and insatiable buying public is precisely that which has been spawned by the permissive society in such a timely way. For a society in which 'anything goes' is also one in which anything sells.[1]

---

[1] The young today, commanding as they do discretionary income and credit on a scale undreamed of by the young of earlier generations, are both prodigal and promiscuous in their consumption, especially so in the United States.

According to Arthur Kempton, 'In the last twenty years or so the kinds of business for which teen-aged labor had value – fast foods, convenience stores, services of all kinds – proliferated. . . . Soon more high school students were working more than ever before, some nearly as many hours as they spent in school. . . . As people in the selling business caught a fresh scent, they lifted their

III

So much for the genesis and the economic rationale of the permissive society. In what other ways does it act to undermine the moral infrastructure of our civilisation?

Some are implicit in its description: a decline of commitment and loyalty. For who can care much about the future of an increasingly unheroic admass society chiefly dedicated to engorgement, one in which popular taste is persistently debased in the name of emancipation, in which promiscuity is extolled as 'fun-loving', in which the quest for novel, whimsical and visceral forms of pleasure has, for many, become the prime purpose of life?

Nor is much insight needed to realise that if the objective really sought is – as it is sometimes called – 'life enrichment', such pursuits are profitless. The idea that, after thousands of years struggling upward toward some beckoning light, we shall attain a plateau along which life will be uninterrupted enjoyment is an infantile fantasy. The fact is that life is too elusive, too paradoxical, to lend itself to simple formulas for 'enrichment'. Its awards are strewn within an intricate mosaic of contrasts, of dark and bright, of joys and sorrows. As the historian Huizinga writes of the Middle Ages, 'We, at the present day, can hardly understand the keenness with which a fur coat, a good fire on the hearth, a soft bed, a glass of wine, were formerly enjoyed.' And it should surely be evident that there can be no real gratification without prior frustration or effort, no real romance without sublimation. Enduring friendships grow between men sharing common hardships and danger: they are not formed on package tours.

Apart from its self-defeating compulsions, however, permissiveness threatens the social order by sapping the moral substructures necessary for its support and cohesion. The pride once taken in personal rectitude begins to falter and, in consequence, the efficient operation of government and industry is subject to the strain and drag of a flourishing undergrowth of corruption. More important yet,

heads and pursued it. A market grew up around the cash the young now had to dispose of; and the young grew prematurely into an adult taste for acquiring deflected status from commodities they had the money to buy but didn't need. . . . Some of these kids by now resonate like tuning forks to changes in pitch caused by the changes in fashions in the culture of acquisition' (*New York Review of Books*, 11 April 1991).

What Kempton says of 'those kids' may in large measure be extended to the population at large. My purpose in stressing this obvious fact of modern life, however, is – as indicated above – to make abundantly clear the extent to which the expanding economy today has come to depend ever more on the production of expendables, of fashionable frippery, and neo-garbage.

within a society in which ideas of right and wrong become ephemeral, diverse and self-serving, in which each person feels free to act on his own privately constituted conscience, intercommunity antagonisms and conflicts will abound. The resulting atmosphere of unease and tension, or the fear of an impending anarchy, will make the populace that much more willing to surrender to the protective agencies of the state's increased powers of surveillance, control and arrest.

Thus as the moral order upon which any enduring civilisation has to be founded is scrapped in the name of emancipation, so, in the name of security, does the state expand its powers. Repressive mechanisms internal to the individual are replaced by repressive mechanisms external to him. It transpires that the Permissive Society is the precursor of the totalitarian state – possibly a populist democratic state for some time, but a totalitarian one for all that.

23 Economic Growth and the Growth of Crime

I

An article of faith among the Established Enlightenment since the eighteenth century is that the basic causes of crime and brutality are to be sought in the poverty and ignorance of people. Hence the certain belief among the apostles of progress in the nineteenth century, and even in the twentieth, that with the diffusion of material prosperity and education, crime would dwindle and die away.

Never has so unshakeable a conviction been more decisively refuted by events. The past four decades in the West have witnessed the most rapid material advance in history and also an unprecedented spread of higher education. Yet over those four decades there has been a six-fold increase in crime. Of particular concern is the yet faster rise in robbery and theft among juveniles, the frequency of mindless hooliganism, the upsurge of crimes of violence, and the indiscriminate killings by dedicated and professional terrorists.

Compared with the period before World War II, we are all of us closer to the edge of violence. Inevitably we are being made uncomfortably aware of its omnipresence; made aware of the lurking threat to our person and property by startling media reports, by public transport notices, by airport search procedures, by cards placed in hotel bedrooms urging us to keep our doors locked at all times, by lectures to schoolchildren counselling them not to speak to strangers, by a marked police presence at sports events, and by the insidious spread of 'No Go' areas in our major cities. Indicators of the rising level of anxiety can be found in the high premia for comprehensive insurance policies, in the popularity of scanning apertures, closed-circuit television screens, more powerful locks and ingenious alarm systems, the greater use of guards in buildings, and the vast number of security organisations and protection agencies in large towns and cities.

Indeed, during the past three decades there have been frequent demands for more police, not only to cope with the massive growth of crime (about which more presently) but also to contend with the spread of violence and hooliganism. We are now accustomed to a conspicuous police presence at routine or festive occasions, and at open air gatherings, political rallies and football matches. Police officers are now to be seen at airports, sea ports and railway stations and – in response to public outcry – they may soon be present on surface and underground trains, and parked close to public houses and nightclubs.

II

How do we account for this extraordinary surge in crime that has confounded the predictions of progressive thinkers? No comprehensive analysis need be undertaken to conclude that in the main the phenomenon can also be traced to the advances made by science and technology. The connections between them will be illuminated in a number of instances.

(1) Consider first those factors that have been most active in eroding the moral substructure of society. Our predominantly secular age is the legacy of a triumphant science. And the best we can hope for in a secular age is that enlightened self-interest may replace divine precepts. Building on scientific discoveries is the technological progress that, along with the enterprise economy, has generated a mass affluence which, in the event, has culminated in the permissive ethos referred to. In consequence, traditional restraints on self-seeking have fallen into desuetude. This liberation from traditional restraints is, as suggested earlier, responsible for the rising trend in family breakdown and the postwar eruption of 'one-parent families' that have contributed so much to childhood insecurity and, later, to emotional instability.

This inceptive amorality is further magnified among the unstable and impressionable by the pervasive influence of popular television and cinema drama which seeks to rivet the attention of the viewer by repeated recourse to scenes of sadistic violence, steamy sex and calculated cruelty. The long-term effect of entertainment that makes cheating, theft, betrayal, torture, violence, murder, destruction, look 'cool', whimsical, clever, 'chic' – that seeks, in effect, to normalise the abnormal – especially among the uneducated young, restless and eager for adventure, bodes ill for the future of the permissive society.

(2) On the other hand, some of the hooliganism of the young today

may also be interpreted as sporadic outbursts in a bid to escape immersion within an atomistic and increasingly anonymous society, one no longer held together by a common pride, culture, religion or patriotism. Once released by the welfare state from the daily grind to eke out a living, the energies of the young are more prone to find vent in seemingly mindless eruptions of violence and vandalism. Such behaviour, however, may have some affinity with the primitive urge to forge a brotherhood through blood; to assert a presence and an identity; at least to make one's mark, to be noticed, to matter.

III

(3) Theft has grown in response to temptation. Before World War II, homes were generally occupied during the day by housewives, by servants, and often by grandparents or other relations. Thanks to labour-saving devices, on the one hand, and greater work opportunities for women, on the other, both parents can be working outside the home even when the children are young. Their homes are generally empty during weekdays from early morning to late afternoon. Again, a large proportion of homes, often in the form of converted flats, are now lived in, or shared, by people of working age, which habitations also remain unoccupied for the greater part of the day.

This radical change in the residential pattern of living clearly offers relatively easy pickings for motivated youngsters who, living as they do in an affluent, secular and permissive society, are less inhibited by shame or fear from breaking in and stealing.

IV

(4) The cooperation of citizens in resisting and exposing crime has declined with the revolution in transport and communications inasmuch as it has accelerated the demise of once settled communities and neighbourhoods within which people knew and cared about each other. In their stead there has come a restless and mobile population, most members of which take up short-term residence in concrete dormitory areas scattered within vast conurbations.

This new foot-loose city-dweller has no commitment to the area within which he is in temporary residence. Nor is he able to count on the support of a community should he be threatened, attacked or harassed. His disinclination to get 'involved' is therefore understandable. More likely than not, he will look the other way if he sees a crime being comitted. Conscious that he and his family have only tenuous support, he feels vulnerable and may refrain from informing the police or refuse to bear witness lest he be victimised. Discretion, he submits, is the better part of valour. If the area in which he has settled looks like becoming more dangerous, he will pack up and move elsewhere.

A related reason why street crime has risen so alarmingly compared with the prewar interlude is that, in consequence of the growing use of the automobile, there are relatively few people on the streets at night, especially in the suburbs. And just because of public awareness of the rise in street crime, people who might otherwise have chosen to stroll about at nights have taken to their automobiles – which, of course, increases the risks that are borne by the remaining people who choose or have to walk.

V

(5) Finally, as an occupation, crime is being facilitated by significant innovations in small weapons technology. Lighter machine guns and missile launchers, radio-controlled explosive devices, infra-red gun sights, letter bombs, laser guns, stun guns and the like are boons to the criminal classes. We may remind ourselves also of the express dependence today on the fast getaway automobile, especially for bank robbery, and the opportunity for a criminal or murderer to escape the country through an international airport within an hour or two of his crime.

VI

Almost every element in the explanation of the rising indices of crime can therefore be traced directly or indirectly to the expanding powers of science and technology. In the event, there can be little hope for the foreseeable future.

As far as one can see, the West will remain predominantly secular and there are no discernible countervailing forces to the Permissive Society it has nurtured. The proportion of housewives in the work-force is expected to grow, as also are the trends in broken marriages, in one-parent families, and in children born out of wedlock. Geographical mobility will increase as will also the size of metropolitan areas. Television channels and video outlets will multiply, the intense competition for the mass market leading to visually more arresting matter – to more overt obscenity (camouflaged as comedy) and more salacious and sadistic scenes. To wind up, one can be sure of continuing technical progress in the design of small weapons. And though the police also will be better armed in the process, the initiative will always be with the criminal, whose reach and destructive ability is increasing.

In the circumstances, the best we can reasonably anticipate are yet more ingenious schemes and devices for our protection and, ultimately, the surrender of greater powers to the police.[1] To be sure, there will be strong resistance by libertarian organisations to further trespassing on individual rights and freedoms, but they are unlikely to arrest the process. For among ordinary citizens there is now a far livelier apprehension of the threat to their freedom from the increasing lawlessness and violence within the cities and suburbs than from the increasing power of the state. And the repercussions do not stop there. To the suffering of the victims and their families, one must add the growth among the populace of anxiety and suspicion that interfere with the normal functioning of its social and economic activities. Indeed, a further rise in the incidence of criminal violence may so intimidate the citizen, so warp and encumber his day-to-day arrangements, as to destroy the very possibility of a civilised life.

Of course, the official statistics may continue to show a rise over time of material standards. But no expansion of material prosperity, no extension of travel opportunities, no entertainment extravaganzas, no frolicsome diversions, can alter the fact that life is a pathetic thing if people, emerging from behind the bolted doors of their homes or automobiles, have to creep about the streets, huddled in convoys, for fear of physical assault. Well may we wonder whether the phenomenal rise of crime, alone and by itself, is not enough to turn the scale of human welfare against all the vaunted economic achievements since World War II. And should the trend continue, as well it may, it would turn to ashes all hopes of a bright future for our children.

---

[1] There is some hope for at least containing the growth of crime by the introduction of more severe penalties and by the re-introduction of capital punishment for terrorist and other categories of murder. Contrary to popular liberal opinion there is ample evidence that punishment does indeed deter. The inquisitive reader may wish to glance through my article, 'The Lingering Debate on Capital Punishment', *Encounter*, March 1988.

PART IX
....

Further Reflections on Things to Come

24 Trapped Within a Growth Warp

I

This new and more realistic conception of the emergent future as a transitional but turbulent phase, with humanity destined to be propelled by irresistible technological momenta through a never-ending sequence of wrenching transformations, material and institutional, is a far cry from the ideals of civility and tranquillity, of harmony and stability, that are invoked by ideas of the good life.

There may indeed be many opinions about an 'optimal' pattern of technology – optimal with respect to human fulfilment – and there may also be general agreement that a society using less advanced technology than is currently in existence or coming into operation would be less restive and stretched, more considerate and caring. But where there is virtually no hope of being able to arrest the cumulative forces set in motion by science – no hope whatever of being able to create and maintain a steady-state economy – it is academic to speculate about alternative worlds.

Such a remark is apt to be judged intemperate, or defeatist, by those who are actively engaged in projects to protect the planet or to effect improvements in a variety of ways. Yet attention to three crucial features of the modern world should suffice to convince the most sanguine among us that this is truly the case; that there is no hope whatever of veering away from the economic-growth path – at least, not while the West survives.

II

First there is the unchallenged rationalisation of the scientific establishment; the unbounded faith that, irrespective of the past record of science and technology, it is to science and technology that we must continue to turn for ultimate salvation. Where they are seen to be successful, it is an argument for more scientific and technological research: where they are seen to fail, there is again an argument for more scientific and technological research.

To many scientists the global risks being incurred do not suggest the existence of limits to empirical research or limits to the expansion of man's mastery beyond which we trespass at our peril. Rather they suggest, at worst, the existence of unsuspected mines strewn along a zone through which, always guided by more research, we must pick our way carefully before triumphant entry into the promised land.

As for members of the larger public in the West, many of them are still high with hopes that sooner or later science will unearth some breathtaking discovery – some new chemical or hormone that rejuvenates the aged and perpetuates youth, that maintains sexual potency, or releases the ducts of euphoric sensation. Perhaps it will effect some genetic breakthrough enabling all of us to give birth to beautiful and brilliant children! Perhaps it will decode signals from outer space telling of wonderfully advanced and superior forms of life which, we hope, will open new horizons of joy and fulfilment for the human race!

The newspapers and the media generally keep these hopes simmering by occasional reports of some impending miraculous scientific achievement or discovery. And although apprehension is also aroused by speculation about the more sinister shape of things to come, so many people today living in a spiritual vacuum suffer from what sociologists call *anomie*, a sense of the purposelessness of life, that they cannot but hope and crave that the future will have something of riveting exhilaration to offer. In fact much of the support of science and of the popularity of science fiction can be attributed to the very restlessness and discontent that is fostered by the economic growth ethos properly regarded as the mainspring of material progress. Indeed, with the spread since World War II of material expectations and 'the entitlements mentality', what is known as relative deprivation – which is coming to include even the ordinary frustrations of life – tends to be regarded by the less fortunate groups in society as intolerable, as indicative of an urgent need of state provision, or else as evidence of insidious discrimination and conspiracy by a ruthless capitalist class.

There is, of course, a growing awareness among the more thoughtful members of society that institutional changes alone may not suffice to usher in the millennium; that much of the inequality among people is inherent; and that much of the tedium and pain of living is ineradicable – notwithstanding which their hopes habitually turn toward the glowing beacon of a science for which, it is claimed, nothing is impossible. From today's massive research ways and means will perhaps, after all, eventually be discovered for removing all pain and frustration from people's lives, for making them whole and beautiful again. Admittedly, then, there is in this discontented world of ours rationalisation enough, arising from hopes and fears, for popular support of continued scientific and technological research.

III

The term 'entrenched interests' is calculated to bring to mind the organised power of wealthy stockholders, business magnates, land-lords, bankers, industrial executives and state bureaucrats – supporters all of the 'Establishment' and fearless growth-men to boot, their vocational purpose (as they see it) being to foster the growth of something or other, whether it be private profit, volume of sales, revenues or exports, or the number of employees, customers or branches of the business. This great numbers game absorbs them thoroughly from day to day and from year to year, the social life they lead being shaped by the game itself and ancillary and subservient to it: indeed, their resultant social life is an extension of it through which connections are made and maintained and through which power is exhibited and exercised. The constitution of the individual caught up in this game becomes expansionist, thrusting and restless, rejoicing in the rise of the relevant numbers or indices and impatient of occasional setbacks. He may, of course, pay lip service at public meetings and conferences to emerging social ideals and environmentalist aspirations, but the idea of a steady-state economy is anathema to him. In sum, the most powerful economic class in the modern nation-state is wholly committed to sustained economic growth. In prudent concession to popular ideals the economic growth to which it is allegedly devoted may be characterised as 'purified', 'humanised' or 'harmonised'. The economic growth it sponsors may sport a new appellation, a new set of credentials: it may be bridled with other goals, or given a 'new direction'. But growth it has to be.

IV

Although their day-to-day occupation is not so charged with expansionist impulse as is that of their executives, the bulk of the working class – using that term to comprehend both blue-collar and white-collar workers, skilled and unskilled personnel, social workers and techniques – have as yet hardly begun to question the growth gospel. What is more, with the latest cost-of-living indices and pay differentials continually being broadcast, members of every occupational group have come to take the liveliest interest in their material prospects from one week to another. After some four decades of gorging themselves from a cornucopia spilling over with 'the good things of life' – enabling them, incidentally, to wreak havoc on the environment in which they are immersed – and of quaffing regularly at the fount of unlimited expectations, workers in the affluent West have come to believe that they are entitled by providence to an annual rise in their earnings.

Indeed, however critical or grim the economic condition of the country, any interruption of this postwar trend, even if only for a year or so, is not to be brooked without every manifestation of displeasure and impatience. The Western world will have to suffer some pretty terrifying experiences before the prosperous working classes will be in a mood to contemplate the implications for their life-style of a steady-state economy.

V

Strong as are the economic interests of both the managerial and working classes, they are not the most powerful. They would not, I believe, prevail against a sustained resistance by today's 'third estate' – the scientific community whose influence on society is still on the ascendant. Despite the growth of dissident voices over the last few years, it is within the scientific establishment that the support for economic growth is most deeply entrenched. This support is not expressed directly as a crude demand for more GNP. It comes disguised as a basic demand for 'freedom of enquiry' which, in practice, is freely translatable into demands for the continued support and expansion of the immense resources and facilities needed for research and development – resources and facilities that are currently provided by industry, by governments and by the universities.

Add to this sacred principle of freedom of enquiry the spur of 'social need' – of the many social problems that in most instances can be traced back to applications of scientific discovery – and the case for maintaining the expansion of research and development appears to be irresistible. Even the idea of imposing some restrictions on scientific freedom or on empirical research, experiment and technical innovation would be anathema to the scientific fraternity. For success in restricting or significantly curtailing the activities of this third estate would seem to threaten the foundations of society. Scores of thousands of scientists might have to move from their prestigious niches in government or industry to humbler occupations. Equally, scores of thousands of academics would have to abandon their hopes of status and recognition. The ambitions of an army of technocrats would be thwarted. Design departments in every industry would close down. Research laboratories would go to rust. Complex and ponderous computers would cease to hum. Stackfuls of learned journals would no longer appear. It would seem to many as if the vital core of society's machinery were being dismantled, and that collapse must surely follow.

One has but to contemplate the consternation produced by any political action to check or repress the progress of science and technology to be tempted to dismiss the idea out of hand – and to conclude, therefore, that scientific research and technological innovation will indeed continue to impel us toward that future of increasing hazard, anxiety and discontent described earlier.

25 Our Shrinking Planet

I

We no longer depend on the advertisements of the oil industry to persuade us to become 'getaway' people. With the unchecked environmental degradation within towns, cities and suburbs, getaway people are continually being provided with more and more places to get away from. But where can they go? When millions of citizens are on the move, ever more eager to get away, it is not likely that many will succeed, or succeed for very long.

One of the more salient incongruities of the age is that while the resources of language are remorselessly exploited to foster expectations of a widening horizon of novel experiences – in the standard euphoric newspeak, all discernible possibilities are 'new and exciting'; all emerging opportunities are 'rapidly expanding'; speed barriers, sex barriers, xyz barriers, are about to be 'crashed'; scientific 'break-throughs' occur every other week; and our lives continue to be mercilessly 'enriched' by a swirling abundance – there is ample evidence that people are beginning to suffer from a sense of claustrophobia.

An obvious cause of this growing sense of claustrophobia is the rapid development of communications, in particular the ceaseless endeavour to increase the speed of travel. Now that we have already succeeded in moving people through the air at a speed exceeding that of sound, in launching astronauts into space, the insatiate spirit of progress demands there be no slackening of our efforts to bring forward the day when we shall sail through space at a speed no less than that of light itself. If today we can foresee a shuttle service of an hour from London to Hong Kong, a yet further reduction of journey time to half an hour would unquestionably be accepted as an improvement. Alas, one of the more manifest and lamentable consequences of bringing distant places ever closer together in this way is that our planetary home, once thought to be immense, now begins to look dwarf-sized.

Not so long ago, no further back than a few years after the turn of the century, the world was still a spacious planet of vast oceans and vast continents. Today one has to return to the sea stories of Joseph Conrad or Herman Melville to recapture the vision of measureless oceans on which seamen ventured. Not that long ago, one could speak with awe and wonder of faraway places to be reached only by perilous sea voyages extending over weeks or months; one could speak of distant lands unknown to men, of uncharted seas, of impassable mountain ranges, of fearsome jungles, of coral islands shimmering in the South Seas, of enchanting islanders far removed from the corruption of a commercial civilisation, of an Africa teeming with wildlife and with warrior tribes, and of exotic and barbaric customs and rituals in distant lands as yet unspoiled by the white man.

True, unless one were a sailor or rich traveller, one might never venture beyond the border or coastline of the homeland. Yet for every one of us there was still this feeling of living in a world of unimaginable diversity of peoples and climates, a world of boundless resources, of inexhaustible variety, of fabulous and undiscovered riches. Although most people could only read and dream about sailing off to far distant shores, they were always fascinated by the tales of travellers and the memoirs of voyagers even where the distances involved amounted to no more than a few hundred miles.

Today no country is more than a few hours away by plane, and the years may see these few hours whittled down to minutes. Not only will the earth appear to our grandchildren as a pitifully diminutive affair, it will also appear irredeemably monotonous[1] – so much so, that they will be driven to seek relief by excursions into the frozen darkness of space or by groping their way over dead planets. Hopes of escape far from the madding crowd, for each of us, are being rapidly extinguished.

The annihilation of distance and of the earth's variety is being accompanied by the annihilation of urban variety in cities the world over. Fashions in clothes, pop music, television programmes, appliances, architecture, are becoming increasingly internationalised. Less than a hundred years ago, there were still striking differences between localities within a country as small as Britain, with

---

[1] Familiar and picturesque scenes of cattle grazing peacefully on meadowland and pastures are destined to disappear. As scientists discover new chemicals and soil substitutes, a growing proportion of livestock will never set foot on grasslands. They will be reared in vast animal factories, there to be blown up to a size, and to be transmuted to a required texture, as quickly and as cheaply as is technologically feasible – no thought being spared by the commercial interests involved for the mute suffering of these helpless creatures.

respect as much to buildings as to dialect. Today a random choice between dozens of new makeshift office blocks to be found in London or in any other large city reveals no perceptible difference from their counterparts in other cities from Buenos Aires to Detroit, from Sydney to Düsseldorf.

II

To this annihilation of distance and the consequent eradication of variety one must add the annihilation of time itself, for the gradual adjustment of society over time to the dictates of economic efficiency and to the notions of continued advancement breeds a temperament and an outlook that create a psychological imbalance between perceptions of the present and the future. The preoccupation of the age with economic growth necessarily fosters a predominantly forward-looking spirit, one that is well illustrated by the automobile and oil advertisements with their steely-eyed young executives, immaculately attired, gazing unflinchingly into the future. No other period in history has produced perorations laden with such wearisome solemnity as 'the future of our nation', 'the future of our people', 'the future of our children', 'the future of mankind', 'the future of the free world'. By contrast with this obsessive concern with the future, any thought given to the present for its own sake must seem reprehensible if not vulgar.

However, the more we are conditioned by the media, by scientists and businessmen, to raise our sights beyond the turmoil of the present and to think in terms of the approaching future, the more insensitive we become about the ugliness spreading around us. The more pie in the sky there is to stare at, the more muted our attention to what is happening right now within the ambient vicinity. If we are daily assaulted by the noise of motorised traffic, the perpetual drilling, and the dust of demolition, we can always turn for consolation to the rising statistics of production and the promise of a brighter future.

This fixation with the future enters our lives and affects our well-being in more ways than one. Each of us, in his own affairs, accepts it as the hallmark of prudence ever to be planning ahead. Whether we are hoarding money, imbibing expertise, building goodwill, seeking promotion, anticipating a vacation (in order to restore the reserves of vigour necessary to move ahead in our career), our thoughts are intent on the future. We are ever scanning our watches. Our calendars are marked for weeks and months ahead. Today's news is barely digested before we are impatient of tomorrow's. The very focus of our experience runs ahead of us. And the here and now is scarcely felt, so pre-empted are our minds by matters to come.

Thus the pure taste of the present eludes us. For in this civilisation that we are bent on transforming as rapidly as we can, the material advantages are to be reaped by those looking farthest ahead – by those who treat the receding present as a jumping-off ground for the future. But this habitual impatience for the harvests of the future is just the characteristic of the age that hastens a man through his fleeting lifespan and effectively cheats him of the spaciousness of time. The ability to immerse oneself today wholly within the stream of the present is given only to children – and to forest peoples, tribesmen, and other small societies governed by settled customs and traditions.

26 The Cult of Efficiency

I

In our routine preoccupation with efficiency and with innovation we neglect or overlook traditional and more potent sources of human gratification. The technocratic mind, for example, focuses on the measurement of output per worker, necessarily ignoring those incidental human consequences of productive techniques that are unmeasurable but which, on reflection, may be held occasionally to contribute far more to the worker's satisfaction than any growth in the value of his output. An easy and open-hearted relationship with one's neighbours and fellow-workers, for instance, is clearly not something that can be produced and bought on the market. Yet insofar as mutual trust itself is nurtured by direct mutual dependence, this more sustaining relationship is more likely to thrive within the smaller-scale agrarian communities which flourished before the advent of the incomparably more efficient methods of modern large-scale agribusiness.

The loss of aesthetic and instinctual gratification sustained by the ordinary working man over two centuries of technological innovation which transformed him from an artisan and craftsman into a machine minder, reading dials, pressing keys and pulling levers, has to remain a matter of speculation. I do not contend that every phase and aspect of this 'industrial revolution' was a change for the worse. It may well be that beginning some time in the first half of the nineteenth century, conditions of work steadily improved over the greater part of the British economy. Yet these conditions of work, including the social facilities provided, may not be supposed to be among the chief factors that contribute to the satisfaction derived by working men from their daily tasks. It is more than possible that the chief source of a man's satisfaction resides in the nature of the work he is called upon to perform and in the overt recognition by the community of the value of his skill.

Two centuries ago, or before factory machinery came into common use, a skilled workman in this country was a craftsman. Whether he worked in wood, clay, leather, stone, glass or metal, he was the complete master of his material. And whatever it was that he created, it grew and took shape in his hands from the elements of the earth to the finished article. The skilled workman was ever mindful that he was also a member of an honoured craft or guild, and he took legitimate pride in the excellence of his work.

Leaving aside the sporadic Luddite flare-up, there is no lack of expressive passages of regret and sadness in English literature at the passing of the skilled hand-worker. One that comes to mind is the touching lament in George Sturt's *The Wheelwright's Shop*:

> Of course wages are higher – many a workman today receives a larger income than I was ever able to get as 'profit' when I was an employer. But no higher wage, no income, will buy for men that satisfaction which of old – until machinery made drudges of them – streamed into their muscles all day long from close contact with iron, timber, clay, wind and wave, horse-strength. It tingled up in the niceties of touch, sight, and scent. The very ears received it unawares, as when the plane went ringing over the wood, or the exact chisel went tapping in (under the mallet) to the hard ash with gentle sound. But these intimacies are over. Although they have so much more leisure men can now take little solace in life of the sort the skilled handwork used to yield them. Just as the seaman today has to face the stokehold rather than the gale, and knows more of heatwaves than of seawaves, so throughout. In what was once the wheelwright's shop, where Englishmen grew friendly with the grain of timber and with sharp tools, nowadays untrained youths wait upon machines, hardly knowing oak from ash or caring for the qualities of either.

And it must be said that the ordinary worker stands in need of more reassurance than the great artist. For the craftsman who meets the express needs of villagers and townspeople there is the inestimable sense of belonging and of being an indispensable element in the daily life of the community. Whatever else may have been lacking in the smaller scale of society in which the yeoman tilled the soil and the master and his apprentices worked with patient skill at their craft, there was always this unassailable self-respect and the abiding sense of security which are not easily to be found in this hurried jostling world of today.

II

What has been said of efficiency in the workplace must be said also of efficiency in the home. It is undeniably more efficient that a child imbibe his amusement from the television screen rather than that his parents' time and energy be diverted to the telling of bedtime stories. More efficient also to press a key in order to capture the music of an internationally celebrated orchestra than to arrange a solo or duet performance by members of the family. On a purely aesthetic plane, the reproduction on a modern record-player of the voice of some world-famous singer is incomparably superior to the voice of a man's daughter at the piano or harpsichord. Yet with the passing of these once-common domestic occasions, victims of technical progress, some essential sweetness in the lives of men has also passed away. Admittedly these old-time options are not necessarily closed to us simply because we now have, in addition, transistors, compact discs, videos and the like. But their relevance to our lives has been submerged; their reality overshadowed.

Just as the occasional sight of a village blacksmith or stone-carver may provoke a wistful curiosity in a visitor, who regards him as a surviving relic of the England of a bygone age, we are also bound to recognise that such activity, picturesque though it be, is of no consequence whatever to the viability of the modern economy. In the same vein of reflection, it must be acknowledged that family evenings of not-so-long-ago when, perhaps gathered around a blazing hearth, the company entertained itself with song and stories, with music and games, were indeed evenings of merriment and gladness. But when the sound of music or voices can flood a room at the flick of a finger, nobody depends for his comfort or cheer upon the affection of his family, upon the cordiality of his neighbours, or upon the animation of the assembled company. It must be owned then that efficiency has triumphed and the pleasure that once flowed between player and listener in the home, and the singing in which the family joined and warmed to each other – these things, in the West, belong to the world we have lost.

III

Passing on to the language laboratories, closed television techniques, video programmes, computers and teaching machines, currently being developed for use in all educational establishments, it is readily granted that the high hopes placed on them by spirited pace-setters will eventually be fulfilled: their continued refinement will enable future generations of students (particularly those in science, medicine and engineering departments) to be taught more efficiently than students today. As surely as efficiency will remain the touchstone, classroom lectures are destined to diminish in the not too distant future. After all, it does not require much intelligence to pose the question: why pay several score, or several hundred, lecturers to teach the identical course in the many different universities in the country when the growing army of undergraduates – all eager to possess the degree that opens for them the door that leads to well-paid positions in industry and commerce – could all be simultaneously tuned in to some silver-tongued super-lecturer? And these televised lectures or video cassettes would obviously be supplemented by auto-instructioned programmes in the home, these being an efficient and highly economical substitute for conventional tutorials and seminars. Indeed, in view of the existing technological possibilities it is legitimate to doubt whether the university as traditionally conceived will survive much longer in its present form.

Yet although teaching will be more efficient in the future there will also be a loss – the unmeasurable loss arising from the deprivation of human contact. Just as television, video, etc. have already succeeded in impoverishing the common fund of mutual experience through which family and friendship are nourished, so is the revolution in teaching equipment destined to dissolve the tutor–student relationship in schools and universities. As he will be seen by a future generation, the youngster of today is a victim of the inefficacy of contemporary teaching methods and is consequently less proficient. But today at least he is held together in companionship with his classmates – together with them to exult or despair, to groan or to laugh – sharing with them the interchange of sympathy that accompanies their daily lessons through a teacher with whom, whether they like or dislike him, whether they love or hate him, they are none the less led to explore the resources of human feeling.

IV

Although scientists and scholars may still form an international community and share intellectual experiences at meeting-points along the extending frontiers of knowledge, for the common man no equivalent prospect exists. For him, the doors of communication with his fellows, indeed with members of his family, are gradually closing as his overt need of their services and their company recedes before the relentless advance of an all-embracing technology.

With this depressing consequence in mind, one may appreciate the acknowledged difficulties of giving impetus in newly built suburbs and towns to something resembling community spirit – something that was common enough in yesterday's slums which, for all the dirt and distress, had in them much that was yet warmly human. One can hardly expect a community to take root in urban or suburban districts teeming with cars, transistors and television sets, where people have no real need to know, and generally do not care to know, anything about their itinerant neighbours.

In the older forms of social organisation which began to disappear toward the close of the nineteenth century it was just this inescapable fact of material and psychological interdependence that held together the family and the community. The centrifugal forces of modern transport had yet to emerge. In the meantime, in village or town, the lives of the inhabitants were dominated by local affairs and local events. Limited though their lives might appear by current megalopolitan standards, all of them – rich and poor, young and old – had their place in a more natural order of things; a settled relationship with one another guided by a network of custom and mutual obligation.

Doubtless there were occasions when some restless or pensive individual found the atmosphere somewhat stifling. But against such chance non-conformism, one must set the individual's sense of belonging to and being an essential part of the life about him. For they were all at the centre of interest and gossip, absorbed in the daily business, the functions and events, of the community into which they were born.

V

Generations have passed and, like the woods and hedges that once sheltered it,[1] the rich local life that centred on township, parish and village has been uprooted and blown away by the winds of change. Today there is no escape from the universal pressure for more efficiency, no escape from the clamour for more excitements and more novelties that goads us on; competing, accumulating, innovating and

---

[1] Since World War II, half of Britain's ancient woods have vanished, and over 100,000 miles of hedgerows have been destroyed.

inevitably destroying. Every step forward in technological progess, and particularly in those things most eagerly anticipated – swifter travel, depersonalised services, all the push-button comforts and round-the-clock media entertainment – effectively transfers our dependence on other human beings to dependence on machines and unavoidably constricts yet further the direct flow of feeling between people.[2]

[2] While skilled workers and office staff are being automated into obsolescence and executives are being replaced by sophisticated decision-making computers, game-playing contrivances are rendering human partners unnecessary. For procreative purposes the sexual act is already something of an anachronism: advances in genetics are making fathers expendable and soon, with progress being made in the design of the synthetic womb, mothers will also become superfluous.

27 Salvation by Science

I

The image of scientists as a fraternity dedicated to the pursuit of knowledge for the ultimate benefit of mankind is a comforting one. Many a popular book on the scientists of yesterday and today presents a picture of men of vision struggling against the prejudices of the age, of men from whose inspired theorising and patient probings into the nature of the universe will come a millennium of supreme enlightenment and universal beneficence. The names of Newton, Darwin, Pasteur, Mme Curie, Einstein, are rich with associations. Not only were they devoted scientists, they were good people, uninterested in worldly things. The scientific establishment is seen as in fact having all the attributes of a priesthood: arcane knowledge, immunity from wordly temptations, prophetic vision, and unwavering faith.

This popular impression, however, does not stand up to scrutiny. Collective knowledge does indeed continue to grow in extent and complexity but, as indicated in Chapter 16, it is scattered among the growing army of specialists. In the past, when the world moved at a more leisurely pace and the sum of man's knowledge was substantially smaller, scientists were few in number and their success sprang from genius rather than from arduous study and specialised training. Of the scores of thousands of scientists to be found today in all countries, only a small proportion are sufficiently gifted to keep in advance of developments along a broad frontier of knowledge. But for those comprising the far greater proportion of the world's scientists, there is nothing for it but to plod along fired by ambition or compelled by anxiety. Whether young or old, whether employed in institutes, state agencies, research establishments or the universities, scientists are now subject to growing pressure both on their time and on their innate capacity simply in consequence of the sheer output of current research, theoretical and applied. Not only must the aspiring scientist struggle to keep abreast of the avalanche of journal literature in which, generally, the writing has become increasingly concentrated and increasingly technical. If he is ever to achieve some modicum of recognition he must himself contribute a learned paper from time to time to the accumulating weight of knowledge within his adopted field of competence. Thus, more than other professions perhaps, the ordinary scientist, and for that matter the ordinary academic also, tends to become overextended and his faculties too polarised to respond easily to other aspects of life, be they intellectual, aesthetic or emotional.

One need not wonder how a person of modest talent becomes a scientist or a university teacher at a time when the sum of knowledge is growing apace and when standards of scholarship are undeniably higher than they ever were. Two factors make it possible: one is the longer period of study and training during which the serious student has to neglect all but the minimal indulgence in social activity. Indeed, few students approach the frontiers of their chosen speciality before the age of twenty-five and most of them not before they are thirty. The other factor, no less obvious, is the secular trend toward ever-increasing specialisation. With the growth in numbers crowding into the field, the specialist sooner or later feels the pressure. Sooner or later, then, he will be tempted to hive off a smaller patch of the field and to devote himself to its more intense cultivation. Thus, as we move along the boundary of any discipline we find thousands of trained workers, each assiduously sifting his thimbleful of earth.

It is this continual splitting and re-splitting of a subject, science or discipline, by which process a myriad of workers may eventually be accommodated over the expanding spectrum of knowledge, that has brought about this state in which only a handful of men can be expected to comprehend more than a fraction of the broader discipline in which they work. Editors of learned journals frequently have difficulty in finding scholars able enough to appraise the quality of some of the highly specialised papers submitted to them. And the recent trend towards learned papers authored by two, three or more names bears further testimony to the growth of specialisation and, therefore, to the difficulties of keeping abreast of the technical literature in closely related fields. Indeed, such are the demands today upon their time and capacity that few scholars are able to read more than a fraction of the output of professional papers published within their particular area of competence. It has been estimated that the average scientific paper is read by less than two people – for while some are read by many people and a few by hundreds, a large number are read by nobody but their authors. One may well wonder what the situation will be like a generation hence. The possibility that our complex and intricately jointed civilisation will soon begin to disintegrate under the weight of its uncoordinated knowledge – knowledge that, in impressionistic terms, seems to be growing at an exponential rate – is not to be dismissed as pure fantasy.[1]

II

Nor does the picture of scientists as being a group largely immune from worldly temptations bear looking at closely. Certainly there is no obvious reason why research in the sciences should appeal only to the pure in mind and motive. After all, the prestige of science has never stood higher. And upon the more successful of its practitioners it confers not only status but also substantial material rewards. Even those of modest ability are able to find profitable positions in government and industry. In the event, scientists have been drawn – along with corporation executives, actors, artists and politicians – into the unending scramble for recognition and material rewards. A man may be coarse-grained, petty, avaricious or paranoid and yet do well enough as a scientist or scholar. He may well write a paper simply because of the intrinsic interest of the subject. He may in fact become so absorbed in the problems it presents as to ignore its relevance completely. But he is no less likely than any other person to discover interest in a subject that happens to carry with it some sizeable research grant. Moreover, whatever aspect of the matter engrosses his attention, he will be spurred on by the prospect of publication; for the scientist counts his published work as ardently as a miser counts his gold. They are his kudos, his claims to professional recognition. They also serve as encashable certificates within the competitive world of science.

Such observations are offered in order to temper the hopes inspired and regularly renewed by popular legends about 'science in the service of mankind' sported in the full-page advertisements of giant corporations. And the scientist himself never questions the assumptions that, on balance and sooner or later, his discoveries will confer benefits on

---

[1] The capacity of computers to store incredible amounts of detailed information, and their speed of retrieval, will indeed save time for professionals and research workers. But the point at issue is not that of speedy access to the storage of data but the innate capacity of the scientist himself, his ability to survey and to manipulate in his own mind a vast swarm of ideas, motifs and constructs that grow out of the remorseless advance of knowledge in his field.

humanity. He may be tempted to assert that increased knowledge of any sort is its own justification. But he is more likely to accept as a self-evident proposition that any additional knowledge entails an extension of man's power over the universe – and therefore an extension of his range of choice and of an opportunity to improve his lot on earth. And should it transpire that in consequence men are made less happy should they become prostrate before some ecological catastrophe or destroy themselves in a chemical or nuclear conflict, why this surely is the fault of society, not of the scientist! For, as indicated earlier, the standard response of the scientist to any failure or misapplication of science is that of urging the application of yet more science.

If the commercial use in agriculture of some new chemical pesticide is found to have wiped out several species of benign organisms, or to have caused ecological disequilibrium, the scientist can be depended upon to remark that more research is imperative. This sort of response is indeed one of the salient characteristics of the age. If men and women become increasingly maladjusted in the modern world, there is a call for more research. So much seems self-evident and surely legitimate. Psychologists, neurologists, sociologists, sexologists, will all be eager to diagnose any new disorders of mind and body that may be traced back ultimately to the extent and speed of the technological transformation of our civilisation. And the more calamitous the afflictions the greater the fascination for the experts – the greater the challenge! We may console ourselves with the conceit that although the application of science succeeds occasionally in ripping us apart in some ways, it is equally untiring in its efforts to sew us back together again.

III

The innocent layman, surrounded as he is by an array of experts of all kinds, is deluded into believing that his welfare is in safe hands whereas, in fact, there is no social science or discipline expressly concerned with human welfare in the round, nor can there be. For we are all of us helpless spectators to the continuance of a technological and economic transformation that is fraught with incalculable and far-reaching implications for our sensory system, our life-perspective, our aspirations, our morale and temperament, and hence our capacity to enjoy life. Thus whereas an institution expressly dedicated to the enhancing of human welfare would indeed demand that technology be evolved expressly to meet the needs of men, the fact is that in the continued pursuit of material progress ends and means have been reversed: men have now to be adjusted in order to meet 'the needs of the economy'. They are indeed being continually exhorted to do so by economic advisers, by politicians, chancellors and Eurocrats, addicted as they are to the all too familiar rhetoric about 'keeping abreast in the race' and 'meeting the challenge of the future'. It has to be accepted then that the dominant influences bearing on social welfare are those that are generated incidentally and accidentally as the foreseeable and unforeseeable side effects of an unsuppressible stream of innovations and discoveries.

It may well be suspected that the human frame and the human psyche are ill-adjusted to the style of living that the new technology is forcing upon us and that – restricting ourselves only to the physical aspects – it is placing ever greater strains on our eyesight and hearing, on our heart and lungs and nervous system. But willy-nilly, technology plunges on, leaving to the medical profession the fascinating and rewarding task of treating the increasing number of casualties unable to cope with the accelerating pace of change.

IV

As a collective enterprise, science itself has no more social conscience than the problem-solving computers it employs. Indeed, like some ponderous multipurpose robot that is powered by its own insatiable curiosity, science lurches on, its myriad feelers peeling away the flesh of nature, probing ever deeper beneath the surface, forcing entry into every sanctuary; inexorably compelled to chart every breathing pulse, to capture every fluttering beat, to uncover every stitch of the living universe, to expose every molecule, cell and particle to its merciless glare. Thus while this unquenchable lust for knowledge masquerades as dedication to the altar of truth, it rips away the warm mysterious darkness that is the soul of the earth and in its place spins a computerised web that mantles the globe with a myriad of flickering lights, electronic bleeps, shimmering images and grinning symbols: nothing to be left unslit or undissected.

The jaws of science are set to crunch open every secret of nature, to chew to tatters the veils of mystery, to scotch every flight of fancy, every source of myth and magic that once gave hope and comfort. All has now to be prised open, the temple treasures ransacked, the juice of life spilt, and the earth's fragrance dispersed. On it must go until there is nothing left to transfix and dissect, nothing left to be discovered – save perhaps the road back.

Long before the final consummation, however, we shall have learned that man does not live by truth alone. Already science has stripped men of the comfort of their cherished illusions; of the uniqueness of the world they inhabit, once believed to be the centre of God's universe, of the immortality of their souls, of their faith in the life everlasting. In the place of myth arise the heroic truths of science: that man dwells on a small planet lit by an insignificant star somewhere near the rim of an immense galaxy that is only one of a countless number of galaxies scattered through the infinitudes of space; that far from being created in the image of his Maker, and like unto the angels, man has evolved from primeval slime, an accidental by-product of the blind operation of natural selection; and that therefore life itself is but a fluke, a chance flicker in eternity.

V

Disencumbering men of their faith is not the only service conferred on mankind by science. Insofar as men cling to the remnants of a moral tradition and, therefore, to a belief in their intrinsic value as human beings, they are fated to be disabused. Having uncovered the secret of the genetic code, having mastered the art of genetic splicing, science presses on breathless for the day when it will enable us to predetermine the genetic composition of the unborn infant and, with luck, to dispose of any need of a mother's womb. Already science is opening for us a wonderland of supercomputers and cybernetic robots. Almost anything a man can do will in time be done better by a machine, and be done infinitely faster. Scientists are busy at work on machines that can translate from the spoken language, machines that can produce poetry, machines that can compose music, and machines that can make complex decisions and generate new hypotheses.

To be sure, by affirming that the marvels of modern science are the creation of man himself, we are being tacitly invited to share the pride and the glory. But such metaphysical crumbs of comfort will not sustain us long. For once we turn from the idea of *man* as the abstract embodiment of the overarching expanse of human knowledge and move toward recognition of the palpable vulnerability of ordinary men and women, we are impelled to acknowledge that in one attribute after another they are being outdone and replaced by sophisticated contraptions of wire and chemicals.

In the meantime, the ordinary layman – and beside the sum total of scientific achievement we are, nearly all of us, ordinary laymen – is daily becoming more of a bewildered spectator to what is happening about him, unavoidably having to adapt his way of life to an urban environment that is actively being transformed in response to an irrepressible flow of technological innovation. Flattered by the press for his readership, wooed by the politician for his vote, canvassed by charities for his donation, cajoled by the salesman for his money, how can he escape the darkening suspicion that he is little more than a unit of exploitation, one of a countless multitude, as near anonymous as makes no difference?

As he is shunted unerringly into the era of automation and freed further from mental and muscular effort, all the syrupy sounds of television, all the baubles and paraphernalia of soft living, and all the eupeptic drugs at his disposal, will not suffice to conceal from him the naked facts of his predicament. He may be taught new sports to maintain his health and new pastimes to soothe his thwarted instincts, but as an ordinary human being, the reins will have slipped from his grasp. He lives by the grace of the scientific establishment, destined to become a drone, protected for a time by institutions left over from an older tradition, but transparently expendable like some thousand millions of others heaped like ants over the earth.

PART X

....

By Way of Epilogue

28 Faint Glimmers of Hope

I

Bearing in mind the self-sustaining momentum of science, the institutionalised compulsion to innovate, the driving expansionism of modern industry, the postwar communications revolution, and the growing pressure of world population, we concluded in Chapter 23 that there is no hope of escape from the thraldom of economic growth in a bid to create a more humane and harmonious civilisation. The many infelicitous consequences, in particular the ecological perils, arising from the scale of rapidity of the technical transformation entailed by economic growth have been outlined in Parts VI and VII. And in the preceding four chapters, I ventured into uncharted waters to return with yet more disquieting impressions of the sort of future we are about to enter.

Well may the thoughtful reader demur at what looks like a wilful and elaborate delineation of a panorama of unrelieved gloom! Well may he protest at this pessimistic piling of Pelion on Ossa! Even though he may feel impelled to agree with the greater part of the arguments of this essay, he is sure to wonder if there are not also some countervailing developments to be set against those gathering forces, shaped and directed by scientific and technical progress, that admittedly are active in endangering human survival and in debasing the quality of life.

II

Some comfort may be gleaned when contemplating the advances being made by medical science. We may, for example, confidently anticipate improved methods of diagnosis and therapy. The eventual discovery of an effective cure for such scourges as cancer or, more recently, Aids would certainly count as a blessing to humanity. The promise of laser surgery and other refinements in surgical techniques, and of new skills in the design of replacements for, and transplantation of, human organs that would prolong life and make it less irksome, is likely to be fulfilled in the near future. Any contribution towards better means of reducing physical pain or raising health standards is not lightly to be dismissed even though, when placed in perspective, it rates only as a modest contribution to the sum of those constituents that are included among the preconditions necessary for the good life.

Neither should we overlook the increase over time of better-equipped emergency wards even though we may suspect that for the most part they will be employed, alas, in coping with the greater number of accidents which we can anticipate with equal confidence in an increasingly mobile affluent society and in a high-technology economy having continual recourse to new chemicals and synthetics and therefore also to more efficient but more hazardous methods of production. And for what solace it affords, we can count on an extension of psychiatric facilities and counselling agencies that are needed to cater for the growing number of people who experience difficulties in adjusting to the demands created by the pace of change and by other abrasive features of modern life.

The costs of medical services, however, will continue to rise if only because of the greater costs of the new drugs coming on to the market and the heavier capital costs of the more complex medical equipment to which, over the future, the medical profession will have more frequent recourse.

III

Aside from the progress expected in the fields of medicine, and assuming that somehow we manage to survive the gauntlet of global perils, there is little prospect of any communal, spiritual or aesthetic resurgence in the foreseeable future. As far as one can foresee, there is for the peoples of the West only more of the same – duly supported by routine exhortation for greater economic effort and impelled forward by innovative research and industrial rivalry. We have in fact reached a stage where it is no exaggeration to say that – notwithstanding the perennial rationalisation of economic growth as a means of reducing the numbers of the relatively underprivileged – further technical progress in already affluent economies is purposeless or worse. For the most part, innovation is channelled into commercial ventures with the aim of titillating or otherwise entertaining a restless consumer society that is already morally disoriented and habitually impatient for the 'new and exciting'.

Among the exciting things that are in the pipeline are vacational innovations; the planning of spectacular amusement parks on the Disney World model, vast pleasure dromes, super-marinas, elaborate fantasy-enactment arenas, and more lavish and all-inclusive holiday resorts. These and other ventures into extravagant recreational facilities and luxurious entertainment will indeed afford surprise and pleasure to masses of people who will brave the congestion, crowded airports and incidental discomforts in order to indulge themselves. And who would begrudge them the opportunity of some reprieve from the stress of modern living! Yet other than this, other than some temporary immersion in a never-never land of wanton carousal, of sensuality, of visceral exhilaration, nothing of enduring value is to be salvaged. Such escapist opportunities do perhaps enable people to cope the better with the more jostling, unruly and disharmonious world they inhabit. Yet escapist opportunities themselves are not to be counted among the components of the good life. Moreover, a constant succession of new impressions and sensations takes away the individual's power of feeling anything deeply or persistently.

What else then can we look forward to but an assortment of tinsel novelties and refinements in 'mod cons'? From breakthroughs in genetic engineering, we can expect hardier and meatier cattle, pest-resistant vegetables, synthetic fruits such as strawberry-flavoured bananas and other 'taste thrills' to tickle the palate of an adult population most of whom are in any case perpetually on a diet and perpetually overweight. Advances in microchip technology will take us into further computer miniaturisation, and from other technical spin-offs we shall come into possession of a new generation of high-definition and three-dimensional television contrivances. Visual telephones will become standard equipment in an increasingly automated world with finger-tip and remote control of more versatile and efficient home appliances and, sooner or later, the creation of domestic robots programmed to be responsive to all routine commands. At the same time, of course, ever larger numbers of citizens will throng to more elaborate gymnasia or enrol in expansive courses designed to wear down the fatty tissue accumulating in consequence of the increasingly sedentary mode of living.

Admittedly the purchase of one or more new machines in the home is likely to occasion some brief elation, but just as clearly it can be realised that it leaves no residue of enduring value to our lives. To boot, it goes to increase our dependence on machines, to build more complexity into the daily routine, and – in increasing the frequency of servicing, maintenance, and also of breakdowns, repairs and replacements – to encroach further on the limited spare time at our disposal.

IV

A foreglimpse of other perquisites to be bestowed on humanity by a beneficent technology need not detain us long. The technocrat's vision of universal telephone ownership by the year 2020, enabling anybody in the world to communicate with anyone else at any time, is not one that is likely to stir up much enthusiasm at a time when citizens of the West are busy removing their names from telephone directories and installing answering machines in their homes in order to reduce interruptions, save precious time, and guard against the occasional obscene call and the persistence of telephone salesmen. Again, the prospect of being able to condense the entire contents of the *Encyclopaedia Britannica* within the space of a cubic centimetre may cause palpitations in the breast of some frenetic entrepreneur. But does anyone believe that it is only the effort required to visit the local library which has so far deterred the ordinary citizen from conscientiously ingesting the mass of information stored within these august volumes?

More generally, the reader may be reminded that absorption by citizens of the industrialised nations of an ever larger volume and variety of goods and services is absorptive also of their time, and so acts to compress the remaining margin of leisure available to them. And, along with the global growth of population, concentrated mainly in the Third World, the rising tide of consumption must inevitably quicken the depletion of natural resources and move us closer to the brink of ecological catastrophe.[1]

---

[1] It is of course quite possible that for some materials, and over some future period, the physical state of the world, and the unbounded potential for technical discoveries, will accommodate the forces set up by market mechanisms and enable us to overcome or postpone incipient scarcities. But there is no warrant whatever for deducing from theoretical possibilities any empirical conclusion that the physical opportunities are unlimited; that economic history can be depended upon to repeat itself indefinitely; and that, somehow, just because such possibilities can be visualised, the world economy will in fact be able comfortably to circumvent any prospective shortage. There can be, and there already appears to be, evidence of diminishing returns to research both for new sources and for substitute materials. And were such evidence not conclusive, we should remind ourselves that there is no prospect whatever of discovering substitutes for the earth's space, its atmosphere, and ozone layer, which may be in the process of being irrevocably damaged.

V

Finally, some of the forms to be taken by a large part of consumption expenditure in the West can be predicted with as much dismay as confidence. Notwithstanding the interest being shown in public transport as a means of alleviating congestion on the roads, the next decade at least will see a steady increase in the ownership of second and third cars and also of second and third homes – so choking the highways and cities with traffic and cluttering the vanishing country-side with more housing developments. And, as mentioned in Chapter 19, over the same period a massive expansion of jet travel is expected, promoted as it will be by continuing mass affluence, by lower costs and lower journey times, and by international competition for new air routes and concessions – and therefore a more extensive and intensive destruction of the earth's natural environment.

29 Signs and Portents

I

We end this part of the book by taking a closer look at what are commonly held to be some of the more hopeful developments emerging in the West: a more equitable distribution of income and wealth, a better-informed public, an expansion of higher education, and a concern among the young about environmental and Third World problems. The comfort they afford us, however, may have to be qualified in view of an imperfect understanding of such phenomena and, therefore, of a failure fully to realise their implications.

We may begin with that rather trite declaration that since World War II Western democracies have become more egalitarian and, especially in Britain, less class-conscious. Although the relevant definitions are elusive and the trends, however defined, are difficult to plot, there can be no doubt about the broad levelling tendencies operating within these societies. And such is the spirit of the times that it is a bold man who can roundly declare that we are the worse for it. None the less, it is undeniable that the growth in social mobility has been accompanied by a growth in informality of address and behaviour which, over time, has brought about a perceptible decline in courtesy, manners and mutual respect.

What is more, whatever the arguments in favour of the less hierarchical and more democratic structure of society which now characterises the Western democracies, it is equally undeniable that the levelling process over time has not been a levelling upwards. It could hardly have been otherwise. For notwithstanding facile taunts about class snobbery and bourgeois hypocrisy by left-wing writers, the middle and educated classes in the decades before World War II exerted on the whole a benign and salutary influence in maintaining standards of taste and propriety. This influence was reinforced and diffused through the existence of a large servant class. Given the standards of address and conduct required of servants, their ubiquitous presence in the home had a restraining influence also on the temper and behaviour of the members of the family themselves.

With the disappearance in the West of a professional servant class and with the gradual economic ascendancy of the moneyed multitude eager for 'the good things of life', this moderating influence exerted by the middle and educated classes has been virtually swept away. In planning the production of all consumer goods, including banking services, travel itineraries, media programmes and popular literature, it is the rapidly expanding purchasing power of the newly affluent masses that now dominates the markets of the West, that rivets the attention of store managers and corporation directors, and fires the imagination of innovators and advertising personnel. But, as pointed out in Chapter 21, this new mass market needs to be malleable, indeed promiscuous, if it is to engorge the products of a modern innovative economy that can survive only by expanding. In the ruthless dynamic expansionism that has taken over the economies of the West, traditional ideas of taste, restraint, discretion and moderation can only be obstacles to economic survival and progress. In consequence the prevalence everywhere of a Gresham's law of culture is apparent – bad taste driving out good.

II

The popularity of the media, in particular television and radio, is often considered to be one of the more promising developments of the latter half of the twentieth century in the belief that, apart from their entertainment value, they serve over time to raise the general level of knowledge of the citizen. The sort of general knowledge offered to listeners and viewers consists in large part of programmes on topics of current interest and news reports, the latter enabling the public to keep abreast of the parade of disasters, conflicts, crimes and misfortunes that afflict communities all over the globe plus a review and commentary on political issues and sports events. No one need question the public's fascination at being witness to the daily quantum of outrage and horror, to the drama of world affairs, or to the unfolding of seemingly momentous events. Whether such current interest and news programmes succeed in augmenting the citizen's fund of knowledge about the world, whether they enlarge his mental capacity or sharpen his critical faculties, is quite another matter. Certainly the occasional random testing of the public's general knowledge discloses the most appalling ignorance. And the notion that the many special reports devised to increase our awareness of the customs and traditions followed by communities in foreign parts, or to acquaint us with the hardships and misfortunes they suffer, must act over time to promote international understanding and so contribute to the ideal of universal peace and brotherhood cannot produce a shred of historical evidence in its support.

There are indeed excellent newspaper articles and excellent television programmes, and there can be no doubt that the media have a limitless potential for raising standards of popular culture.[1] But even if all television programmes were brilliant on any criterion, the net effect on our lives would not be good, and this for a number of reasons, some obvious, some less so.

First, although television may be said to have an unlimited potential for good, there can be no doubt that it also has an unlimited potential for keeping people inert for hours on end. And insofar as it realises this potential it makes a contribution to the sedentary life that is the support and solace of the medical profession.

Secondly, in the absence of television some part of the twenty-seven or so hours a week that the average viewer currently spends before his television screen would be spent in intermingling and conversing with others. As suggested earlier, an unavoidable consequence of this innovation has therefore been the drying up of the direct flow of communication and sympathy between people. As dependence upon the television for entertainment has grown, so has there been a diminution of hospitality. Absorbed as people become in their television or video programmes of an evening, they no longer encourage the informal dropping in of a friend or neighbour for a chat or a drink. Inevitably we know less and care less about them.

Thirdly, it may seem evident that the presentation of panels of specialists and other eminent personages who address themselves to problems in science, history, ethics, literature, sex, politics, education or family care must do something to enlighten the mind of the viewer. But this sort of intellectual pageantry, this parade of expert opinion on every aspect of the universe, tends also to inhibit the range of men's discourse and speculation. Whereas a century ago the civilised man might express himself without diffidence on any subject

---

[1] Though they may raise standards of taste and popular culture, it cannot seriously be contended that specialised knowledge can be acquired or an academic discipline mastered simply by repeated exposure to television programmes. One does not learn a subject by osmosis, but only by prolonged and persistent study.

that took his fancy, his spirit today would be muted in deference to an omnipresent establishment of experts.

Worse, although people who are attracted to television programmes that are dedicated to the continual re-examination of fundamental questions about religion, psychology, aesthetics, philosophy and morals may appear to become more open-minded, their seeming liberality will have more to do with doubt and perplexity than with enlightenment. As they expose themselves to successive groups of savants in an age of eroding moral consensus, the distinctions in their minds between good and evil, vice and virtue, truth and falsehood, religion and ideology, become blurred and re-blurred and virtually dissolve. Any confidence they once had in their own judgement and sense of right begins to ebb. Thus the resulting growth of tolerance or rather of acquiescence – especially in the manifestly vulgar and obscene – though apt to be interpreted euphemistically as an element of 'moral pluralism', is in fact nothing less than a symptom of moral paralysis.[2]

So much by way of misgivings even if the quality of programmes were uniformly high. But it is almost certain that, on balance, television standards will deteriorate as the number of channels grows and as the ensuing competition to capture the largest chunk of the mass market increases the temptation to produce more arresting episodes and scenes, with more frequent recourse, therefore, to features and fiction depicting violence, horror, carnality and sadism, or to 'laugh-track' comedy richly admixed with smut.[3] It has been estimated that the average American youngster takes in some 6,000 scenes of mayhem, sadism and murder before reaching the age of 14. To argue that it does not signify, that the difference between the real

---

[2] Moral paralysis may be said to encompass the petrification of social attitudes, and therefore also the obstruction of critical thinking about current issues, that results from the media's frequent recourse to emotive and ill-defined denunciatory terms such as 'racism', 'sexism', 'discrimination', 'exploitation', 'imperialism' – a part of the flotsam of the pseudo-enlightenment of the left.

Their use of language also serves to impress the seal of approval on aberrant tendencies. Thus unwed mothers now come under the rubric of 'one-parent families'. Pornographic films take on the euphemism of 'adult movies'. And homosexuals are continually referred to by the newspeak term 'gay' – a term that is incidentally an effective weapon in the struggle against the as yet predominant heterosexual establishment. For the resort to this once-popular adjective 'gay' is surely calculated to impart to what, in plain language, is the practice of homosexuality an air of carefree defiance, a dash of colour, a touch perhaps of the exotic, so making the practice that much more attractive and fashionable to the disoriented young. Thus the term comports well with 'the new sexual pluralism' aspects of permissiveness ardently promoted by 'advanced' manuals which exhort the young to discover their own innate 'sexual orientation'.

[3] A deplorable instance, at the time of writing, is the unseemly excursion of BBC television into the crudest of sexual burlesques in a desperate bid to raise guffaws among the feeble-minded.

world and the screen world is readily recognised, is to beg the question. The desensitisation of character that sets in over time is indicated by the diminution of disgust and outrage experienced by the viewer.

There can be no doubt that sexual promiscuity, homosexuality, hooliganism, cruelty, vulgarity, obscene language and, indeed, sporadic violence would be far less prevalent today were it not for the media which in exploiting the compelling powers of these aberrant tendencies have also succeeded in normalising them into the popular culture.

Nor do we need to be reminded that television cameras are ever at the disposal of the more disruptive elements in the community. More than other media, television is repeatedly used by agitators, rioters, hijackers, terrorists, kidnappers and fanatics to impress their message, their grievances, or their demands on a world public, and also to incite supporters or sympathisers elsewhere to lawless or insurrectionary action. In these respects, television's power of instant visual communication acts also to encourage protest and defiance, and therefore to increase the incidence of violence and political assassination.

To be sure, there are still producers dedicated to excellence. Good music and opera, good investigative reporting and good entertainment can still be enjoyed, even though they are supported only by an enthusiastic minority. But the overriding influence of television on taste and on behaviour has been for the worse.

The spoken word itself has been one of the worst casualties. The unceasing endeavours to attract the viewer's attention occasionally issue in a veritable frenzy of verbiage and, along with the daily interviewing of semiliterate individuals, words are mispronounced, misused, overused, pounded together, broken up, and incongruously combined. And the sheer volume of output and the interminable repetition of words are themselves destructive of the beauty of language. Words of delicate sentiment come to lose their fragrance. Phrases, once stately or solemn, poignant or poetic, to be unveiled only on rare occasions, get dragged about in the dust of sales campaigns, rolled in with crude imperatives until they become stale and sullied and shorn of the joys of evocation. Even obscene remarks, which once might issue forth only under the most trying provocation, have become so common as to forfeit their power to shock or amuse.

III

Moving on to formal education at university level, it is hard to avoid scepticism when reflecting on the greater educational opportunities made possible, and indeed demanded, by the expanding 'high-tech' economy.

Among the mid-Victorian reformers we may pick out Matthew Arnold as one of the more enlightened public figures who agitated for the reform and spread of education in the secure belief that with the growth in the nation's prosperity the treasured cultures of the world would be accessible to all, providing 'sweetness and light' and edification to ordinary men. Alas for those far-off innocent days! It is as well that Arnold has been spared a visit to the modern mega-university so popular in North America where young philistines now stalk the campus, with pocket computers at the ready, and where the bulk of the genuine students come to have their plastic minds pounded into the shape necessary to fit into some part of the transitional structure of the high-technology economy. In these sprawling 'knowledge factories' humming with technical equipment, the original conception of the university as a community of scholars, and the idea of higher education as a civilising process, has a distinctly nostalgic air.

The plain fact is that so-called higher education is nowadays predominantly technical and vocational. It is not education in the classical sense. It is not education in the humanities. It has no obvious connection with the graces of civilised living. And to face the sad truth, the nineteenth-century ideal of a rounded education in both the sciences and the arts, though it does linger on, is wholly impractical at a time when the average scientist, specialised as he is within a narrow field of his chosen subject, has only vague ideas of developments in related fields of research. Within any one of the broad disciplines, the scientist or scholar is able to master but a fragment of the growing knowledge. Moreover, as contributions continue to pour into the growing number of increasingly specialised journals at what must seem an alarming rate, his fragment of expertise becomes yet a tinier part of the advancing frontier of knowledge within a broad discipline.

Thus the man of liberal education today is a figment. He may be literate. He may be 'well read' with respect to the popular classics. But he can be really learned only over a minute segment of the expanding horizon of knowledge, learned enough at any rate to take his place among the faculty of a university, or rather a 'multiversity' – one of the highly organised teaching establishments collectively referred to by the cynics as 'the knowledge industry', whose chief function it is to churn out the specialists needed to keep the complex economic machine in motion.

In brief, the educational system is no longer geared to produce educated men or men of cultivated intelligence. In the main, it is geared to produce scientists and technicians. Indeed, the minute specialisation generally involved in postgraduate research, which tends to cramp the spirit and warp the judgement, is the antithesis of the traditional education in the humanities.

And this is not all that is to be deplored about the tendencies manifest in the new knowledge industry. Over the last three decades ideological doctrines have infiltrated the curricula of many of the larger universities. Spurious academic subjects such as 'black studies' and more recently 'women's studies', putatively designed to 'raise consciousness' and strengthen commitment to credos of 'emancipation', manifestly fail to meet the stringent requirements of scholarship: certainly the doctrines of these ideologically inspired 'studies' are not regarded by their proponents as provisional and refutable hypotheses. Clearly arrangements being made for their systematic propagation in these circumstances do not comport well with the idea of a university as a forum for open-minded enquiry and impartial scholarship.

Finally, to move from the absurd to the pernicious, a high proportion of the universities in the United States have begun to forsake what academic standards they once strove to maintain in the novel (though, so far, unsuccessful) endeavour to comply with the official policy of 'affirmative action' – a policy which requires that the gender and racial composition of students and staff be brought into relation with a proportional representation of the 'protected minorities' (which group, incidentally, also includes the women of America). Selection on the basis of merit has therefore now to be tempered by considerations of both gender and race.

We may conclude with the observation that with the unprecedented expansion in the student population since World War II, and with the rise of the new permissiveness, the traditional role of the university as the guardian of civilised values has become an anachronism. Developments have made it abundantly clear that it can no longer be regarded as a sort of secular cathedral conducive to detached reflection and unfettered enquiry. In many ways the university has transformed itself into a microcosm of the outside world. Into it are imported the political passions, the prejudices and the trendy deviant movements of the larger world, and often on a scale that gives it a reputation in the popular mind as being a hothouse of pseudo-radicalism and student intolerance. It is sad to reflect that on so many occasions in the last few years the one place where a controversial issue could not be debated was the university.

IV

Notwithstanding the soaring incidence of hooliganism and teenage crime, optimistic voices can be heard on both sides of the Atlantic announcing a new awakening among the young. The impression that, taken as a whole, the younger generation evince more environmental concern than their parents is not altogether surprising, if only because the unflagging attention of the media to environmental matters is of recent provenance. For all that, and however unavailing their efforts may prove to be in view of the powerful institutional forces arraigned against them, idealistic stirrings among the young about humanity's obligation to conserve the earth's environmental resources form a welcome contrast to the cultivated avarice that is the leitmotif of the age. Also welcome is the eagerness with which many young people respond to appeals for aid to relieve the many communities in Africa and Asia suffering from famine or disease, or afflicted by plague or other disasters. And it would be churlish to dissect the motives and emotions of the many young people who participate in the campaigns, and in the entertainment and sports events, organised to raise funds for numerous charities at home and abroad.

Yet it must be said that their contribution to the good life, or even to a more worthwhile existence among the impoverished peoples of the Third World, cannot amount to much; a drop in the bucket, no more. Insofar as famine, disease and ecological catastrophes arise from population pressure on limited land resources, it is the offspring of those enabled to survive and breed – because of the food supplies that filter through – who are earmarked as potential future victims of the famine and disease which are likely to erupt in a yet more crowded Third World. And if we are concerned more with the outcome than with the intentions, we are going to have to conclude that whatever good can be salvaged from the greater environmental awareness of young people, and from their eager participation in events organised to relieve distress at home and abroad, it is heavily outweighed by the consequences of their other and more self-regarding activities.

Admittedly, generalising about the attitudes, values and aspirations of the younger generation in the West is fraught with pitfalls. But one may reasonably affirm that the new freedom to experiment in life-styles, to do one's 'own thing', to travel the world talking to anyone, sleeping anywhere, trying anything, is unlikely to shunt us toward the good life as conceived in Chapter 16. Whatever advantages may be claimed for these jaunty treks into foreign parts, the indiscriminate fraternal hobnobbing has no affinity with those more enduring friendships that can only grow with time and care.

In comparison with their elders there may seem to be some shift of emphasis from absorption in material considerations, though such difference is plausibly attributable merely to a difference in age. Certainly they show no diminution of appetite. Whatever it is that the young seek, the more of it the better. From crown to toe they, too, are 'maximisers'. Their outlook marks no real exception to the ethos of an age whose chief characteristic is not materialism but insatiability.

It is not too cynical to see their apparently unbounded tolerance as being largely the product of the moral vacuum in which they were reared. At any rate, their inordinate fondness for mixing with the world takes them by land, sea and air in every kind of vehicle and in every kind of company to every city and resort over the globe during the summer months – there, like disoriented termite colonies, to swarm into the parks and squares, to pour through castles, palaces and galleries, and to squat and sprawl, smoke and munch, over the once hallowed steps of spired cathedrals. Travelling in groups, large or small, they extend their experience from the best hotels to the sleaziest pensions, seeking consciously to be equally at home everywhere; to slum with the poor and slum with the rich; to ape the apparel both of other countries and of other periods of history; to eat the foods, borrow the accents, play the instruments, and adopt the customs of other cultures; to enter the tabernacles and to revel in the rituals, alike of primitive tribes and of ancient civilisations – in short, to be excluded from nothing that might pass for experience, whether bright or dull, good or evil, sublime or seamy.

Thus the young of the affluent countries are today among the most ruthless and persistent plunderers of the earth's vanishing variety. Their unchecked gluttony, magnified by commercial interests, is currently one of the more potent forces at work combining with others to diffuse an admass civilisation and to promote a cultural entropy – one that is in the process of dissolving all hierarchies, flattening all barriers, blurring all distinctions, erasing the mosaic pattern of centuries, transforming the once rich diversity of our universe into an inextricably blended monotony.

V

At the end of our journey, then, what remains of the once inspiring vision of man's progress toward perfectibility? The glimmers of hope are fading. Naught is left but a dogged belief that, notwithstanding the many unforeseen and untoward consequences, the struggle cannot be entirely in vain. Should everything else fail, man's extended mastery over nature can be vindicated by his greater power to alleviate suffering and physical hardship.

But even here we must demur. Is it so certain that such a prospect offers consolation? An affirmative answer is not at all self-evident. Let us recall in this connection the pampered denizens of Aldous Huxley's *Brave New World*, artificially procreated and systematically conditioned to fit comfortably into predetermined occupations. Happily there were no sexual taboos, no anxieties, no doubts. Any incipient apprehension was dispelled by swallowing a euphoric tablet, 'soma'. Indeed, since the synthetically created humans were programmed and conditioned to fit perfectly into the brave new world, Huxley's mock utopia can be interpreted as the nemesis of the fuzzy-minded progressive, with his touching faith in salvation by science, his rejection of the notion of sin, and his negation of the value of sacrifice or suffering. For in this beautifully tailored civilisation, presided over by a benevolent technocrat, the concepts of good and evil were entirely obsolete. All activity, economic and social, being guided by a trained elite, nothing was left for choice or chance and, therefore, no scope either for vice or virtue. The only relevant categories in such a dispensation were health and sickness, these being associated respectively with efficiency and inefficiency.

And what are the consequences for the inhabitants of achieving so ideal a state of adjustment? Imagine a potential Juliet of this Brave New World accidentally stumbling into the arms of a potential Romeo. The first flicker of desire would be quenched by instant fornication. And if, owing to some distraction, Romeo vacillated, Juliet could be depended upon to console herself at once with a couple of soma tablets.

In a world purged of all frustration – in a world, that is, of instant gratification – there can be no sublimation and therefore there can be no passion. In a world of sexual licence there can be no romance. In a perfectly conditioned world, where appetite has free rein and nothing is left to want, there can be no conflict, and therefore there can be no drama. In such a world there can be no suffering, and therefore there can be no tragedy; there can be no great issues to galvanise the community, no call for sacrifice, and therefore there can be no heroes. In such a world, bereft of transcendent emotion and idealism, there can be no poetry and neither then can there be any aspiration toward the good and the beautiful.

Thus, even if we somehow survive the approaching hazards, social, military and ecological, that is, the fated creation of an irresistible technological momentum, the future, the most favourable future, is not an inviting one. For if the conscientious endeavours of science and technology – directed as they are toward realising the dreams of countless visionaries to free mankind from all the frictions and frustrations of the world – eventually bear fruit, the resultant civilisation will be one that is mockingly comparable with Huxley's Brave New World of emotional cretins.

30 In Conclusion

I

From this ambitious endeavour to expose the more significant features of modern economic growth and to uncover their implications for fulfilment, a bleak and sombre picture has emerged. In broad outline, the pattern of things that is materialising about us centres upon a highly complex industrial civilisation, albeit one that is becoming more vulnerable and more unstable owing in the main to the rise of mass affluence and mass mobility, to the decline in the West of moral consensus, and to other infelicitous consequences of rapid technological change discussed at length in the preceding chapters.

In his search for mastery over nature, then, and addressing himself to specific ends, it transpires that man has been all too successful. And his appetite has fed on his success. There are no bounds to his ambitions and, until very recently, only tenuous restraints on his rapacity. He appears to be foredoomed to wreck the social order as surely as he has begun to wreck the ecological order.

A dawning recognition of this scenario has come to us belatedly – over the last three decades only. Something akin to apprehension and dismay is creeping over the West. As must be expected, the mood of the public fluctuates with the political and economic events, but the whiff of foreboding persists. Something serious seems to have gone awry, something that transcends the regular litany of economic afflictions and the vicissitudes of political fashion. Certainly we are all of us aware that the joys of jet travel have brought with them a destruction of the spaciousness and variety of our planetary home; that, owing to advances in technology, ecological devastation cannot be confined within the borders of any country; and that, owing to the advances made in lethal weaponry, none of us is safe today from attack by massive forces directed by tyrants and fanatics.

Yet should we somehow survive all the perils originating in new technologies and their products, the prospects for humanity are far from auspicious. For one thing, the public's anxiety about the uncertain side-effects of thousands of synthetic substances appearing on the market, about the growth of internecine antagonism, and about the phenomenal upsurge of crime and violence, is sure to augment the power ceded to governments and therefore to constrict personal freedoms. For another, the metropolitan scale, mobility and anonymity of our civilisation breeds mutual estrangement and distrust. And belatedly we are also discovering that a rational humanism, the product of the Enlightenment, cannot of itself impart a sense of purpose or meaning to our lives; that the current flight into wanton superstition, new bespoke religions and revivalist carnivals only bears witness to the pain of living in a spiritual vacuum.

Indeed, in this regard we may look back far beyond the last four decades or so. Since the eighteenth century and ever more rapidly as time wore on, the leading luminaries among the Western nations became active in disencumbering society of the myths and traditions that had flourished over centuries and millennia. Urged forward under the twin banners of science and progress, generations came to discard their faith in a divine lawgiver and in a divine purpose transcending the material universe. The rich tapestry of heraldry and festivals, of customs and ceremonies, of rituals and benedictions – all that, in spite of hardship and suffering, gave purpose, pageantry and ultimate dignity to the smaller communities of an earlier age – has had to be relegated to the rubble of history in the universal drive to quicken pace and to give free rein to appetite.

Thus we have paid dearly for the material plenty and for the technological toys bequeathed to us by science. Having sundered the filaments of this once intricate web of custom and tradition, we are now compelled to recognise that an earlier and pervasive sense of kinship and loyalty, of pride and propriety, of the unquestioned acceptance of duties and privileges, and the common acknowledgement of mutual obligation – distinctive features all of an earlier age – have all but vanished.

And with the passing of that age there has emerged on the scene the etiolated and synthetic creature that is bound to, and essential to, the continued expansion of a high-technology economy: the new economic man, the man-in-the-automobile, the insatiate denizen of a supermarket civilisation, garlanded with gadgetry, festooned with technical frou-frou, besotted by promiscuous media, unhinged by futuristic fantasies, daily anointed with the holy oil of motivation, heir apparent to a glittering cascade of electronic all-sorts – and inevitably assailed now and then by pangs of despair and foreboding.

Obstructed everywhere by material impedimenta, the flow of sympathy and feeling between people runs thinner. Personal arrangements once rooted in trust or custom give way to formal contracts: once conceived as a sacrament, marriage today is conceived as the legalisation of a relationship, a tentative experiment. And even within the family, just and proper treatment has come to depend less on natural feeling and accepted obligation and more on statute law, on new rights, and enforcement agencies. In general, as respect for custom and tradition declines, legislation perforce expands and litigation thrives.

And what hope is there then for the political community? An emerging population of self-seeking, hyper-mobile citizens can hardly be said to constitute a nation. Nor will the spread of enlightened self-interest, of equal opportunity, of material abundance, and generous state welfare services – agenda that are priorities for all political parties – serve to impart national cohesion. It is in fact doubtful whether any of the liberal democracies of the West can be held together much longer as a free people simply by economic policies alone, no matter how successful; held together, that is, without a pride in their common history, without esteem for their insitutions, without respect for their leaders, without a common culture, without a common code of ethics – and without faith, hope or purpose.

Once more we are led to conclude that within its territory the increasingly fragmented political community can be held together as a nation or a commonwealth only by an engirdling structure of legislation administered by an expanding bureaucracy, enforced by the courts and ultimately by the police.

II

To punish mortals for their sins, the gods grant their wishes. But whether seen as Nemesis or Fate, the vision evoked by our interpretation of events is a frightening one: that of Western civilisation, a civilisation tracing its lineage back to the Enlightenment, to the Renaissance, to medieval humanism, a civilisation born of high hopes and auspicious heralding, today frothing with power and glee, and yet tormented by pangs of despair. For this prodigious economic power that came with the Faustian bargain has now visibly begun to wreck the social order as surely as it has begun to wreck the natural order – and in its blindness corrupting and undermining the very institutions that once sustained it. And when we raise our sights to discover its effects on the world at large, we can no longer evade the harrowing spectacle of already bloated populations in various parts of the Third World continuing to multiply and in their desperation devouring and despoiling the habitat that once supported them.

III

A final reflection.[1] The human adventure just might have turned out otherwise. If one speculates on the connection between the Judaeo-Christian religious tradition, on the one hand, which confers on man, as God's chosen creature, dominion over all forms of life, and, on the other hand, the exploratory and exploitive nature of his activity that has extended his power to an awesome degree, quite another history is imaginable, one that does not lead to the present predicament.

Tribal religions did not, for the most part, envisage man as the paragon of the universe, but as no more than a component part of nature; one creature among an uncountable number of different creatures, one form of life among a limitless variety. As such, the tribesman was possessed of a reverence for all forms of life, indeed, for all things found in nature. A tree, a spring, a rock, was not simply an inanimate object. It, too, had a spirit of its own, and a place in the universe. Therefore, whatever a man needed from the earth for his own survival had to be taken with respect, with care, and sometimes with conciliatory prayer and ceremony.[2] One had to placate the spirit within all things to ensure that one's own spirit in its turn would not be scorned or violated.

Had such a religious attitude toward life prevailed throughout the ages, organised communities would not have advanced very far when judged by the lights of modern achievement. Such communities today would be referred to as 'static' or, worse, as 'stagnant'. But it would be parochial to refuse to entertain the idea that a necessary condition for continued survival on this planet of ours is that all civilisations – after advancing to some viable level of technology – should remain static or

---

[1] A reflection I owe to my reading of an admirable monograph by Lynn White the title of which, to my shame, I cannot recall or trace.

[2] In Carlos Castaneda's *Road to Xtlian*, Don Juan lays a net to trap birds for a meal, and succeeds in catching six. To the consternation of the author, however, Don Juan lets four of the birds free since, as he explains, the remaining two would suffice to remove their hunger. One does not take life from a creature simply in order to gorge oneself.

stationary. Indeed, a dynamic civilisation – dynamic in the sense of a persistently advancing technology – looks to me to be inherently unstable. For it is impelled ever onward, eventually reaching a stage where it cannot draw back – even when the precipice comes into view.

We are told in the scriptures that 'the love of money is the root of all evil'. And this is surely so in the diurnal drama of human affairs. But in today's global context – and thinking poignantly of this small planet earth that is man's heritage and his only refuge in the vast frozen darkness of an inhospitable universe – it is surely the love of knowledge, the love of scientific knowledge, that is ultimately the root of evil, and the seed of his own destruction.

Appendix A The Balance of Payments

The substitution of government exhortation for economic policy is a feature of our national life particular to the postwar period, and though fairly popular in other countries whenever economic difficulties are encountered, it has had so great a fashion in Britain that one discerns a tradition in the making. As we cry wolf at the drop of an index, discover ourselves edgily perched on the precipice every other year, are lectured round the clock about our shortcomings as 'economic men' (while in between times being taken to task for our crass materialism), are continually being warned that we cannot go on much longer 'living beyond our means'[1] – and yet in some mysterious manner are able apparently to put off the dread day of reckoning – it is not surprising that our responsiveness, alike to pep talks and to crisis talks, has waned over the years. We seem to have learned to live comfortably in an atmosphere of vague but persistent economic foreboding.

This is as well as may be. What is amiss is the common belief that the concern with growth, with inflation and with the balance of payments is the very stuff of modern economics; furthermore, that the figures for annual productivity, interest rates, exchange reserves, are the indicators *par excellence* of our material comfort, the very substance if not the sum total of our national achievement. It is just this sort of belief that makes economics so exasperating a subject to the layman and acts over time to cramp the vision of men in authority. It is this sort of belief that imbues otherwise intelligent people with a

---

[1] Any excess of imports seldom represents more than between 1 and 2 per cent of our total national income, generally well below the average per annum real increase of national income. The notion, therefore, that only hard work and austere living will enable us 'to pay our way' in the world is nonsense. It may be difficult to coax foreigners to buy that little extra of our goods that would bring us into balance, but if they were willing to buy the extra, we would not need to endure any hardship in supplying them. If not, again without hardship, we could directly reduce our excess imports, or, as we shall see, invest abroad less than we have been doing.

compelling sense of urgency, so that once in office they cannot forbear to warn, cajole, bribe and threaten us about increasing this, that and the other. It is this sort of belief that prevents ministers and officials from thinking anew and critically about our existing economic institutions. For despite pop journalistic phrases about 'new thinking', 'cool looks', 'radical reorganisations', 'agonising reappraisals' and the like, there is hardly an unorthodox idea about economics to be found lurking in the 'Establishment', or for that matter in the 'anti-Establishment'. Especially is this true about our notions of foreign trade.

To touch, by way of example, on a minor issue first – the connection between economic growth and the balance of payments. If we are exhorted to export more, we are no less exhorted to grow faster. More exports and more productivity are both 'good things' and, what is more, the success of either, it is believed, is promoted by the success of the other. If we grow faster we shall, we are told, improve our export position. And if we export more, this will surely enable us to grow more swiftly. We seem, therefore, to have good reasons for keeping our attention riveted on either.

These supposed connections do not, however, stand up to cursory examination. Suppose we are so charmed with the speech of Mr Shovehard, the Minister for Exports, that we all decide to abandon our union or private demarcation rules and instead to work overtime to make our goods more attractive in price and quality to the foreigners, and suppose also that we succeed thereby in reversing the present trade imbalance into one of a large export surplus. However, in making such goods attractive to foreigners we have also made them more plentiful and attractive to ourselves, a factor which must be chalked up to the growth account. But this increase in our exports has not caused the increase in growth; rather it appears as an incidental effect of economic growth as evinced by reduced prices and improved quality. We seem to have shown the reverse causal relationship: that growth leads to exports. This, however, is an incomplete account and we shall return to it in a moment. In the meantime, in order effectively to isolate the exports-help-growth thesis, suppose instead that by some happy accident, unforeseen by economists, exports grow rapidly so that soon we are able to show a large export surplus year after year. Does this of itself promote economic growth? One reason why it may do the reverse is that while our export surplus is maintained it will be financed by an equal reduction of our available gross domestic saving and, therefore, a reduction to that extent of investment in domestic industry. Conversely, so long as an import surplus is maintained it enables us to release domestic resources in order to add to the new investment already made available by domestic saving. Economic analysis can go further than this, of course, but enough has been said to suggest that a statement that economic growth is itself helped along by an expansion of exports is not a self-evident piece of reasoning.

As for the reverse relation, that of economic growth stimulating exports, although the assertion has a superficial plausibility – as, for instance, in the first half of the above paragraph – this relation, too, tends to wilt under scrutiny. The effects on our balance of payments of an increase in the rate of economic growth may be considered under two main headings, (1) the aggregate and (2) the technological. Under (1) we include two general propositions: (a) inasmuch as this country spends a given fraction of its income on imports, a faster growth of its real income from any cause – increasing population, increasing per capita income with, or without, technological advance – results in a faster growth of its imports from the rest of the world; (b) insofar as the level of our prices rises compared with the price levels of other countries, this fraction of our income spent on imports itself tends to rise (and the fraction the world spends on our exports to fall), thus aggravating further an adverse balance of payments. And our price level may well rise, both absolutely and relative to world prices, if the increase in our rate of growth is accompanied by attempts to push further into our 'full-employment zone'.

Under (2) we take account of the effects of improved technology on the prices of our import substitutes and on the prices of our exports. (a) If the spurt in productivity chiefly takes the form of innovations in the domestic production of new or cheaper substitutes for our imports, the volume and the value of our imports are thereby reduced. (b) On the other hand, if our productivity advances are concentrated in our export industries, then although the *volume* of our exports will tend to increase, their *value* will increase only if, despite our lower prices, foreigners spend more of their currency on them. Should they spend less on them (increasing their purchases by a proportion that is smaller than the fall in our prices), the value of our exports will fall.

As it happens, the quantitative information necessary to strike a balance of tendency for the UK is, as yet, unavailable. Until it becomes available there can be no acceptable presumption that, in general, a faster rate of economic growth in the UK would improve the balance of payments position. In the meantime, however, it is my guess that it would be likely to worsen the balance of payments.

Let us then turn to a more fundamental problem, the importance to our economy of a large volume of trade. The public, long conditioned by their newspapers, are in no doubt that we must export to 'survive'. If we have managed to survive for so long without exporting enough to 'pay our way' in the world, it is presumably because the world has been lenient with us so far. The transition from export-mindedness to mercantilism is, however, short and easy. It is not uncommon for large export orders, gained or lost, to make front-page news. Apparently goods exported emit an odour of sanctity denied to common or garden goods that remain to be consumed inside the country. The impression persists that by exporting we pile up reserves of economic strength along with foreign currencies, and that by importing wc dissipate them. An announcement from the Board of Trade that the country's exports are breaking all records has a regenerative effect on our spirits: we begin to feel proud, confident and very respectable. (One dare not imagine the general acclaim and exhilaration that would follow the discovery, at the end of the year, that we had in fact exported the whole of our national output.)

Now businessmen need seldom trouble to push their ideas to their logical conclusions. They know that more of some things is good and more of other things is bad. Without a shadow of doubt, exports are one of the good things: it follows that we cannot really have enough of them. The trained economist, however, has at the fore of his mind the notion of an 'optimum' quantity or flow of things. The 'optimum' volume of trade would be the 'just right' volume – more or less than which is to be avoided. Though this concept is straightforward enough, as we shall see, owing to a highly volatile economic environment this optimum volume of foreign trade is practically impossible to measure with a pretence of anything approaching exactness. For all that, the notion of an optimum volume of trade as a goal of attainment could with advantage replace the current mercantilist view rampant among businessmen, journalists and politicians. It would increase their receptiveness to the possibility, the likelihood even, that the volume of our foreign trade is too large; that we should be more comfortable with a smaller volume of trade.

It is not necessary here, however, to burden the reader with the theory of optimal tariffs which demonstrates that, starting from a free trade equilibrium, there exists a set of tariffs that (in the absence of retaliation) would enable the community to exploit the maximum advantage from its foreign trade and, in any case, attain a higher level of potential welfare than would exist in a completely free trade situation. Nevertheless, by translating into welfare terms the two related effects of a tariff – a reduction in the domestic demand for imports and the consequent improvement in the terms of trade – such theorems do serve to combat parochial doctrine about the advantages of increasing foreign trade.

In the existing circumstances, however, it is more relevant to consider ways of reducing the volume of imports,[2] and of stabilising its composition, with the object of diminishing the magnitude and recurrence of balance of payments crises in a world of fixed exchange rates. A discussion of this possibility has the incidental merit of exposing in another crucial context the falseness of the no-choice myth. There are no 'musts' in international trade, as in fact there are none in the field of economic policy. 'Export or perish' slogans are a misleading form of rhetoric. Economics is concerned, *inter alia*, with investigating the implications of *alternative* choices that are open to us. And if presumably honest men talk to us as if there is in fact no choice, they do so either in ignorance of the opportunities that are open to us or else from the conviction – which occasionally, at least, ought to be made explicit – that we should concur with them in rejecting all the alternatives did we but know them.

Turning, therefore, to the volume of foreign trade, we might begin by agreeing that, given the already outsize population of these islands, there would be genuine hardship for a long time if we could not import some minimum assortment of goods from abroad. Whatever our conception of this minimum assortment, once we extend the import ration from this bare minimum we move out of the range of discomfort and enter a range of diminishing frustration. The ration now includes goods that are generally admitted to be highly desirable. We move on from there to include the range of fashion and luxury goods: French cheeses, Italian shoes, German cars, Belgian chocolate, American cigarettes, Japanese toys, Dutch tomatoes, and so on; things not to be spurned, and important for a variety of reasons to some people, but which could be called 'essential' only by a misleading use of language. Yet if a sizeable proportion of our import bill does consist of goods such as these that cannot reasonably be classified as 'essential', and indeed may more usefully be classified as 'expendable', it is surely perverse that responsible ministers should

---

[2] It is generally recognised that the elimination of a deficit by import controls is less 'burdensome' than its elimination by exports promotion.

continue to exhort us as though such imports were a matter of life and death to our economy. Of course, they do not say this in so many words; rather they talk about the country's *need to export*, and labour us with patriotic duty to strain to the utmost to sell abroad. But the additional exports we must strain ourselves to sell can be properly regarded as 'essential' to our 'solvency' only if our imports of close substitutes, luxuries and quasi-luxuries are persistently regarded as 'essential'.[3]

Ordinary honesty should make it clear to the public that we have, for one reason or another, adopted the policy of allowing the import of 'expendable' goods, and in consequence we are now seemingly up against the wall trying, at the given rate of exchange, to pay for them with exports. For all I know, such a policy if understood by the public might be universally approved – another challenge, perhaps! But since these simple implications of our current foreign trade policy are never put to the public in this candid fashion, we have no means of knowing what the response of the public would be.[4]

One of the things that we import to the tune of some £900 million a year (taking an average over the last six years) that cannot by any stretch of the imagination be called essential is foreign securities[5] – in other words, lending abroad or the export of capital.[6] Moreover, this is one kind of import which, if curtailed, is not in the least likely to cause reprisals.

In addition, there are longer-term allocative implications that suggest a reduction of our capital exports, at least if we are concerned with the economic position of the domestic economy.[7] It may well be that the British investor's immediate expectations are realised and he

[3] In general, it is misleading to assert that we 'need' to export, say, an additional £200 million in order to meet the excess of our imports unless it is also agreed that *everything* we import is 'needed' in that same sense.

[4] While it is true that we have certain international commitments and that unilateral action of some sort and on some scale would invite retaliation, there is no reason to speak and act as though we were tied hand and foot by the rest of the world, and unable to move a joint save by international consensus. It is possible that the continuance of our traditional policies carries more depressing consequences than those that would follow our opting out of international agreements (if necessary). However, as we shall see, there are other, more radical choices yet available to us.

[5] It is true that the import of securities may lead to export orders. But the fraction of exports thereby generated qualifies the magnitude only, not the essential argument.

[6] Any interest or dividends collected in this country over the future do feature as part of our invisible exports. They must therefore be taken into account in any long-term policy. But we are concerned here with the immediate and short-term balance of payments problem.

[7] If, on the other hand, we are concerned quite selflessly with the welfare of the world at large, we should seek to increase international factor mobility – encouraging the export of our capital especially to underdeveloped countries and importing their labour – until some international equilibrium is reached.

obtains a higher return from his capital abroad than he does by investing it in the home economy. However, as additional capital is exported its yield abroad diminishes. In general this causes the yield on all the intra-marginal units of capital, already exported, to diminish also. Thus, the net return to a marginal unit of capital is less than what is received by the investor of that marginal unit by an amount equal to the fall in the return on all previously exported units of capital. Indeed, the net return to the domestic economy of the additional unit of capital exported might well be negative.[8]

There are two other reasons why investment abroad tends to be too high relative to domestic investment. The first arises from the process of innovation. Insofar as technologically more advanced capital equipment is introduced in the production of specific goods, the prices of such goods (relative to other goods and relative to wages) tend to fall. As a result, the return on any previous investment of now obsolescent capital also tends to fall. The investor is aware of this risk of obsolescence but is indifferent to incurring the risk at home or abroad. But the domestic economy ought not to be indifferent. Within the domestic economy such losses suffered by the domestic investor represent a gain for the domestic population. If, on the other hand, the investment is placed abroad, any such subsequent loss represents a transfer from the domestic capitalist to the foreign population.

The third reason for the tendency to overinvest abroad arises from institutional factors. The rational investor compares the returns to his investment at home and abroad net of all taxes. Now the return to the *British economy* of an increment of investment abroad is in fact no more than the return received by the British investor after paying taxes to the foreign government. The return to the British economy of investment at home, on the other hand, exceeds the net return received by the British investor by the amount of the tax he pays to the British Government.

The case for the control of foreign investment is even stronger than these long-term considerations suggest, when such investment is seen against the backcloth of continual balance of payments difficulties. For this search by investors for larger profits abroad is what ultimately

---

[8] For the world economy as a whole this reduction in the returns of all intra-marginal units represents a transfer from the owners of capital to the rest of the population. But from the standpoint of the capital-exporting country, the fall in the return on the intra-marginal units of capital already exported is to be regarded as an external diseconomy. For the additional investor unwittingly inflicts a loss on all the existing holders of foreign capital. Such a loss would be taken into account, however, only if the export of capital were in the hands of a monopoly.

contributes to bringing about the credit restrictions at home, to say nothing of our government having to borrow abroad, on short term, at very high rates.[9]

Another practical way of reducing our imports is to grow more of our foodstuffs at home. Increased self-sufficiency in foodstuffs (after allowance for the import-content of increased home production) may save us well over £300 million of imports and, possibly, without much increase in costs. Farming is one of Britain's more efficient industries, and if there were some initial rise in costs it would probably be absorbed within a few years. In the short run, moreover, import restrictions might well lower the foreign price of our remaining food imports since some time must elapse before foreign supplies find other suitable outlets.

Finally, as one looks down the list of items imported into, and exported from, the UK, one is invariably struck by the close resemblance between them. Textiles, clothing, footwear, hardware, automobilies, ships, trucks, aircraft, paints, machinery of all kinds, cameras, toys and vast quantities of chemicals are both imported and exported. One could reasonably surmise that a large proportion of these things, in particular the finished goods, are very close substitutes, and that although their further restriction might cause some occasional resentment – and would certainly incur the charge of being retrograde among the doctrinaire – it would not be likely to inflict hardship. At any rate, increased restrictions on these luxuries, quasi-luxuries and close substitutes would, in the immediate short run at least, reduce the apparent need to whip ourselves into 'viability'. Moreover, this proposal to examine ways and means of reducing our present import bill, it should be stressed, is not for the purpose of gaining any ephemeral trade advantage. True, the immediate effect of implementing the proposed measures might be regarded as an attempt to cut our foreign purchases to what we could comfortably afford, and as such one need not alarm oneself with exaggerated expectations of retaliation. But the larger objective is to reduce permanently the volume of our foreign trade and, perhaps, to induce other Western European countries to do the same. By eliminating much – just how much can be left to discussion – of the trade in luxuries, close substitutes and such goods as one might reasonably

---

[9] It does not follow from these remarks that no foreign investment should be permitted; merely that the bulk of our foreign lending should not be determined by the profit expectations of investors, but rather by more comprehensive welfare criteria and/or by considerations bearing on the country's long-term economic policy.

classify as expendable, one could hope for greater stability in the pattern and volume of trade over the future. One might hope therefore to check the present trend towards an increasingly fluctuating pattern of foreign trade – especially as by far the greater part of world trade takes place between the affluent countries of the West and, as a proportion of world trade, is increasing.

On the supply side, more rapidly advancing technology entails a swifter shifting to and fro of short-lived technological advantage in closely competitive products – and, with larger productive units, the competition is likely to be pretty ruthless. On the demand side, as the margin for non-essentials grows over the future, one may surely anticipate more impulse- and fashion-buying, features that can only aggravate the increasing vicissitudes of international trade. Of course, there will always be those who view the fierce competitive struggle with enthusiasm. To others, who see in life more serious objectives than a perpetual jockeying for position, the opportunity of permanently reducing the least stable, or most expendable, components of our imports by some sacrifice of variety and perhaps cheapness, in order to remain free from perpetual anxiety, may have a stronger appeal.[10]

[10] It will always be argued by the inveterate free trader that the competition of such foreign goods, whether Italian Fiats or French perfumes, helps to keep down domestic prices. However, the size of the British home market alone is, for practically all of those sorts of imports, large enough to exploit fully the economies of scale. Where the efficient plant size is small enough it is up to the government to make much more use of the Monopolies Commission and the Restrictive Practices Court in promoting competition. Where not, product standardisation, either voluntary or government-inspired, may enable us to reduce costs without much sacrifice – or, indeed, with some welcome sacrifice – of variety.

Appendix B Technological Unemployment

Owing to careless exposition in some elementary textbooks, the casual student of economics is frequently left with the impression that technological innovation cannot lead to unemployment – the unfortunate Luddites, imagining themselves displaced by machinery, being regarded as the victims of vulgar error rather than of historical circumstances. In extenuation of this belief in the impossibility of technological unemployment it must be conceded that until not so long ago the dominant view was, and had been for over a century, that neither could unemployment arise from a deficiency of total demand. For with the great equilibrium systems of the classical economists in mind, it was not easy to evisage underemployment *equilibrium* arising from insufficient demand.

A brief word about the latter. The very existence of involuntary unemployment, it was believed, exerted a downward pressure on money wages. And if wages were in the process of decline the position, by definition, could not be one of equilibrium. Moreover, the gradual decline in money wages, it was argued, tended to restore full employment, since any reduction in money wages implied a corresponding reduction in the price level and, through the operation of (1) the cash-balance effect in reducing interest rates (which were imperfectly stabilised by speculative activity) and of (2) the asset-expenditure effect in reducing the real volume of saving, the level of employment would rise until all underemployment-pressure on prices ceased. The conclusion that involuntary unemployment could exist only in the short run did not, however, satisfy Keynes, simply because the time required for market forces effectively to reduce such unemployment might be very many years. What is more, this tendency to long-run equilibrium is valid only provided other things remain equal: in the real world, then, this tendency is diverted by continual economic changes, and therefore cannot be depended upon, no matter how long we are prepared to wait. The long-run solution was therefore irrelevant: 'In the long run we are all dead!' The practical thing was for the government to intervene immediately in stimulating effective demand by the several means open to it.

There is also something of this older long-run-equilibrium complacency in the popular fallacy that technological unemployment cannot exist. Thus (even if we ignore production functions with regions of negative marginal returns to the abundant factor) a labour-saving innovation may well be such that the existing supply of labour in the economy could be employed only at a real wage materially below that in existence. In a competitive economy in which wages were completely flexible the new technique and the new wage would come to prevail, and anyone who attempted to continue with the old technique would (paying the new wage and rentals) cost himself out of the market. Again, therefore, in some 'long run', full employment would be restored at this lower absolute wage. But if, for institutional reasons, there were determined attempts to maintain the real wage at its pre-automation level, technological unemployment could continue for many years.

Even this argument, however, concedes too much, for two reasons: (1) because with the new method of production, factor substitution may be negligible. True, there may be several alternative ways of producing a set of goods, but if they are all highly labour-saving then unemployment with near-zero wages, as the market solution, is consistent with each method – at least, such a solution would prevail in a market with completely flexible factor prices. However, if institutional forces could determine wages and rentals, unemployed labour would continue to exist until capital accumulation reduced the labour–capital ratio to the point at which the existing supply of labour could be employed again at positive wages. A possibly 'academic' solution for highly labour-saving innovations might be to reduce drastically the hours put in by each labourer, though such a solution might well act to reduce technical efficiency.

The other reason (2) is that the assumption of homogeneous labour is too abstract a concept for the relevant economic models. In automation, complex capital equipment is combined with skilled 'brain labour' both in the producing and the operating of the machinery: the whole idea is to dispense not only with unskilled labour but also with highly skilled manual labour and clerical labour. Thus, the proportion of such labour required in any automated process must be expected to decline with the evolution of technology.

Again, it is open to people to be complacent and talk of a long-run 'transformation' of old-type manual labour into new-type brain labour – though even here, since substitutability is likely to be small, it may be a long time before there were sufficient capital to employ the transformed supply of labour. However, it is far from being impossible that in the not too distant future a large proportion of the adult population will also be *unemployable* simply because they will not be endowed with the innate capacities necessary to acquire the more highly developed mental skills which may be called for by a more complex technology. In these circumstances, no matter how far the wage of the *unemployable* may fall, they could not be profitably employed in industry. Of course, they may all be comfortably maintained by some transfer of the increased output produced by the reduced working population. There need be no economic crisis, only a social one.

Appendix C Interpreting the Benefits of Private Transport

I

In this note I construct a hypothetical situation to reveal some of the circumstances under which consumers' surplus, when used as an index of the benefit to be derived from private automobile travel, may give perverse results – a rise in the index being accompanied by a reduction in the benefit experienced by motorists. Less surprisingly, it will also be shown that the use of consumers' surplus in determining optimal traffic flows, in cost-benefit studies, and in estimating rates of return on road investment, results in overinvestment solutions in road construction unless the alternatives to private automobile travel are properly priced.

Although not essential, it will simplify the analysis to assume (1) that in all sections of a fully employed economy, except those under examination, price is already equal to social marginal cost, and (2), provisionally at least, that there are no neighbourhood effects external to the transport industry that affect the amenity of the public. We can circumvent the appropriate-rate-of-discount problem by estimating the consumers' surplus for each individual in terms of present discounted value of expected surpluses over the future. A measure of this consumer's surplus (based on the Compensating Variation) on the purchase of a new automobile requires the individual to anticipate, at the time of purchase, the total number of miles for which the car will be used, valuing each mile at its maximum present worth to him (net of all variable costs, including fuel and maintenance), and arranging the values in descending order to the point of zero maximum worth. This arrangement produces a function $V(m)$ of total expected mileage. After completing M miles the car is to be sold for a sum having present value £T. If the car when bought costs £B, including tax,[1] the present

---

[1] This tax may be an underestimate or overestimate of the costs incurred by the community (exclusive of the costs of mutual congestion) in keeping the existing traffic moving on the existing system of roads. The analysis assumes that the tax is exactly equal to the costs incurred.

discounted value of the compensating-variation measure of consumer's surplus, CS, is equal to $\int_0^m V(m)dm - (B - T)$, this sum being the maximum the individual would be prepared to pay in order to secure a permit to buy the car at the price £B, given his expectation of re-selling for the sum mentioned after motoring M miles.

Phase I of the situation is one in which there is no private traffic whatever, an efficient system of public transport, say a bus service, linking together all parts of the city. Individual A, typical of others, uses the bus daily to take him to the centre of the city in about ten minutes. Public transport is also used for his occasional outings.

Phase II is the transitional one in which A buys a new car that, in the circumstances prevailing (which he, short-sightedly, projects into the future), is expected to take him to the centre in five minutes. On his anticipation of the future he makes a CS of, say, £800. Provided that only A buys a car, and nothing else changes, A is to that extent better off in Phase II than in Phase I.

Phase III occurs after a large enough number of others follow A's example. Within two or three years, we may suppose, the increase in the number of private cars is such that it takes A fifteen minutes to drive to work. He realises now that he was better off in Phase I, but this opportunity is now closed to him; for owing to the build-up of private traffic the congestion is such that it would now take him twenty-five minutes to reach his office by bus. Moreover, since bus drivers have had to be compensated for the increased difficulties and risk of driving, the bus fare has risen.

Phase III' is the situation which exists when public transport has been withdrawn altogether, as may happen if commercial considerations alone prevail. Analytically, however, it differs from III only in being a more extreme case of it.

II

By assumption, A is now worse off in Phase III than he was in I. He would, of course, prefer II to either III or I. But II is a transitional phase only: it is no longer open to him, and could be reserved for him only if he exercised the powers of a dictator.

Since A is typical of other individuals who have changed from being passengers to being motorists, we can assume that I is *socially* preferred to III. Dealers in motorcars and accessories may, themselves, be on balance better off, but we suppose that they could not compensate the rest of the community and remain as well off as they were in I.

There are two things to notice. First, that under existing institutions there are no self-generating forces that can restore to the community the socially preferred Phase I. Only a collective decision could return the community from the existing III or III' phase to the original I situation. Second, that A's CS on his automobile in Phase III will exceed that in Phase II, notwithstanding that he gets less benefit from his automobile in Phase III. It was, in fact, just because public transport was so cheap and efficient in Phase I that the maximum amount he was prepared to pay for successive miles of private driving was lower than it was in Phase III, where the public transport alternative was unattractive. If now, for example, we move to Phase III', in which the public transport alternative is completely withdrawn, a loss of welfare will certainly be experienced by the remaining passengers. Some of these ex-passengers will have little choice but to purchase automobiles. Compared with their new alternatives, of either walking to work or not working in the city, the CS on their purchases will be positive, and may even be large. Since we may assume that the cars used by the displaced passengers in Phase III' take up more road space than did the displaced buses, the motorists in Phase III', of which A was a typical member, will also be worse off than they were in III.

If the benefit conferred by the private automobile on its owner is measured by his CS, or any proxy measure, the chronological change through II, III and III' will appear to register a continuously increasing benefit notwithstanding the continuous deterioration in his welfare in this respect.

A similar development could of course arise in other situations, for instance in a suburb linked by rail to the city. At the given rail fare, n commuters are required in order for the railway to 'break even'. If, therefore, owing to an initial change from rail to road, only m commuters remain $(m<n)$, the railway service must close down. The closure clearly makes the m commuters worse off. But it also makes those who were, before the closure, travelling by private automobile worse off, (1) because m commuters now have to travel by road and increase the congestion there; and (2) because even though automobile travellers made no use of the railway, or used it infrequently, it did provide a form of insurance in the case of the car being out of service – or for such occasions when, for one reason or another, the motorist did not feel up to driving.

Again, however, despite the fact that everyone going into the city is adversely affected by the railway closure, the community's demand for road travel will be seen to have expanded, so each individual consumer surplus, and therefore the collective consumers' surplus of automobile owners, will reveal a gain. Each ex-train commuter who has now perforce to purchase an automobile must reveal a positive CS. As for the remainder, once the railway service has been removed the only alternative, we may suppose, is walking to the city. The maximum amount any individual would be willing to pay for the ith journey by car is consequently greater.

III

These simple illustrations may serve to remind the transport expert that there are difficulties other than those of statistical measurement. Not only can the index of consumer's benefit rise over time without any actual experience of benefit – simply because 'real' income is increasing, and therefore people are prepared to pay more for the ith unit of any good, or service, whose actual utility to them in fact remains unchanged – but such an index can rise concurrently with an actual reduction of benefit. The more significant parts of the *ceteris paribus* of all consumer's surplus (and rent) analysis relate to the constancy of the prices, and/or availabilities, of the close substitutes, and complements, for the good or service in question. The more effective the good y as, say, a substitute for x, the smaller will be the consumer's surplus on purchases of x at the given prices. Raise the price of y, and ultimately withdraw it from the market, and this simultaneously reduces the welfare of the consumer and increases his measure of consumer's surplus on purchases of x.

The same illustrations also serve to show that any allocative recommendations flowing from such estimates of the demand curve for automobile travel are invalid in the absence of optimal outputs in the alternative services. In the first illustration, as the community moves into Phase III the transport expert may continue to revise upward his estimate of the 'optimal traffic flow',[2] which expands, therefore, along with the fall in motorists' welfare. Of course, in the

---

[2] By calculating the marginal congestion cost of traffic $dc/D = dC/dT \cdot dT/dS \cdot dS/dN$, where C is total congestion cost, N the number of vehicles, T the total time taken by the traffic over the given route ($= tN$ where t is the average time taken per automobile) and S is the average speed of traffic over that route, the optimal traffic flow is that which equates marginal congestion costs dC/dN to the demand price $P(N)$ for that route.

event of Phase III' being reached, there remaining no alternative but to walk to work, the elasticity of demand may be so low as to make little difference, if any, between the actual traffic flow and the optimal traffic flow.

The transport expert may also use the data in III and III' to justify investment in road-widening, in fly-overs, freeways and bridges in the attempt to accommodate the expanding number of private auto-mobiles.

Now if there were effective methods for imputing congestion costs in the first place, other recommendations would follow which, under our assumption that in all other sectors price was equal to social marginal cost, could be justified. Beginning with a satisfactory public transport in Phase I, such a mechanism would require that full compensation for any inconvenience caused to every passenger and bus driver by the marginal car be imputed to the marginal car. Such a scheme would ensure that no additional car be allowed on the route(s) in question unless it were able to effect a Pareto improvement – the owner of the car being at least no worse off after compensating everyone else using the roads (bus passengers, bus drivers and intra-marginal automobiles). Such a requirement, which would ensure growing benefits from traffic, might well entail an optimal flow with very few private automobiles.

Be that as it may, it is only *after* this optimal flow is established that one may proceed correctly to estimate the returns to investment in road-widening, freeways and other traffic-accommodating projects. A traffic flow that has *not* been corrected implies that marginal congestion costs exceed marginal benefit for some part of the existing traffic flow: total congestion costs incurred being, then, so much greater than the optimally determined congestion costs, the saving by traffic investment will *appear* to be correspondingly greater. It is possible, therefore, that an initial optimal traffic flow might reveal no economic case for traffic investment, whereas failure to establish this optimal flow would allow traffic to pile up congestion costs and would therefore enable investment to *appear* profitable – in effect by reducing excess traffic costs that were not warranted in the first place.

Similar remarks apply to our second illustration. If as a conse-quence of rail closure congestion occurs on the road connecting the suburb to the city, the establishment of an optimal flow of motorised traffic must precede any estimate of the benefits of road investment. More important, the rationale of the proposed rail closure itself should be scrutinised before the requirement. A fall in the number of fare-paying passengers below some critical number n is generally irrelevant in this connection. The line should be kept running for the time being, if, at any number of passengers for which price is equal to marginal operating costs, total benefit exceeds total operating costs.[3] Benefits may be reckoned as the sum of three items: (1) the fares that could be collected of all those willing to pay the marginal cost price (as determined by the existing demand schedule) plus the consumer's surplus of every such individual; (2) the insurance value of the railway service to those who do not anticipate any particular railway journeys; and (3) the sum total of any (additional) congestion costs that would be inflicted on all motorists having to use the suburb-to-city road after the railway closure.[4] It would not be surprising if many of the railway services closed or due for closure could prove economic viability by meeting these conditions. At all events, closing a railway service that, on this criterion, ought not to be closed entails a misallocation of shiftable resources currently being used by the railways. After the misallocation of resources by the closing down of the railway service, investment in roads that would otherwise (if the railway service were available) be clearly seen as wasteful might well appear profitable.

IV

We have confined ourselves in this note to external diseconomies that are internal to private motoring, i.e. to the mutual congestion costs of motorised traffic, following the popular custom of relegating to a parenthetical remark the unmeasurable, though probably much more important, effects on the physical environment. The private car carries along with it, however, a much neglected disamenity-potential through its being the chief agent of rapid urban sprawl and ribbon building. As 'developers' set up estates farther and yet farther from city centres, in the assurance that wherever they site their buildings families with private cars will be prepared to make the longer journey in order to live in country areas, the advantages of those families already settled in these areas are diminished.[5]

---

[3] Largely the earnings of *necessary* personnel, fuel and maintenance charges.

[4] To be more exact, (3) should be included insofar as this contingent addition to congestion has not been anticipated. If it had been wholly anticipated, it would have raised the consumer's surpluses of existing and potential railway users, and would have raised the value of the railway to motorists who make no regular use of the railway.

[5] Again, however, if some institutional mechanism could be established whereby each additional home-buyer (who adds to the existing number in or near the area and so contributes to its transformation into a suburb) were obliged to compensate existing householders for the loss of

Even if we restrict the analysis to a given area, say the city and its dormitory areas, the continual visual disturbance, the pollution of the air by exhaust fumes, the incessant engine noise and vibration generated by any n travellers using private transport are very many times those generated by the same number using public transport instead, in particular if public transport were electrically powered. Hence, although an optimal flow of traffic calculated with respect only to mutual traffic frustration already favours public transport at the expense of private transport (comparing this optimal flow with the usual free-for-all that makes road investment appear so profitable), an optimal flow that also takes into consideration these other environment-damaging consequences – no less relevant or significant for being statistically elusive – would further reduce the warrantable flow of private traffic. If the number of private-car journeys consistent with this more comprehensive measure of the optimal were believed to be few, the costs involved in their regulation might well suggest prohibition within a given area of all private traffic as the most economic solution – allowing, perhaps, for a given number of private taxis within the area for emergency purposes.

It may well happen that, contrary to our initial assumption, the existing public transport was adequate in the first place with respect to coverage, speed and frequency. However, an analysis that yields a Pareto optimal solution requiring the provision of an efficient public transport service does not depend upon the chronological sequence posited for its validity.[6]

amenity endured by his settling there, the criterion for a Pareto improvement could be met. Such external diseconomies would then be automatically corrected and urban sprawl be subject to a built-in check.

[6] In general, if each vehicle differed in size and other relevant characteristics, and if the value attached by the occupants of each vehicle to travelling the distance in question differed for any ith journey, we should determine the optimal traffic flow, and its composition, by maximising the social surplus. This is got by ranking the individual journeys by the excess of CV over the marginal congestion cost until the excess is zero. In the absence of welfare effects on the CV measure, which would be brought into operation by compensatory payments, the optimal flow and composition of the traffic is uniquely determined. For any flow having a social surplus smaller than this maximum indicates a potential Pareto improvement. Thus some journey(s) currently excluded by the composition of the existing traffic could replace some journey(s) currently included, and thereby increase the social surplus. The additional gain from such exchange operations could, of course, be distributed among the participants so as to make each of them better off.

Appendix D The Rationale of Marginal-Cost Pricing

I

Before talking about an improvement in the allocation of resources, we require certain ethical premises on which judgements of better or worse are to be raised. In the West they have usually been of a libertarian character: nothing is good for society unless it is held to be good by the individuals who form that society. And while it is true that there are people who appear to be incompetent judges of their own interests, this is usually regarded as an argument for education rather than for paternalism. Be this as it may, since there is no providential method of determining the true interests of any persons which would command general assent, it would be impolitic at this early stage to premise propositions about social welfare on anything other than each man's view of his own interest. Though aware then of its occasional falsehood, we follow, provisionally, the liberal convention of regarding each man as the best judge of his own welfare.

Let us define an improvement in the allocation of society's resources in a way familiar to economists – as an economic reorganisation of those resources, involving a change in the collection of goods produced and in their distribution, which could make some people better off (in their own estimation) without making anyone else worse off. An 'optimal', 'ideal' or 'summit' position – the adjectives are used interchangeably – is therefore defined as one from which no economic reorganisation can qualify as an *improvement* in resource-allocation: in other words, an optimal position is one from which no economic reorganisation is possible that makes some people better off without in the process making at least one person worse off. Alternatively, an optimal position may be interpreted as one that does not contain any 'slack', inasmuch as there is no way of reorganising production and distribution as to make everyone better off than he is.

Such an optimal position of the economy has associated with it a well-known property: that the collection of finished goods valued at the prevailing prices has a higher value than that of any alternative collection of goods that could be produced with the existing resources of society. This property is, indeed, a corollary of the definition of an optimal position. For if it were otherwise, if one could reshuffle the existing resources so as to produce a collection of goods with a yet *greater* value at the initial prices, then it would, after all, be possible to give everyone the same value of goods as he enjoyed before and still have some goods left over. The value of these goods left over could then make one or more persons better off. But this implies that an allocative improvement is still possible. Therefore the so-called optimal position was not, after all, optimal as defined. It cannot then be otherwise than as stated: an optimal position has the property that, valued at its prevailing prices, no other collection of goods producible with the same total resources of society can be worth more than the optimal collection.

How can we know when the economy is at an optimal position? In general, when no resource – no type of labour, machinery or land – can be made to yield a higher value when transferred to some other employment. If we follow the custom of regarding these resources as divisible into very small units – an expository convenience – and also, to some extent, substitutes for one another, this highest-value property of an optimal position, mentioned above, can be expressed by saying that the value contributed by a unit of any type of resource will be the same at the margin for all goods in which it is used. For example, in an optimal position, the value contributed by an additional, or marginal, unit of a given type of labour in textile production, in fishing, in barley cultivation, and in every other process in which it is used, must be the same. If it were otherwise, if it were still possible to transfer a resource from its current occupation to some other occupation in which the value of its contribution were larger, we should have succeeded in increasing total value at the prevailing set of prices. It would, therefore, follow from our first optimal property that we could not have been in an optimal position to start with. Hence the standard optimal rule, or allocation rule, that the marginal value contributed by any type of resource be the same in all its uses to which it can be put.

We may take a further step by supposing that the market functions well enough to set a single price for each type of resource. If now production is so organised that everywhere output is expanded to the point at which the marginal value contributed by any type of resource is equal to its price, the allocation rule must everywhere be met. For if in all uses the marginal value produced by any kind of resource is equal to its market-determined price then, clearly, this marginal value contributed by any type of resource must be the same in all uses. Hence, assuming a single market price for each type of resource, we may express the allocation rule as requiring that the marginal value of any resource be equal to its market price.[1]

It is necessary to recognise, at this stage, that by dividing both the marginal value contributed by a resource and the market price of that resource by the number of units of any good contributed by the marginal resource, the above allocation rule (that the marginal value of a resource must equal its price) is transformed into the rule that the price of the good be equal to its marginal cost. Thus we arrive at the common recommendation of marginal-cost pricing in industry as a means of establishing an optimal position.

There are, however, two complications we must face up to in connection with marginal-cost pricing.

The first has to do with the distribution of the national product, or the national income, among the members of society. We have shown that once an optimal position is reached the value of the goods is as high as or higher than the value of any other producible collection of goods, *provided* we value all alternative collections of goods at the particular set of prices prevailing in the initially optimum position. But the relative prices of these goods arise, in principle, from the pattern of demand that emerges from the distribution of income associated with the collection of goods that is being produced in the optimal position in question. A change in individual tastes which changes the pattern of demand can obviously move the economy to a new optimal position. But, from what we have just said about distribution, there can also be a change to a new optimal position without any change in individual tastes taking place. For instance, any redistribution of income – arising, say, from alterations in taxation and government expenditures – may change the overall pattern of demand and, therefore (unless supply prices happen to

---

[1] It is interesting to note in passing that a so-called perfectly competitive economy tends towards such an optimal position. By definition of such an economy, firms accept the market prices of all goods and of all resources as beyond their power to influence. Each firm will profitably expand so long as the value contributed by employing an additional resource of any kind exceeds the price of that resource. In equilibrium there is no incentive of additional firms to come in, or for expansion or contraction of existing firms. Each firm is, in fact, producing an output at which the marginal value of each resource is equal to its price. If all industries are organised in this way, the value of the marginal contribution of each type of resource is the same in all products, so establishing an optimal position.

remain everywhere constant irrespective of quantity produced), the set of prices also. If this happens, then the particular collection of goods that was previously optimal will not, in general, have the highest possible value at these new prices – though, as we have already shown, any *new* optimal collection of goods will certainly have this property. One may therefore assume, in general, that there is an indefinite number of optimal collections of goods that can be produced with the existing resources of the economy, each one generated by some particular income distribution and associated with a distinct set of product prices.

The neglect of this interconnection between income-distribution and resource-allocation has been a potent source of confusion in the past. Notwithstanding all that has been written in recent years on this subject, unsophisticated writers venturing into the field of resource-allocation frequently argue as if these two considerations, distribution and allocation, can always be treated separately. Under certain conditions – constant costs in the production of all goods and services – the set of goods *prices* will be the same for any optimal position, each optimal position being distinguished from the others only in containing a different collection of goods. Under other conditions yet more far-fetched – each person buying the same proportions of all goods as everyone else irrespective of his income – no conceivable distribution of income makes any difference to the resulting pattern of demand and, therefore, to the optimal collection of goods which, in these conditions, is uniquely determined. These are special cases, however, and though in the real world the universal-constant cost case may be important, as a general proposition it must be affirmed that an optimal position is optimal only for a given distribution; also the value of the optimal collection is a maximum only when valued at the resulting set of prices.

The second complication is the apparent all-or-nothing character of the applicability of the allocation rule. If for any reason we are unable to meet the allocation rule in each and every sector of the economy, its application in the remaining sectors may not improve matters: thus, an adopted procedure of meeting the allocation rule whenever it can be met need not move us closer to an optimal position, and may even move us farther away from one. If, to illustrate, the output of the steel industry were such that all steel products were priced at twice their corresponding marginal costs and, for institutional reasons, this situation could not be altered, we should not be doing the best we can in the circumstances by strict marginal-cost pricing in the remaining sectors of the economy. In this simple case, as it happens, we do know what to do: we can come closest to an optimal position by adjusting the output of all other goods so that their prices also are twice as large as their corresponding marginal costs. This arrangement is, in fact, optimal since it ensures that the marginal value contributed by each type of resource is the same in all goods. However, in less simple cases – where, for example, several industries produce unalterable quantities of goods having quite different price–marginal cost ratios – the 'second-best' allocation rules for the remainder of the economy are not easy to determine. Even where they could be determined they might be far too complex to be of any practical use.

II

Let us consider these two complications in a little more detail.

The interconnection between resource-allocation and income-distribution seems to suggest, on the surface of things, that a bias in favour of the *status quo* enters whenever one aims to bring the economy closer to an optimum using the existing set of prices, since this set of prices itself emerged from the existing income-distribution. Unless we have special reasons to be satisfied with the existing distribution of income the optimal position corresponding to this existing set of prices has no more claim on our attentions than any other 'efficiently produced' collections of goods.[2] For each of these efficiently produced collections could be made optimal by some appropriate distribution of income. The only satisfactory solution to this problem seems to be that of choosing an optimum collection of goods which corresponds to some distribution of income that is, in some broadly accepted ethical sense, more satisfactory to the community than any other.

Suppose, however, that there are political limits to the degree of income redistribution that is feasible over the foreseeable future, must we waive any pronouncements about resourse-allocation? Not necessarily. The less we are able to alter, for institutional reasons, the existing structure of income-distribution the more likely is it that all discernible movements towards any optimal position will be such that everyone is made better off. But even where the distributional structure of incomes is allowed to vary widely, it may turn out to be the case that the resulting pattern of demand, and therefore the

---

[2] An 'efficiently produced' collection of goods is one produced with existing resources and techniques and with such economy that it is not possible to produce more of any good without reducing the output of some other good.

optimal collection of goods, remains substantially unaltered. If the world were like that, we could quite logically pursue allocative improvements independently of their distributional effects, even though it may be ethically unacceptable to ignore these effects. If we did so in such circumstances, however, we would be enabled to say without ambiguity that gainers in a movement to an optimal position *could* always fully compensate losers and themselves be better off than they were in the existing non-optimal position.[3] Now if the gainers did *not* compensate the losers, the resulting distribution might well be worse than it was in the non-optimal. We might then require either that no move towards optimality be made unless the resulting distribution was judged to be no worse, or else that losers be fully compensated in moving towards the optimal position. In the latter case nobody is actually made worse off and some are made better off. Since progressive taxes are a means of redistributing gains, the more highly progressive is the tax structure the more warrant there is for pursuing optimality without regard to distributional considerations. In the limiting case of taxation that equalised all incomes, any movement to an optimal position will actually make everyone better off.

Turning to the 'second best' problem which arises, say, when in several sectors of the economy there is no prospect of being able to enforce the allocation rule that outputs be adjusted to bring prices into equality with corresponding marginal costs, there is, as indicated, no simple and general rule to guide industrial outputs. But does this mean there is no practical guidance available to the policy-maker concerned with improving allocation? Again, not necessarily, for if we had information to suggest that, after meeting the marginal-cost pricing rule in all those sectors in which it could be met, the residual movement of resources that would yet be necessary to bring the unaccommodating sectors into line was slight, we could proceed to enforce the rule in all the accommodating sectors with a good conscience. By doing so we attain a position that is at least close to an optimal position. And for practical purposes this is very satisfactory. True, we know that there exists some conceivable reshuffling of

---

[3] In virtue of the definition of an optimum position we can already say that no movement from it, to any other position, is able to make everyone better off. What is more pertinent, however, to the idea of an allocative improvement is the stronger statement that in the movement from any non-optimal position to an optimal position everyone could be made better off (alternatively, some could be made better off and no one worse off) – that is, gainers could more than compensate losers. And this statement, as indicated above, is true only in special cases.

resources that would enable us, if we could discover it, to reach yet a higher position – the elusive second-best position itself. But we also know that the margin of hypothetical gains is narrow.

Again, if several of the alterable sectors are severely out of line with all the other sectors – say prices in these alterable sectors are far below their corresponding marginal costs compared with all other sectors – we may almost certainly improve the situation by operating on these several sectors alone. For a contraction of the outputs of these several sectors, to the point at which their price–marginal cost ratios increased to the extent necessary to equal the *average* ratio of the remaining sectors of the economy (without increasing the spread of these ratios among these remaining sectors), would effectively narrow the spread of price–marginal cost ratios for the whole economy. The new position would then be closer to an optimum than it was before we reduced the outputs of these several low ratio sectors. In general, the further is price in one sector below its marginal cost compared with the range of price–marginal cost ratios in the remaining sectors, the more sure one can be that the gain from transferring units of resource from this sector to the others – a movement of resources towards sectors in which their value is higher – will overcome any countervailing repercussions on other prices.

This same argument may carry more conviction if put differently. Starting from a non-optimal position, we count as an improvement any economic reorganisation that enables everyone to be made better off unambiguously. If we effect some reduction of output in, say, the automobile industry, which alteration would enable us to make unambiguously better off all those people directly concerned with automobiles – the producers, employees, purchasers, and all those affected by the manner of producing and utilising automobiles – the definition of an improvement has been met *provided* that people not directly concerned with automobiles remain relatively unaffected. This condition is met if in the remainder of the economy (the R sector) there are negligible changes in the prices of goods and resources in consequence of the reduction of output in the automobile sector (the A sector). The less likely is this latter condition to be met, however, the more important is it that the repercussions in the R sector be taken into account before attempting to strike a balance of gain or loss. Thus the crucial assumption which, if met, would justify the partial approach followed in the text (in Book I) is that the gains from curtailing output in any A sector are large relative to the repercussions in the R sector. For the discussion of the disamenities inflicted on society by motorised traffic I shall be assuming this condition is easily met.[4]

---

[4] This same condition permits us, if we wish, to ignore or to treat separately any incidental benefits conferred on society by economic activity. I happen to believe that such benefits that remain to be exploited are of limited significance and, therefore, that there is little social welfare to be gained by prescribing for them. None the less, an attachment to the contrary opinion need not prevent any reader from agreeing with my arguments: if adverse spillovers are large and uncorrected, an increase in social welfare follows their correction whether or not there are, in other industries, beneficial spillovers remaining to be properly exploited.

Index